The Beautiful Game?

The Beautiful Game?

The Stories Shaping the Future of Soccer

Nicholas M. Watanabe

BLOOMSBURY ACADEMIC
NEW YORK • LONDON • OXFORD • NEW DELHI • SYDNEY

BLOOMSBURY ACADEMIC
Bloomsbury Publishing Inc, 1359 Broadway, New York, NY 10018, USA
Bloomsbury Publishing Plc, 50 Bedford Square, London, WC1B 3DP, UK
Bloomsbury Publishing Ireland, 29 Earlsfort Terrace, Dublin 2, D02 AY28, Ireland

BLOOMSBURY, BLOOMSBURY ACADEMIC and the Diana logo are trademarks of
Bloomsbury Publishing Plc

First published in the United States of America 2026

Copyright © Nicholas M. Watanabe, 2026

Cover image: © istock/catalby

All rights reserved. No part of this publication may be: i) reproduced or transmitted in any form, electronic or mechanical, including photocopying, recording or by means of any information storage or retrieval system without prior permission in writing from the publishers; or ii) used or reproduced in any way for the training, development or operation of artificial intelligence (AI) technologies, including generative AI technologies. The rights holders expressly reserve this publication from the text and data mining exception as per Article 4(3) of the Digital Single Market Directive (EU) 2019/790.

Bloomsbury Publishing Inc does not have any control over, or responsibility for, any third-party websites referred to or in this book. All internet addresses given in this book were correct at the time of going to press. The author and publisher regret any inconvenience caused if addresses have changed or sites have ceased to exist, but can accept no responsibility for any such changes.

A catalog record for this book is available from the Library of Congress.

ISBN:	HB:	979-8-216-37600-2
	ePDF:	979-8-216-37602-6
	eBook:	979-8-216-37601-9

Typeset by Integra Software Services Pvt. Ltd.
Printed and bound in the United States of America

For product safety related questions contact productsafety@bloomsbury.com.

To find out more about our authors and books visit www.bloomsbury.com and sign up for our newsletters.

Contents

Introduction 1

1 Messi Mess: Why Did the World's Best Player Join MLS? 5

2 The Americans: Who Are the Owners Taking Over the World's Top Clubs? 27

3 Soccer's Biggest Mystery: Why Are So Many Women Tearing Their ACL? 51

4 The Pyramid: What Is Happening in the Lower Tiers of Soccer? 73

5 Cristiano in the Desert: Is Saudi Arabia the Future of Soccer? 97

6 Expecting Goals: How Are Analytics Changing the Game? 119

7 Too Much Soccer: Is Expansion Killing the Sport? 143

8 Who to Support: Which Clubs Deserve Our Attention? 165

9 The World's Game: Who Is Taking Over Soccer? 189

Acknowledgments 211
Notes 212
Index 248
About the Author 251

Introduction

We live in an unprecedented time for soccer.

Soccer is the most watched, played, and consumed sport on the planet. Today, more people follow clubs, post about matches on social media, and purchase tickets and merchandise than at any point in history. Fans can recite the starting lineup for matches played twenty-five years ago, tell you the exact type of boot that David Beckham wore in the 2006 World Cup (Adidas Predator Absolute), and how many dogs Arsenal's Kai Havertz has (three). As such, federations and leagues have prioritized the strategic growth of the game in order to take advantage of this unparalleled interest from fans. In the 2024/25 season alone, UEFA expanded the Champions League—the tournament that crowns the champion of European club soccer—from 125 to 189 matches and FIFA (the global governing body of soccer) revamped the Club World Cup from a small seven-match competition into a sixty-three-match spectacle spanning across North America.

For soccer fans, this should be the golden era of soccer, as there are now more matches and content for them to consume than ever before. However, the industry is currently in a strange position. Although the influx of rich investors and revenue generation have reached an all-time high, there are indications that fans may be losing interest in the sport to some degree. The top brass at FIFA and the major European leagues continue to highlight they have billions of viewers around the world; however, television viewership for the Premier League declined by 10 percent in 2024-25.[1] And this is just the tip of the iceberg, as top leagues around Europe have had their media rights revenues stagnate or decline in recent years.

As such, questions are now being raised by fans and the media about how the sport is being managed and controlled. Why are all the major tournaments expanding? Can the players handle playing so many games? Are rich investors ruining soccer? Why is the World Cup being held in Saudi Arabia? And most importantly, who really is in control of soccer?

Within the chapters in this book, I attempt to answer these and other important questions through an in-depth examination of the powers that control the soccer industry. Indeed, while fans are intimately familiar with their favorite players and teams, many are left wondering what happens behind the scenes and how this impacts the clubs they support. While most will know major players in the industry like Gianni Infantino who currently serves as the President of FIFA and David Beckham who owns Major League Soccer club Inter Miami CF, there are lesser-known figures like Tony Bloom, Yasir Al-Rumayyan, and Michele Kang who are all playing prominent roles in shaping the future of the sport. As such, this book provides readers with insights backed by detailed research to better understand the business side of the soccer industry.

One of the central themes throughout this book is the essential role that money and power play in soccer. Although economic power and politics have always been present within the sport, the global expansion of the game has entirely reshaped the dynamics of the industry. Where a few decades ago soccer was dominated on and off the pitch by Europeans and South Americans, the rapid expansion of the game has attracted investment from around the world. As such, business and political leaders from countries such as Qatar, Saudi Arabia, and America now wield immense influence over the sport.

This has manifested in American financiers battling one another in the French soccer leagues rather than on Wall Street, the Saudis proposing to build a stadium hundreds of feet in the sky to attract the World Cup, and Hollywood actors purchasing near-bankrupt fifth division clubs. In addition to these topics, this book covers a wide range of questions including: why did Messi transfer to Major League Soccer? Why are there so many knee injuries in women's soccer? Can lower league clubs survive the commercialization of the sport? And how are soccer clubs using analytics to improve their squads? These discussions not only reveal the figures and organizations that run soccer but also analyze the reasons and motivations for their involvement in the sport.

At the same time, while soccer may be the most accessible sport in the world, with each passing day the business side of the industry slips further under the domain of the rich and powerful. The sport that was once known for teams being integrally connected to the communities they originated from has now become one of the most exclusive clubs in the world. Perhaps the best example of this is the English Premier League—widely considered as the pinnacle of the game—whose clubs are predominantly owned by real estate moguls, private equity firms, and nation-state-backed investment groups. The Premier League is not alone in this. As is discussed in later chapters, billionaires are not only buying teams in top European leagues, but are even investing in third, fourth, and fifth-tier clubs.

Understanding how the soccer industry functions has been a lifelong passion for me, and this book is the culmination of a life spent watching, observing, and researching the sport. While attending college, I began working for a Major League Soccer club where I was able to gain first-hand experience in how professional soccer teams operate. Knowing that I wanted to continue working in soccer, I went to graduate school and focused my studies on examining the economics of sport leagues, with special focus on soccer. I am now entering my sixteenth year as a professor of sport business, where I spend my days teaching students and writing research articles about soccer.

In researching this book, I have learned more than I ever thought I would about the soccer industry and continue to love the sport despite all its issues. Likewise, I hope that it provides you, the reader, with new insights into the beautiful game and the forces that control it.

As one final note, throughout this book I will use the term "soccer" to refer to the sport. Although I prefer to use the word "football" in my everyday conversations, I must acknowledge that I am the product of two countries (Japan and America) that both call it soccer. Moreover, as there are various types of football, including the American, Canadian, and Australian versions, it will reduce the potential for confusion by using the word soccer. The term football does appear in this book but is mostly for organizations that have football in their name, such as the English Football League or Football Association.

1

Messi Mess
Why Did the World's Best Player Join MLS?

Publix—a major supermarket chain dominates the American South. On a humid summer night, a family speaking Spanish made their way through the cereal aisle. The kids excitedly dropped various colorful boxes of sugary treats into their shopping cart. A standard Sunday evening trip to the grocery store, except the unassuming man in a dark t-shirt and flip-flops pushing the cart was Lionel Messi, perhaps the greatest player in soccer history. A photo appeared on Instagram and immediately was reposted by people around the world. The word was out; Messi had arrived in Miami. On June 15, 2023, Major League Soccer (MLS) club Inter Miami CF announced they had signed Messi to a two-and-a-half-year contract, leading people to ask, how did Messi end up playing in America?

The simple answer follows the theorem laid out by Nobel Prize economist Ronald Coase—Messi signed for Miami because they are the team that valued him the most. In other words, workers, whether they are baristas, soccer players, or accountants tend to work for the employer who is willing to provide them with the most compensation. While Messi was an aging star coming toward the end of his career, his deal with MLS paid $65 million (USD) a year, plus another $70 million from outside endorsements and commercial activities.[1]

The story of Messi's move to MLS gets to the core of why teams buy and sell players and highlights the philosophical differences that exist in how teams value players. In extreme cases, these differences can lead to domination and glory for some, and utter ruin for others. And as with most soccer stories, this one begins with a young child playing with a ball.

The Beginning

Two figures stood in a field. One of them, a man in his late 30s, grabbed a ball and with the force of a slightly overweight adult, punted the ball high into the air.

"CONTROL IT!" He yelled at a young boy. The kid watched the ball arcing through the air, his blond hair damp with sweat. He quickly maneuvered his body and cushioned the ball as it sped toward the ground, settling it gently at his feet. For a boy of his age, this was not an easy feat. He was clearly gifted.

"NOT GOOD ENOUGH!" The father shouted at his son, bending down to pick the ball up. He lined up another punt, and yelled "AGAIN!" rifling the ball back into the sky.

It's 1983, four years before Lionel Messi will be born. On a field in East London, David "Ted" Beckham was putting his son David through another training session. While other families enjoyed the beautiful day, taking walks, smelling the fresh spring air, the two Beckhams repeated drills for hours to teach young David how to properly kick a ball. And young "Becks," as he will eventually be nicknamed, did learn how to hit the ball properly. As most soccer fans of my generation will tell you, he became one of the most dangerous set piece takers in the entire world.

But the story we are concerned with is not Beckham's development from a soccer prodigy into a Manchester United icon. Instead, what is of interest is Beckham's transfers between clubs, and how he started a chain reaction that would alter the future career paths of numerous soccer stars, culminating in Messi heading to Miami.

Fast forward to 2003. Manchester United were hosting Arsenal in the fifth round of the FA Cup on a sunny February day. The rivalry between the two teams was the stuff of legends. Hard tackles, amazing runs, flying fists, crazed celebrations, scrums of adult men wearing shorts pushing and screaming at each other. By all measures, this FA Cup match was a relatively tame affair. Arsenal opened the scoring with a deflected free kick that trickled into the United net while their keeper watched helplessly. The same keeper, Fabien Barthez, was left helpless again in the second half as Sylvian Wiltord slotted home cooly from close range. Two-nil to the Arsenal.

In a fit of anger, United's fiery manager Sir Alex Ferguson stormed into the dressing room and began to berate the players for their performance. Beckham was having none of it and swore at Ferguson. Incensed, Ferguson charged Beckham and kicked a pile of clothes. Out of the pile, Ole Gunnar Solskjær's boot began to spin through the air and smacked straight into David Beckham's left eyebrow. The metal stud gashed through skin, Beckham's hand instinctively shot to his eye, and he started to charge Ferguson. Other players held Beckham back, but it's too late. A line had been crossed. Paparazzi snapped a photo of Beckham with a bandage covering a bloody scar above his eye fueling speculation—Would Beckham leave United? Would Ferguson be forced to resign?

United managed to win the league title, but all was not well at the club. The boot incident, though a freak accident, was the proverbial straw that broke the camel's back. For years, Ferguson had exhibited absolute control over his team, including checking the love lives of his players. And this was the source of the friction between Ferguson and Beckham. Rather than marry a "proper" local girl, in 1999 Beckham wed Victoria Adams—better known to the rest of the world as Posh Spice. Thus, rather than the stay-at-home mom that Ferguson desired, Beckham chose an international pop-star and fashion icon who at the time was probably the second most famous English woman on the planet behind Queen Elizabeth II.

In his autobiography, aptly titled *The Boss*, Ferguson ruminated about how Beckham's marriage transformed him from a hard-working player into a celebrity who wasn't focused on soccer. Only a year into their marriage, Beckham requested to stay at home to take care of his sick infant son. The team permitted this, but when Victoria was photographed attending London Fashion Week that same night, Ferguson exploded. David was dropped from the squad for a crucial Premier League match and fined two weeks wages—the maximum amount allowed by league rules. In Ferguson's mind, Victoria should have stayed at home to care for their son so that David could train with the team and focus on winning a title. Forget that Victoria, like David, also had a demanding career performing live in front of tens of thousands of screaming fans.

So, as much was made about how a kicked boot forced Beckham into leaving United, it was not really about that one moment. The writing was on the wall from the instant the Beckhams said "I do." Indeed, there had been several years of speculation that David would leave United, with the boot simply serving as the flash point that persuaded United to sell him in the summer of 2003. United initially came to an agreement to sell Becks to Barcelona, but the deal was hijacked by Spanish rivals Real Madrid who paid €35 million to complete the transfer. Though it would not be evident for more than a decade, this moment played a critical role in the future of both Spanish clubs.

Galácticos to Galaxy

Beckham was now a part of the Galácticos, a team of superstars assembled by Real's infamous chairman Florentino Perez. Becks was not just joining one of the best teams in the world, he was now part of the most talented roster ever assembled by a single club. Where does one even start? Ronaldo, perhaps the greatest striker in history, paired with Spanish legend Raul. Midfield? Oh, just Zinedine Zidane who powered France to a World Cup title, with the attacking creativity of Luis Figo. Defense? Roberto Carlos overlapping with the most powerful shot in the game. On paper, this was not a club; they were the Avengers of world soccer.

And yet, things never really worked out on the field for the Galácticos. In Beckham's four seasons with the club, they were limited to a Spanish Super Cup and one La Liga title. While Real could afford this collection of superstars, the addition of Beckham was rather superfluous from a squad-building perspective. Beckham previously had been the undisputed right midfielder for England and United, but at Real he was in direct competition with Luis Figo who just a few years earlier had been named the best player in the world. What Madrid really needed was a more defensive player in the midfield like Claude Makélélé who they sold to Chelsea shortly after Beckham's arrival. Zidane was critical of these transfers and equated the addition of Beckham and departure of Makélélé to buying an extra layer of gold paint for a Bentley that had just lost its engine.[2]

But none of this really mattered to Florentino Perez. He had not purchased Beckham to improve the Real squad, he brought him in to sell tickets, shirts, and sponsorships. And in this aspect, Beckham was a great success, with commercial revenue for the club tripling after he moved to Madrid. As fans, we tend to value players based on their performance on the field and ability to produce wins. While these things are certainly important for teams, as more wins generally lead to an increase in revenue, teams truly value players based on the revenue they create compared to other players—or what economists call Marginal Revenue Product (MRP). In this sense, Beckham's transfer fee and presence at the club was justified in his ability to generate a greater MRP than almost any other player on the planet.

Over the next several seasons, Real Madrid became the highest grossing soccer club in the world. Despite this financial success, Perez came under intense scrutiny for his approach to running the club, with fans noting that the club seemed to be more of a marketing project than a sporting one—that Perez was more concerned with signing players based on how many shirts they sold rather than the number of goals they scored.

On February 27, 2006, Perez resigned as President of Real Madrid. Focused on rebuilding Madrid into champions, Madrid's new leadership brought in former Juventus manager Fabio Capello to helm the team for the 2006/7 season. Capello, known as much for his authoritarianism as he was for his defensive style, immediately benched Beckham and Ronaldo, essentially bringing the Galácticos era to an end.

Nine thousand kilometers away in Los Angeles, Tim Leiweke, CEO of Anschutz Entertainment Group (AEG) smelled an opportunity. As the head of AEG, Leiweke oversaw the company's vast portfolio of sport and entertainment organizations and venues, including multiple MLS clubs. And as he watched Beckham sulking on the Bench at Real, he hatched an audacious plan that would transform the sport forever.

Leiweke flew to Madrid and arranged a lunch meeting with Beckham on the very first day teams were legally allowed to talk to David about leaving Real. During the meal, the pitch was made—Beckham should come play for the Los Angeles Galaxy. By Beckham's own admission, he blew off the offer as he was focused on trying to regain his spot with Real. But behind the scenes, the Galaxy and numerous other clubs were actively negotiating with Beckham's agent. Furious at reports of Beckham potentially leaving, Real's board of directors declared Beckham would never play for the team again, and Capello dropped him from the squad.

This was the final straw; Beckham was ready to leave.

On January 11, 2007, Beckham signed a contract. The LA Galaxy officially announced that Beckham would be moving to America to become the highest paid soccer player in the entire world.

That League

When David Beckham signed with the LA Galaxy, Major League Soccer was an entirely different league than it is today. Soccer fans around the world are still quite condescending toward MLS and its quality of play, bloopers from the league are quickly shared on social media, as fans laugh at how the Americans have tarnished the beautiful game. On the other hand, the list of star players who have played for the league is an impressive collection of icons of the game. Arsenal legend Thierry Henry played five seasons for the New York Red Bulls. Zlatan Ibrahimovic, the narcissistic Swedish striker, shocked fans around the world as he scored a forty-five-yard volley in his debut for LA Galaxy. World Cup winners such as Kaka, Bastian Schweinsteiger, and Andre Pirlo all played in the league. And none of this would have been possible without Beckham and Leiweke.

Today, when a player moves to MLS, the common refrain is that they are past their prime. That they are joining a retirement league, a place where they can kick up their legs, take it easy in training, score a few goals, and make a fortune in endorsement deals from American corporations. When Beckham made the move, it was not just a retirement; it was moving to the backwaters where one would be forgotten forever.

Before Beckham's arrival, MLS imposed strict cost controls for all teams. The fear was that the league would repeat the mistakes of its predecessor, the North American Soccer League (NASL), who went broke after lavishly overspending on stars like Pele, Johan Cruyff, and Franz Beckenbauer in the 1970s and 1980s. In 1996, the league's inaugural season, MLS teams were capped at $1.2 million (USD) of salary for their entire team. To put this into context, the highest-paid player in the Premier League at the time was Newcastle United striker Alan Shearer who earned around $2.7 million a year, or more than twice what an entire MLS team was being paid.

Even with the salary cap rising to $2.1 million in 2007, it was clear that spending restrictions would prevent MLS clubs from fielding offers for top players that would rival those from European clubs. At the same time, the league and owners knew they needed to attract star players to grow. One only had to look at the success of other leagues playing in the same cities, such as the National Basketball Association (NBA), who became a global phenomenon on the backs of superstars like Michael Jordan, Kobe Bryant, and Allen Iverson. And thus, MLS was faced with a conundrum: How to pay superstar players without letting wages spiral out of control.

The answer to this wage issue came in the form of a new regulation instituted before the start of the 2007 season—the Designated Player Rule. At the time, this rule permitted every MLS team to sign one player at a salary above the established individual maximum, with only $400,000 of the salary counting toward the team's wage budget. For example, David Beckham's salary in 2007 was approximately $5.5 million, meaning that $400,000 of these wages counted toward the Galaxy's salary cap, with the remaining $5.1 million exempted from the league's salary rules. Although not a perfect solution it solved the two main concerns of being able to access superstars without causing budgets to inflate too rapidly.

And thus, Beckham was the first Designated Player (DP) signed by MLS, leading to the rule commonly being referred to as the "Beckham Rule." The door was now opened for players from around the world to consider MLS as a financial alternative to major European leagues. The Beckham Rule would also end up being the mechanism that allowed Inter Miami to offer a large enough compensation package to entice Lionel Messi to sign with them.

But we're not quite at Messi's story yet. To get there, we need to dive further into the deal that brought Beckham to America. In the five years he played for the LA Galaxy, Beckham's average salary was $6.5 million. Although a large sum of money for most of us, this was only a fraction of what many of the top soccer players were being paid in Europe. For example, Chelsea midfielder Michael Ballack was paid £121,000 per week in 2007, or around $12.5 million a year. As much as the Beckhams loved America, taking a massive pay cut to play in a league that most players considered inconsequential didn't make sense.

The reality is that the $6.5 million a year that Beckham received in salary from the LA Galaxy was just the tip of the iceberg. As CEO of AEG, Tim Leiweke knew that despite being an astronomical offer from the perspective of an MLS club, it would not be enough to convince a top star to play in the league. Instead, what Leiweke and executives at AEG and MLS did was to come up with one of the most innovative offers in soccer history.

In total, it was announced that Beckham was due to make $250 million over the span of his five-year contract, with a large portion of this coming from endorsements[3]. By partnering with corporate sponsors, MLS and AEG had put together a compensation package that made Becks the highest-paid soccer player in the world. At the same time, AEG also crafted their own deal with Victoria by becoming the promoter for the upcoming Spice Girls reunion tour[4] including fourteen nights in the O2 Arena in London, a venue where Leiweke had personally overseen the construction.

No other soccer club in the world could offer such a complete package to the couple. To Manchester United, Real Madrid, and others, David Beckham was there to kick a ball, and his wife was just someone who helped draw a little extra media attention. But to Leiweke and AEG, the Beckhams were so much more than that. Yes, David was there to help the LA Galaxy win matches and raise the profile of MLS and American soccer. But as a couple, the Beckhams were valuable assets whose celebrity status could be attached to AEG projects, venues, and other business ventures around the world.

The Clause

Major League Soccer operates using a unique business structure called a single-entity organization, a fancy business term that essentially means the league owns and oversees all its member clubs and players. An investor who is interested in purchasing an MLS club will pay money to gain the rights to operate the club, but they do not own the club. What they own is a stake in the league as a whole. The single-entity structure also means that clubs do not own the players. Rather, a player joining MLS will sign a contract with the league, and the player is then allocated to the specific team that has negotiated the deal and has first rights to the player. Thus, when Beckham signed with the LA Galaxy, he was really signing with MLS.

This single-entity structure provided Beckham with a unique opportunity that most professional sport leagues could not offer—a guaranteed path toward ownership. In negotiating the contract, Beckham's agent Simon Fuller proposed that David should be given the option to purchase his own MLS club in the future as a reward for taking the chance to play in the league. The argument was that Beckham was risking his future professional and international career by moving to LA, and thus he should be compensated for this gamble. The league, which clearly had assigned a high MRP to Beckham, agreed to the proposal and inserted a clause that Beckham could purchase an MLS franchise at the guaranteed price of $25 million once he retired. At the time, this was fair market value for an MLS franchise, as the San Jose Earthquake owners had just paid an expansion fee of $20 million to join the league in 2007.

As such, when Beckham officially announced his retirement from soccer in May of 2013, negotiations immediately began to make him an MLS owner. When Beckham signed his contract with LA in 2007, it was speculated that he was targeting New York as the location for his future franchise as he even named his son Brooklyn. However, by the time he hung up his boots, the league was already in the final stages of negotiating with the owners of the New York Yankees and Premier League club Manchester City to bring a new franchise to the city[5]. Miami was considered the next choice, and Beckham quickly assembled a team of investors including multiple telecommunications billionaires from across the globe.

In January 2018, Beckham's ownership group was officially awarded a new franchise in Miami, making them the twenty-fifth team to join the league. As agreed upon in his 2007 contract, the price tag for the franchise was $25 million, an amazing deal considering the Nashville expansion franchise had to pay $150 million to join MLS one month earlier. Now as an owner, Beckham begins to plot his own shocking transfer move.

And there is only one person in the world he wants.

The Legend

Celia called out to her grandson from the sidelines. She almost never missed training or matches, making sure that she was there to support young Leo. He was small, much smaller than the other boys his age. And even though they could easily push him around, Leo had something special. When they went to tackle him, first one, then two, then a gang of three, they found themselves missing, nutmegged, colliding with one another as the diminutive Lionel Messi dribbled past them with ease. Despite his lack of size, Messi became a member of his hometown club, Newell's Old Boys who were known for producing some of the most talented players in Argentina.

And yet, at the age of ten, Messi already faced the end of his career. Doctors diagnosed him with a deficiency in growth hormone, explaining his tiny size. His own coaches at Newell's called him a dwarf. Messi began growth hormone therapy, but the cost was too high for his family, and insurance only covers a part of what was needed. With Newell's refusing to pay for the rest of the treatment, Messi's family began to look for other options. No other club in Argentina would take a risk on the tiny boy. The last course of action to save Messi's soccer future was to hire Horacio Gaggioli as his agent in the hopes of getting a contract overseas.

Gagioli went to work, and enlisted Josep Minguella to convince Charly Rexach, the director of Barcelona's first team that they should give young Leo a trial. Minguella told Rexach that Messi could be another Maradona, and Rexach agreed to arrange a trial. How could he not? Two decades earlier, it was Minguella who brought Maradona to Barcelona[6]. Messi didn't just impress; his talent was at a different level, and Rexach wanted to sign him immediately. But the board hesitated. They didn't usually sign players from overseas at such a young age, especially ones so tiny. Leo continued to train with the Barca youth teams, but his father grew restless. Angry that his son had been left without a contract, Messi's father told his son's agents to deliver an ultimatum—sign Leo or he would go to another club … maybe even Real Madrid.

Rexach refused to let Messi leave and signed young Leo on December 14, 2000. Messi was sent to La Masia—"the farmhouse"—Barcelona's legendary youth academy. At first, his teammates thought there was something wrong with Leo. He was shy and so quiet that his teammates believed he was mute. On the field, Messi was anything but quiet. In 2002-3, his first full year with the youth team, he scored thirty-six goals in thirty games. The entire squad was full of young talent who would go on to become icons of soccer, but Messi was on a different level. Arsenal tried to sign Messi away from Barca, but he refused to leave.

Leo quickly advanced through the ranks. At sixteen, he was brought into a first team training session during an international break. The young Messi started dribbling past professionals twice his age. French soccer legend Ludovic Guily remembered how starters for Barcelona started kicking and fouling Messi to try and stop him. Instead, Messi kept getting back up, dribbling past them and scoring goals[7]. After that first training session, Ronaldinho, who was about to be named the best player in the world in 2005, declared that Messi would eclipse him someday[8].

In 2004-5, Messi was assigned to play for Barcelona B. Several members of the senior squad approached manager Frank Rijkaard and convinced him that Messi should be with the first team. Messi was promoted by Rijkaard, and the rest was history. In 2008-9, new manager Pep Guardiola gave Messi the number 10 jersey, the number worn previously by Maradona, Ronaldinho, and even Guardiola himself. Soccer fans know the rest of the story. The dominance of Messi and Barcelona for the next decade. While at Barca, Messi won ten league titles, four Champions League trophies, seven Ballon d'Or awards naming him the best player in the world. He set records for the most career goals, assists, and hat-tricks in La Liga, the top-flight of Spanish soccer.

The Cost

At the time when Real Madrid was bringing in David Beckham to boost their commercial appeal and financial resources, Barcelona was also engaged in its own attempt to build a soccer dynasty. Rather than focusing on marketing and sponsorships, Barca's emphasis was directed at player development, recruitment, and retention. Essentially, while both clubs were vying for soccer greatness, their philosophical approaches on how to achieve this were antithetical to one another. This meant that when Messi emerged as a generational talent within their own academy, Barcelona would stop at nothing to keep him. With Messi as their talisman, Barca achieved greatness, but it came at a cost.

In 2005, Messi turned eighteen and Barcelona signed him to his first professional contract that would keep him at the club until 2010. A few months later, upon realizing that Leo was one of the greatest young talents they had ever seen, the club quickly extended his deal until 2014. Generally, soccer clubs tend to sign young players to relatively short deals, as they are unwilling to make large investments on unproven talent. In this sense, Barca's move to lockdown Messi for ten years was a testament to the faith the club had in the young Argentine's abilities.

Where most players would have been happy with a ten-year contract because of the prolonged financial security it guarantees, superstars are quite the opposite. As rich clubs are willing to risk large investments to obtain their services, superstars could potentially lose value by locking themselves into a long-term contract. And thus, even though Barca were not obliged to change the terms of Messi's ten-year deal, the club clearly realized it would only be a matter of time before he became disgruntled with the contract. As such, in

2007 Barcelona negotiated a new deal with Messi to increase his base salary to €100,000 a week, or just over $7 million a year. The following year, Barcelona renegotiated to make him the club's highest-paid player and then extended his deal in 2009 to run till 2016, while also adding a €250 million release clause[9]. Barcelona appeared to have appeased the world's best player and locked him into a long-term commitment to the club.

Everything seemed to be smooth sailing, and then 2014 struck. The season was a total disaster on the pitch, Barca went trophyless, and Messi vented his anger toward coach Tata Martino to the press. Realizing that Messi was Barcelona's most valuable asset and at the pinnacle of his abilities, an internal debate began within the club as to whether Messi's €250 million release clause should be activated to sell him to another club. But selling their best player was not the Barca way, that was something the businessmen at Real would do. Instead, Barca moved quickly to placate their superstar, increasing his salary from $17 million to $27 million a year.[10]

This didn't put an end to the rumors that Barca might sell Messi. Fed up with the speculation, Barcelona President Josep Bartomeu announced in 2016 that they were currently working on a new contract and that it would make Messi a Barcelona player "forever."[11]

He couldn't have been more wrong.

Negotiations dragged on for over a year on the "forever" contract, and finally in November 2017, the club announced a new deal that would keep Messi with Barcelona until 2021.[12] The details of the contract were leaked to Spanish newspaper *El Mundo* who then published the headline "555.237.619" on January 30, 2021. The nine digits represented the amount that Barca was paying Messi in his new contract—€555,237,619 over four years,[13] or almost $170 million a year. Included in this deal was a renewal fee of €115 million and a loyalty bonus of €77 million that was paid just for signing the contract. The amount is astronomical, especially considering that Barcelona announced they were over a billion euros in debt[14] a few days earlier. *El Mundo* did not mince words, describing Leo's new deal as "pharaonic," not as a compliment of greatness, but instead comparing him to an all-mighty ruler who used an entire kingdom's resources for his own personal glory.

The Debt

How did Barcelona, one of the top revenue-generating clubs in the world, end up in such a dire financial situation? There were numerous individuals and reasons that could be blamed for the fiscal mess, but the core of it lay with the club's philosophy of signing the best players in the world. For Barca, it was not enough to just be one of the best teams in the world; fans and executives demanded winning at all costs. As such, this philosophy necessitated Barcelona to engage in an arms race against the richest clubs in Europe—competing against billionaire backed Premier League clubs like Manchester United and Chelsea to sign players. But the team that likely had the biggest impact on Barcelona's spending was archnemesis Real Madrid. Armed with the financial windfall from the David Beckham signing, Real was one of the few clubs in Europe that had both the resources and prestige to lure players away from Barca. Thus, as Madrid built another superstar team backed by booming commercial revenue, Barcelona recklessly tried to outspend them.

By the early 2010s, Barcelona's financial approach to acquiring new players was haphazard at best. The strategy seemed to simply be to identify the best player in the world and offer more money than anyone else. This was exactly what happened with Barca's signing of Brazilian prodigy Neymar in 2013, when they outbid other top clubs with an astronomical fee of £48 million for an untested teenager. The deal sparked further controversy with rumors of back-room dealing and third-party ownership leading to charges of tax fraud from the Spanish government, as well as several Barca board members taking the club to court over the misappropriation of funds. In the midst of the scandal, club President Sandro Rosell resigned and was immediately replaced by Josep Bartomeu in January 2014.

Although the Neymar controversy tarnished Barcelona's reputation to some degree, it was only a side act to the real issue that was about to plague the club—Bartomeu's presidency.

Under Bartomeu's reign, Barcelona began an unprecedented campaign of spending to attract and retain star players at the club. Since their previous Champions League title in 2015, the club spent an enormous amount on transfer and wage bills[15] trying to return to the pinnacle of European soccer. Notably, in 2017/18, the club spent €389 million to bring in Coutinho, Dembele, and Paulinho after losing Neymar, who departed to PSG for a record €222 million. To put into context how out of control Barca's spending and financial situation was, despite the record amount received from the sale of Neymar, the club only registered €32 million in profit. What is notable about this is that soccer clubs use an accounting technique called amortization, where debt is paid off over a set period. For example, if Dembele cost €145 million to purchase and his contract was for five years, then the club would distribute this amount of costs equally over this time. In other words, Dembele was on the books for about €30 million plus his wages and other compensation.

Thus, with Barcelona able to log €228 million in transfer revenue and only about €97 million in new player expenses, the club should have registered around €130 million in profit just from the sale of Neymar. The fact that Barcelona only reported €32 million in profit meant that the club would have had losses closer to €100 million if Neymar hadn't been sold. As Jaume Roures, who previously helped Barcelona with their finances stated in an interview with ESPN, if you were only able to turn a profit of €32 million after a world record sale, you would be fired in any other business.[16] All of this was indicative of a larger malaise that plagued Barcelona—financial mismanagement and overspending.

If we dive further into the club's 2017 finances, we can see the club's management even attempted to put a positive spin on their financial situation by publicizing[17] that they were the first professional sport team in history to make over $1 billion in revenue (€914 million). The club that had brought in the most revenue in history had somehow only made a profit of €32 million largely thanks to the accounting practices used by soccer clubs. The simple math reveals that Barca made about €686 million from business activities outside of player sales and had expenses of €882 million. Although this wasn't the exact number, as a soccer club's accounts are a complex dance of moving assets, debts, taxes, amortization, and other accounting procedures, it revealed that without player sales Barca was spending about €200 million more than they were earning.

Any business losing €200 million a year is not just overspending; they are on a path toward bankruptcy. And yet, despite knowing this, Barcelona's leadership continued to put out press releases talking about record revenue figures, Messi's "forever" contract, profits, whenever there were signs that the ship was beginning to sink.

Though the *El Mundo* article cast a lot of blame on Messi for the financial state of the club, Messi's yearly cost was likely around €139 million, or about 15 percent of Barca's total expenses. While this is a large amount of a club's expenses to be spent on any single player, even if Messi was sold for €250 million, it likely would not have solved the larger financial issues. The reality is that even without Messi's salary the club was still running a €60 million deficit, and would likely have spent even more money trying to replace him. Moreover, considering Messi was the club's most marketable asset, his departure would have caused a decline in revenue leading to even greater losses.

As such, Bartomeu had essentially bet the club's future on the cult of Messi without any attempt to cut spending. His only hope was that Messi would generate enough revenue to outpace the cost of running the club. In 2017/18, the club reported a debt of €157 million, which more than doubled to €488 million in 2019/20 as the club borrowed money to cover a cash flow shortage because of the shutdowns from the COVID-19 pandemic. Entering the 2020/21 season, Barca faced ballooning debt, out of control spending, and a hotly contested election for club president. And yet all of this was a backdrop to a bigger drama that was unfolding—Messi's contract was due to expire at the end of the season.

The Transfer

Despite these financial troubles, Barcelona was confident they would be able to convince Messi to sign a new deal. But there was a major roadblock. In 2013, La Liga introduced spending regulations, called Economic Control, which limited how much could be spent on players in relation to the financial resources of a club. With steep declines in revenue due to the COVID-19 pandemic, many clubs were forced to tighten their wage budgets. But for Barcelona, the past decade of overspending on players had pushed the club past the point of no return. Seeking a solution, Messi and Barcelona began negotiations, with Messi agreeing to take a 50 percent salary cut to help meet financial regulations.[18] But even with these sacrifices, Barca's wage bill was too high. On August 5, 2021, Barcelona announced that even though they had come to an agreement with Messi on the terms of a new contract, La Liga financial rules prevented them from registering him as part of their squad.[19]

Messi was leaving Barcelona.

A tearful press conference. Leo broke down, emotions swelling at the realization that after more than twenty years with Barca, he had to leave. The mute little boy who could dribble past everyone was now a sobbing bearded man in his 30s heading toward the twilight of his career. Three days later, Messi appeared in Paris where he had officially joined Paris Saint-Germain (PSG) on a two-year deal. These two years flashed by. Messi was still at the top of his game winning the Ballon d'Or in his first year with PSG, but there was friction within the team. PSG had amassed their own version of the Gálacticos with Messi, Neymar, and French superstar Kylian Mbappe, but the team crashed out in the first round of the Champions League knockout rounds two years in a row.

It was almost a carbon copy of Beckham's ending with Real. In May 2023, Messi went on a trip to promote tourism in Saudi Arabia. PSG were furious with the unauthorized trip and suspended him. Messi refused to renew his contract with PSG, and a few days later, the club announced Messi would leave at the end of the season. Halfway around the world, a businessman in America began forming a plan to bring the most popular soccer player in the world to MLS. This time it was Beckham's turn to entice a superstar to come to America.

In the decade-and-a-half since Beckham had signed with the LA Galaxy, the global soccer market had gone through significant changes. Back in 2007, MLS seemed an unlikely landing spot for one of the best players in the game, especially as the league was encumbered by strict spending regulations. Now it was the imposition of financial controls in European leagues that made MLS and other previously overlooked leagues attractive destinations, especially for aging superstars with high salaries. Thus, it seemed destined that Messi would be joining MLS, especially as he had previously stated that he wanted to live and play in America.

However, signing Messi would not be as easy as Beckham had hoped for. In the changing market order of global soccer, a new competitor emerged in the form of the Saudi Pro League. A few years earlier, one would simply have laughed at the suggestion that Messi would play in Saudi. But that changed in 2023, when Al Nassr signed Cristiano Ronaldo to a $75 million a year contract.[20] Like Beckham's MLS contract, Ronaldo's deal with Public Investment Fund backed Al Nassr also included commercial opportunities that raised his potential yearly earnings to $200 million. The Saudi Pro League had essentially stolen a page out of MLS's playbook, except the Saudi league had the backing of a sovereign wealth fund worth almost a trillion dollars.

Now they were trying to steal Messi away from MLS, with reports indicating he had been offered $1.6 billion dollars over three years.[21] From an economic perspective, the amount being offered by the Saudi Pro League was more than anyone else could offer and would allow Messi to triple his net worth in return for a few years of kicking a ball in Riyadh. But as we know, Messi turned them down and instead accepted a two-and-a-half-year deal with Inter Miami worth $150 million including bonuses and other compensation.[22] Messi's deal with MLS was only one-tenth of what Saudi had offered, so what had Becks and the league cooked up to convince him to come to America?

The basic details of Messi's contract were nothing special, with his guaranteed salary listed at $20.4 million a year.[23] Inter Miami co-owner Jorge Mas also confirmed Messi would earn around $50 to $60 million a year from a unique profit-sharing deal that had been signed with league partners Apple and Adidas.[24] What was truly exceptional about this deal was the inclusion of tech giant Apple. Where MLS had partnered with the world's largest venue company to help sign Beckham, the league now turned to the highest valued company in the world to help provide a financial offer to entice Messi. As the exclusive broadcast rights holder for all MLS matches, Apple saws Messi as an amazing opportunity to market and boost the sales of their match broadcasts. As such, Apple offered Leo a revenue-sharing deal where he would get a cut from every new paid subscriber to Apple TV's MLS package. No individual athlete in a major professional sport league had ever managed to negotiate their own individual share of broadcast revenue.[25]

Once again, MLS had produced an innovative deal to attract a global star. Factoring in these additional sources of income, Messi not only became the highest-paid athlete in MLS history but also earned more than any player in the NFL or MLB. Only four NBA players—Damian Lillard, Karl-Anthony Towns, Devin Booker, and Nikola Jokic—had higher salaries than the Argentinian.[26] Messi had already conquered the soccer world while at Barca, now he was ascending to the top of the colossus that was the North American sport industry.

And none of this would have been possible without Tim Leiweke signing David Beckham to the LA Galaxy back in 2007. Without the "David Beckham" rule allowing designated players to be signed outside of league-imposed wage restrictions there was no way that MLS would have been able to acquire Messi. It was even possible that without the special clause allowing Beckham to purchase Inter Miami, that MLS would not have been able to convince Leo that Miami was better than Riyadh. You see, the final part of Messi's contract included an ownership clause like Beckham's. That is, it was expected that once he retired, Messi would join Beckham as part of Inter Miami's ownership group—a union of Barcelona and Real Madrid superstars.

The Cycle

The sequence of events leading to Messi appearing in the cereal aisle of a Florida grocery store is quite remarkable. A small kid from Argentina moved to Europe, became a household name, watched the club he devoted himself to fall into ruin, turned down a billion dollars from Saudi Arabia, and then signed with a club owned by David Beckham.

Money was a critical factor in keeping Messi at Barcelona, and it was a vital part of Beckham's tale at Real Madrid. But the different philosophies behind these business decisions sent Barca and Real in opposite directions. A postmortem into Beckham's time at Madrid would suggest his purchase was not motivated by the need to add another attacking-minded midfielder to the squad. Real President Florentino Perez clearly considered the signing of Beckham as a strategic decision to further transform the club into a machine focused on the monetization of soccer. As much as fans may have hated this, it could very well have saved Madrid from the same fate that might await Barcelona. Before Beckham's arrival, Real earned around £90 million annually in commercial sponsorship, advertisement, and endorsement deals. By 2005, this value skyrocketed to £186 million,[27] (equal to €275 million at the time). Essentially, Beckham made Real the richest club in the world.

But it is also important to note what Real did with all that money and commercial potential after Beckham left. With its wealth of resources, Madrid was able to build a strong roster while continuing to grow revenue. Without Beckham, Madrid likely would not have had the funds to complete one of the most legendary transfer windows in history, where they purchased Cristiano Ronaldo, Kaka, Xabi Alonso, and Karim Benzema in the summer of 2009. This group, the "Second Galácticos," cost €231 million and were pivotal in delivering numerous titles, including an unprecedented three Champions League titles in a row from 2015 to 2017.

On the other hand, Barcelona's strategy was first to give Messi enough money to keep him happy, and then to pay whatever it took to provide him with a strong supporting cast. While Real was also spending large sums to constantly improve the squad, it came with the caveat that there had to be enough commercial revenue to do so. Thus, while both teams were consistently amongst the top spenders on soccer talent, Barca was clearly the worst offender with a budget of over €700 million a year compared to Madrid's €400 million.

And here again, some praise must go to Perez. This is not to say that he was a clairvoyant who foresaw the future of soccer—a world where associations and leagues would implement strict spending regulations on teams. Instead, he understood the economic reality that governs the beautiful game, a capitalistic world where eventually, it would be business metrics such as Key Performance Indicators that dictated the fortune of teams, rather than the goals they scored on the pitch. Barca, may have understood this at some level, but could not give up their focus on winning titles. The club had numerous chances to plot a new course by implementing cost controls, but the refusal to do so led them further into financial despair.

The soccer purist in me finds this reality to be incredibly depressing. A world where a well-crafted press release announcing the official tire partner is just as important as a box-to-box midfielder. A world where you tell a player who has spent most of their life with a single club, that they must leave because accountants have determined that the club didn't charge enough for tickets. Honestly, I couldn't care less if your club has a deal with Asahi Beer or Continental Tires; I want to see the dynamic ballet of soccer that excites the mind and heart. But the reality is no matter how good a center back pairing you have, if you cannot attract sponsors, balance your books, and sell tickets, your club will fail as a business. Real Madrid understood this. Barcelona didn't. In fact, one could argue that the financial gains from signing Beckham not only allowed Real to keep spending on players but also coaxed rivals Barca into overspending leading to their financial demise and Messi's departure.

Likewise, MLS executives understood that soccer was a business, and that to continue growing their fledgling league, they would need a "face" to promote the American brand of the sport. Thus, when the opportunity came to bring the man who had tripled Real Madrid's revenues, rather than be bogged down by league regulations, the LA Galaxy approached Beckham with a unique deal. Wealthy European soccer clubs could offer him more salary, stronger competition, and center stage in the world's most watched competitions. So, MLS offered Beckham a different opportunity, the chance to transcend beyond soccer stardom, and to build his own brand. A decent salary, nonstop endorsement deals, and most importantly future ownership of a club, as Vito Corleone would say, MLS had made Beckham an offer he couldn't refuse.

And it was this exact model that Beckham himself would use years later when the opportunity came to court the greatest player in the game to Miami. MLS may be disparaged for its quality of play, but from a commercial standpoint, the league has leveraged the strength of its business partners better than most other soccer leagues. For example, even though Ligue 1 sold its naming rights to McDonald's, you don't see them getting the fast-food giant involved in contract negotiations. In this sense, MLS embraced the entrepreneurial spirit of its home soil, and though it may make the beautiful game more acquisitive and materialistic, it sparked the chain of events that led first to Beckham and then Messi joining the league. Frankly, it has made MLS more relevant; people around the world now could be spotted wearing pink and black Inter Miami shirts with the name "Messi" emblazoned on the back.

As the soccer industry continues to turn toward a money-oriented consumeristic endeavor, teams and leagues will be forced to evolve their approach to managing the sport. Even Barcelona, in an attempt to escape from its fiscal nightmare, started to adopt innovative ways of generating revenue. In the aftermath of Messi leaving the club, Barca executives started leveraging their assets and partnerships to raise capital, including selling a portion of future licensing and media rights deals.[28] The problem is that Barca are now potentially mortgaging away future income to balance their books, while continuing to engage in player spending they simply can't afford.

So far, Barcelona has managed to stay afloat and remain one of the best teams in Europe, with the club hoping that renovations to their home stadium Camp Nou will provide a much-needed boost in revenue to stabilize finances starting in 2026. But as it stands today, Barca is essentially walking on a tight rope with no safety net to catch it. There is the possibility they will safely navigate their way through this mess, but even the slightest trouble could send them spiraling toward disaster.

In contrast to Barcelona's perilous future, Messi's outlook is much more secure. In addition to amassing wealth that will keep his family financially stable for generations to come, he has also found a new path for after he hangs up his boots—ownership. And who knows, in ten or fifteen years, we may see Messi repeating this cycle yet again, trying to convince Lamaine Yamal, Bukayo Saka, or Vinicius Jr. to leave Europe and play the last few years of their soccer career in America.

2

The Americans Who Are the Owners Taking Over the World's Top Clubs?

In 2005, an argument over the ownership of a horse caused several owners of Manchester United to sell their shares in the legendary soccer club to American businessman Malcom Glazer. Glazer, who made his money through investments in real estate, banks, health care, and various other industries, was no stranger to big-time sports, having purchased the Tampa Bay Buccaneers of the National Football League (NFL) a decade earlier. Despite having run a successful professional franchise in the richest sport league in the world, Malcom's desire was to expand his portfolio to include one of the world's most popular soccer clubs. In 2003, Glazer slowly began acquiring shares of the club with the ultimate goal of launching a takeover bid. As such, when relations within the club became acrimonious as manager Sir Alex Ferguson sued shareholders J. P. McManus and John Magnier over the ownership of championship racehorse Rock of Gibraltar, Glazer swooped in to purchase McManus and Magnier's shares of the club. This move gave Glazer control of about 57 percent of the shares of the club, making him the majority stakeholder and officially launching his campaign to take over one of the most decorated clubs in the world.

What followed is often seen as a cautionary tale in England of what happens if you allow rich foreign investors to take over your club, especially those "bloody yanks" with their disregard for the history and traditions of soccer. Although Glazer was rich and owned an NFL team that was worth $877 million at the time,[1] to buy out the remaining 43 percent of the club required a significant amount of capital. This purchase was completed using a leveraged buy-out of around $1 billion, which is a fancy way of saying that Glazer bought United by using the club's assets as collateral for the debt while putting in very little of his own money. Although United had been one of the top spenders in the Premier League on player transfers and salaries, the club had remained debt free for over seventy years until the Glazer takeover.[2]

The backlash from fans was severe and immediate. When the Glazer family first arrived in Manchester, they required a significant police presence to protect them from a crowd of angry supporters who had come to protest the sale of the club. At the time, there were major fears that the debt-financed takeover would either reduce United into a money printing machine for the Glazers and the hedge funds who helped finance their purchase, or that the massive debt would drive the club into administration (bankruptcy). However, concerns that Sir Alex Ferguson and critical members of the squad would leave because of the new owners were quickly subdued as United won the Premier League in the season after the Glazer takeover (2006/07) and the Champions League the year after that.

Over the next several seasons, while United's continued run of success on the field helped to significantly increase their commercial and broadcast revenue, the club's debt grew to a record high of $1.16 billion in 2010.[3] Although this debt was able to be reduced after the sale of 10 percent of the club on the New York Stock Exchange, media reports indicate that United has spent around $1.62 billion in payments related to the leveraged buy-out triggered by the Glazer's. The fans might have been able to forget about their club being encumbered with massive debt if the team had continued to perform well and win titles. However, since Ferguson's retirement in 2013, the club has gone through nine different managers, none of whom have been able to lead United to a Premier League title. Things hit rockbottom in the 2024/25 season with United finishing in fifteenth place, their worst season since the club was relegated to the second division in 1974.

Under Glazer's ownership, the club that was once the model of success on and off the field in English soccer had been transformed into a laughingstock. Because he was the first American owner in the Premier League, and since United's downfall was so heavily publicized, it set the tone for how fans across Europe would think of the incoming wave of foreign ownership groups. American owners in soccer became synonymous with debt, mismanagement, and rising prices.

At the same time, those supposedly inept Americans have also played a major role in modernizing the business side of the soccer industry. Whether it be ticket pricing systems, enhancing commercial revenue, hospitality and concessions, or enhancing the overall fan experience, these practices have come from years of refinement in the major professional sport leagues in North America. Indeed, Premier League clubs have long modeled many of their business practices based on what is being done in the NFL and National Basketball Association (NBA). In recent years, there has also been an exodus of American sports business executives heading across the pond as their expertise and services are now highly in demand from European soccer clubs who want to refine their business strategies and operations.

In the following, I will profile four Americans who own European soccer clubs. This group represents the good, the bad, and the ugly of American involvement in the sport. They include a disgraced baseball team owner, a visionary leader, a financier who tries to fix problems with money, and a tech guru who is attempting to challenge oil barons and conglomerates at their own game. This motley crew of characters has come to operate some of the most powerful clubs in soccer and is influencing how teams and leagues do business. Naturally, this also has had an impact on the development of the sport across the world.

Frank McCourt

If there was a list of people who shouldn't be allowed to own a sport franchise, Frank McCourt should probably be at the top of that list. McCourt made his money through real estate development, mostly within the Boston area. As he amassed his fortune, McCourt tried to purchase his hometown Boston Red Sox of Major League Baseball (MLB) in 2002, with the aim to move them out of historic Fenway Park and into a new stadium that would be built on land he was developing on the waterfront.[4] When this takeover bid failed, McCourt set his sights on the Los Angeles Dodgers, who at the time were one of the most inept teams in baseball.

In 2004, McCourt purchased the Dodgers from Rupert Murdoch's News Corp for $430 million, a deal which included a significant amount of real estate around Dodger Stadium and training facilities in Florida.[5] As a real estate developer, this purchase seemed like a perfect fit for McCourt, as he would not only take control of a professional sport franchise in America's second-largest market, but he would also be able to further monetize the properties around the stadium for his financial gain.

There was one problem in all of this. While McCourt was rich, he did not have the $430 million needed to purchase the Dodgers just lying around. With much of his assets tied up in real estate, McCourt used a leveraged buy-out to finance this deal, just like how the Glazers purchased Manchester United. Although questions were raised about the amount of debt the Dodgers would be taking on as part of this deal, the sale received final approval after a positive vote from MLB owners.

After the purchase of the Dodgers was completed, McCourt moved his company's quarters to Los Angeles, to develop the newly acquired real estate around Dodgers stadium. Initial plans were to use the existing land to build an NFL stadium with the goal of turning the area into a major sport and entertainment complex. However, due to outside influence and political pressure, these plans were scraped and the parking lots around the stadium were never turned into commercial properties.[6] The lack of revenue from these heavily leveraged properties likely increased the financial stress that both McCourt and the Dodgers were under. Things got worse for McCourt in 2009, as he divorced his wife who also served as the Chief Executive Officer (CEO) of the Dodgers. The divorce, which was considered the most expensive in California history, resulted in McCourt paying his ex-wife Jamie $130 million to give up her share of the Dodgers, as well as $20 million in legal fees.[7]

However, there was bigger drama brewing.

Although the Dodgers improved greatly on the field with McCourt in charge, including four playoff appearances in his first six years of owning the team, the purchase of players combined with the manner in which the team had been acquired through a leveraged buy-out was straining their finances. Short on money, McCourt attempted to sign a new local television deal with Fox Broadcasting in April 2011 that would pay around $2.5 billion over 20 years.[8] Included in the deal was a $30 million loan that would be provided to the Dodgers to help them make payroll.

With both McCourt and the Dodgers in severe financial trouble, MLB Commissioner Bud Selig announced that the league would be taking control of the team and their business operations as of April 20th, 2011. To make matters worse, the Internal Revenue Service announced they were also opening an investigation into the Dodgers and McCourt amidst allegations that both Frank and his ex-wife had effectively treated the team like their own personal ATM, using the club's money for shopping trips and personal expenses.[9]

McCourt immediately released a statement noting that the Dodgers were in compliance with the financial rules set out by MLB. However, the Dodgers were effectively bankrupt at this point and were only able to make payroll in June by borrowing money from friends of McCourt. It soon became clear that the only way the Dodgers would make their July payroll was through the approval of the television contract with Fox, which included the $30 million payroll loan. As such, when Bud Selig rejected the contract in late June, it effectively rendered both the Dodgers and Frank McCourt bankrupt.

In a logical world, this would be the part of the story where McCourt goes bankrupt, sells the Dodgers, and moves back to Boston to resume his previous life as a successful real estate developer. The unfortunate reality is that, rather than being punished for his incompetent management of the Dodgers, in the end, he was actually rewarded for his failures. After fighting a series of court battles against MLB, McCourt finally acquiesced in November 2011, issuing a joint statement with the league that he had agreed to sell the Dodgers. Following a brief bidding war, the Dodgers were sold to a consortium led by former NBA superstar Magic Johnson and Guggenheim Partners for just over $2 billion. This made it the highest amount a professional sport franchise had ever been sold for, surpassing the previous record of $1.5 billion that the Glazers paid for Manchester United.

Somehow, McCourt had driven one of the most popular teams in America into financial insolvency and rather than being flogged in the streets as punishment, he was instead rewarded by becoming an accidental billionaire. In any other industry, including real estate where McCourt had made his original fortune, such mishandling of a company would lead to ruin. But in professional sport, because of the scarcity of franchises and their rapidly increasing valuations, you can make a total mess of things and still walk away as one of the richest people in the world.

At the time, this seemed to be the end of Frank McCourt's foray into ownership of a professional sport team.

On August 29, 2016, just four years after he had to sell the Dodgers in disgrace, it was announced that McCourt had purchased renowned French soccer club Olympique de Marseille—also known as OM—for the paltry sum of $47 million.[10] What was most stunning about this, was that a man who was known for being terrible at managing professional sport teams in America, had been allowed to purchase one of the most famous clubs in Europe. At the time, American investment in soccer was booming, with most of it being directed toward clubs in England. Thus, while there was hesitation over what an American owners could potentially do to a club, Ligue 1—the French first division—and French Football authorities also did not want to let any investments slip away to rival leagues in other countries.

Indeed, where McCourt had been virtually penniless near the end of his reign with the Dodgers, his newly found wealth instantly made him one of the richest owners in Ligue 1, where expectations were that he would open his checkbook to help return Marseille to glory. Despite having previously been owned by billionaire Margarita Louis-Dreyfus, OM was in severe financial trouble. With Louis-Dreyfus having shown little to no interest in using her own money to strengthen the team, Marseille floundered on the pitch, finishing thirteenth in the 2015/16 season.

As such, when McCourt purchased the club, and then promised a cash influx of $200 million over the next four years,[11] it was precisely the news that Marseille fans had been waiting to hear. McCourt kept his word, and in the following transfer windows purchased superstar Dimitri Payet who had previously been sold off to West Ham United of the Premier League to help OM pay off its debts. Under McCourt's ownership, Marseille dramatically improved their form, finishing in fourth place in his first season, and making it to the Europa League final the following year. Although the media has expressed skepticism and even some sarcasm over McCourt's attempts to rebuild Marseille,[12] he has been rather successful at doing it.

This is not to say his ownership has been all roses. While Marseille's revenue increased after McCourt's takeover, the club still found themselves in financial trouble. Notably, the cash influx provided by McCourt was not enough to cover spending on player transfers and salaries. At the time, Marseille's goal was to make it into Champions League which guaranteed at least €30 million in prize money to participants. However, having failed to qualify for the competition for three years in a row, the club's wage bill outpaced the revenue being brought in. As such, when OM's yearly losses rose to €91 million in 2019, the club was charged with violating the European Financial Fair Play (FFP) rules put into place to control club spending.[13] After being found guilty of FFP breaches in 2020, Marseille was fined €3 million and had 15 percent of its revenue from European competitions stripped for the following two seasons.[14]

Despite this bad news, things were looking up for Marseille as they finally secured their return to the Champions League in 2020. McCourt's gamble was paying off.

Indeed, perhaps the description that best encapsulates McCourt's approach to running professional sport teams is that he is a gambler. With the Dodgers, he heavily leveraged the team with the belief that real estate development and a new television deal would allow him to build one of the most powerful sport teams in America. When none of these came to fruition, he lost his seat at the table and was sent packing. Now with Marseille, McCourt is taking a new approach by gambling that investment in players will make the team good enough to consistently qualify for Champions League and generate enough revenue to stabilize the clubs' finances. This is quite the risk, as numerous teams have attempted this and failed, including OM's rivals Lyon who faced potential relegation because of financial issues caused by poor on-field performance and dwindling television revenue.[15]

So far, McCourt's ownership of Olympique de Marseille seems to have been a success. While his drive to build a competitive team has resulted in the club spending beyond its means, McCourt has managed to avoid the same financial blunders he made with the Dodgers. However, McCourt is still gambling with the club's future. Although Marseille managed to qualify for the 2025/26 Champions League which will help to improve the club's financial situation, there is no guarantee that they will continue to do so. Indeed, Marseille's sporting director Medhi Benatia confessed in a press conference that the club would be facing a "disaster" if they had not qualified for the Champions League.

McCourt was given a rare second chance as an owner in professional sport, and so far, has demonstrated that he can effectively lead a professional sport team. However, it is quite clear that the margins he is operating within are rather thin. Though he has been able to rehabilitate his image as one of the most incompetent owners in the history of sport, it does not guarantee that Marseille will continue to sustain their success. Indeed, as Ligue 1 television revenues continue to plummet, OM's survival will become more and more dependent on Champions League qualification. If they were to slip up for a few seasons, it could send the club spiraling toward the same fate as McCourt's Dodgers.

Michele Kang

Yongmee Michele Kang, more commonly referred to as Michele Kang, may be the most important person in women's soccer. She currently serves as the majority owner of the Washington Spirit of the National Women's Soccer League (NWSL), OL Lyonnes of the French Premiere League, and the London

City Lionesses of the Women's Super League (WSL). For those not initiated in women's soccer, OL Lyonnes is the most dominant club in men's or women's soccer over the last twenty years, having won their league in eighteen of the last nineteen seasons, as well as eight UEFA Women's Champions League (UWCL) titles during this time. Kang controls one of the most impressive and decorated portfolios of soccer clubs in the world and has played a critical role in the expansion of the women's game.

And yet, despite owning some of the most important soccer clubs in the world, Kang has been involved in professional soccer for only the last five years. As she admitted, she did not even know who Lionel Messi was when she first started paying attention to the beautiful game.[16] Nevertheless, she has risen to become the matriarch of women's professional soccer and has proven to be a true visionary in understanding and building the sport's potential.

Michele Kang was born in Seoul, South Korea. Despite being the top of her class in business administration at Sogang University, Kang quickly came to realize that even if she was a star in the classroom, there were limited career opportunities for her as a woman in Korea at the time.[17] As such, she made the decision to move to America, where she first got a degree in economics from the University of Chicago, and then a master's in public and private management from Yale University.[18]

With her elite education, Kang quickly rose through the ranks of some of the world's most powerful corporations. After serving as a partner at Ernst & Young, one of the top four accounting firms in the world, she moved to aerospace and defense contractor Northrop Grumman, where she worked her way up to becoming the vice president of the company's Health & Science Solutions division.[19] Ever the entrepreneur, Kang left Northrop Grumman in 2008 to focus on the creation of her own company Cognosante, which specialized in technological solutions for healthcare and governmental organizations.[20] Under Kang's leadership, Cognosante was able to secure more than $300 million a year in government contracts, eventually leading to its acquisition by tech giant Accenture in 2024 for approximately $1 billion.[21] In 2025, Forbes estimated Kang's net worth at over $1 billion, making her one of only thirty-eight women in America who could call themselves a self-made billionaire.

So, the question is, how did this Ivy League educated billionaire entrepreneur get involved in a sport she barely knew anything about? In what is one of the most fortunate moments in the history of women's soccer, US Senator Tom Daschle—who also happens to be on the board of Cognosante[22]—invited Kang to attend the official ceremony at Capitol Hill celebrating the US Women's National Team (USWNT) winning the 2019 FIFA Women's World Cup. In attending this celebration, Kang was able to see firsthand the importance of women's soccer and was also introduced to Steve Baldwin who was the managing partner of the Washington Spirit. Despite being based in the Washington DC area, Kang had been unaware that there was a local franchise until this fortuitous meeting.

Following this event, Baldwin arranged Kang to have dinner with Washington Spirit players Aubrey Kingsbury and Andi Sullivan, where the trio discussed the soccer club, as well as Kang's passion in helping support and develop women leaders in the community.[23] And thus, it was of no surprise when the Washington Spirit announced at the end of 2020 that Michele Kang had joined the ownership group,[24] purchasing a 35 percent stake in the team with Baldwin remaining as the primary decision-maker for the club.[25] It seemed a match made in heaven. A self-made businesswoman using her resources to help support other women to pursue their dreams through soccer and develop into rolemodels for the entire country.

However, the honeymoon quickly came to an end in the following season. In early August 2021, the *Washington Post* published a story with numerous players alleging Spirit manager Richie Burke had verbally and emotionally abused them, including some who had left the Spirit because of Burke's conduct.[26] Although Burke stepped down as coach, the NWSL launched an investigation into the Spirit and several other clubs amidst widespread allegations of emotional abuse and sexual misconduct across the league.[27] This was followed up by multiple reports alleging misconduct on the part of Baldwin, who was accused of running the Washington Spirit as a "boys club" where he had created a hostile work environment for women.[28] Moreover, Baldwin was also accused of enabling Burke's conduct as well as excluding Michele Kang from participating in operations or decision-making within the club.[29]

This was not the first time in her life that Kang had faced bullying, discrimination, and exclusion for simply being a woman. Where before she had to take a loan to be able to escape from such chauvinism, Kang now had hundreds of millions of dollars of assets to fight back with. In September, Kang published an open letter to the investors and fans of the Washington Spirit highlighting her attempts to change the club's toxic culture, ending with a call for Steve Baldwin to sell his shares of the team to her.[30] Kang's letter was followed up by statements from supporters and the players, all of whom asked Baldwin to put an end to this saga and sell the team to Michele Kang.[31]

Rather than simply relinquish his shares of the club, Baldwin instead responded his own letter to investors in the Washington Spirit, where he repeatedly called Kang a liar and said that she had conducted secret meetings with players and staff to stage a coup against him.[32] While all of this was happening, Baldwin was conducting exclusive negotiations to sell the team to Los Angeles Dodgers owner Todd Boehly for $25 million. Refusing to give in, Kang immediately placed a $35 million bid for the Spirit, which would make it the highest amount ever paid for an NWSL club.

However, things had become personal for Baldwin, and rather than accept more money, he continued to push for a deal with Boehly. In response to this, several investors in the Spirit threatened legal action if Baldwin refused to accept Kang's higher bid of $35 million.[33] With Baldwin still refusing to relinquish the club, Kang completed a business masterstroke by asking many of the investors to convert the debt the Spirit owed them into equity, and to either sell her those shares or to vote in favor of her bid for the club.[34] After battling for over a year, Baldwin eventually relented in the spring of 2022, with both Baldwin and Bill Lynch selling their shares to Kang.[35]

Michele Kang was now the controlling partner of the Washington Spirit, making her the first female majority owner of any NWSL club.

Following her purchase of the Washington Spirit, Kang set sights on expanding her portfolio of women's soccer clubs, with her next target being the superpower of women's soccer Olympique Lyonnais Feminin, who recently were renamed OL Lyonnes. On May 17th, 2023, it was announced that OL Groupe, recently purchased by American businessman John Textor, had agreed to sell 52 percent of OL Feminin to Kang for around $28 million.[36]

As part of this deal, Kang was named to the OL Groupe's board of directors, and the club also initiated the sale of their NWSL franchise in Seattle to avoid conflicts of interest due to Kang's ownership of the Washington Spirit.

Fresh from the purchase of OL Feminin, Kang also bought newly formed London City Lionesses at the end of 2023. Although the Lionesses played in the Women's Championship, the second division of women's professional soccer in England, with Kang's backing, the club was able to bring in highly talented players and earn promotion to the top-flight Women's Super League in 2025. Kang herself attended the final match in which the Lionesses sealed their promotion, becoming the first independent club not affiliated with a men's club to reach the top division of English women's soccer.

After the purchase of these three clubs, Michele Kang had one more major announcement. In Paris during the 2024 Olympics, she announced the launch of her newest company Kynisca, which would serve as the parent organization that would oversee all the women's soccer teams that she owned. Moreover, Kynisca wouldn't just simply be a holding company for Kang's portfolio of soccer teams, but also include a $50 million investment to help improve training and sports science for women athletes.[37] Considering that women are six times more likely than men to tear their Anterior Cruciate Ligaments, Kang's investment is a critical step forward in helping to solve this injury crisis and to further build best practices for women's soccer.

In just five years, Michele Kang had built a women's soccer empire. Although all her clubs have won titles under her ownership, Kang's vision is not just about hunting for glory or even profit. Instead, it is an empire that is dedicated to using Kang's own resources to continue developing women's soccer on and off the field, while also focusing on some of the most critical issues within women's sport. In a day and age when every club owner calls themselves a philanthropist and brags about what they give back to the community, most of them pale in comparison to what Kang is doing for women's soccer players around the world.

Moreover, Michele Kang may be one of the soccer industry's great visionaries. She has shown that women's soccer, which has been devalued and mocked through much of its history, can thrive independently of men's clubs with proper investment and leadership. Kang has even made the model of multi-club ownership palatable with the creation of Kynisca. Rather than the typical focus displayed by organizations like City Football Group who seem hellbent on monopolizing talent and dominating soccer, Kang's has reinvented this model into an organization that is dedicated to further promoting women's soccer and protecting the players.

Michele Kang may not have been in the soccer industry for very long, but she is probably one of the best owners in the sport.

Todd Boehly

It is impossible to write a chapter about the influence of Americans on the soccer industry without including Todd Boehly. Boehly has already appeared twice in this chapter, once as the president of Guggenheim Partners who provided the majority of the financing to purchase the Los Angeles Dodgers for $2.1 billion from Frank McCourt, and again as the Dodgers owner to whom Steve Baldwin tried to sell the Washington Spirit.

So, who exactly is Todd Boehly? This was a question many Dodgers fans were asking when news broke that Guggenheim Partners, led by Boehly, had purchased their team.[38] After graduating from college with a degree in finance, Boehly moved to London on the advice of a professor who said it was the financial center of the world.[39] After studying at the London School of Economics, Boehly went on to work for a series of prominent financial institutions including Citibank and Credit Suisse. In 2001, Boehly joined Guggenheim Partners, a Chicago-based investment firm that also specialized in financial advising for its clients across a wide number of industries.[40] At Guggenheim Partners, Boehly helped build the company's portfolio of credit investments—basically a fancy way of saying they loaned money to major corporations.

When it was announced that Frank McCourt was selling the Dodgers, Boehly and Mark Walter—the controlling partner of Guggenheim Partners—formed a consortium of investors including Magic Johnson, American entertainment executive Peter Gruber, and others. With this wealth of financial resources, the consortium was able to offer a record $2.15 billion for the Dodgers, beating out rival bids from Arsenal owner Stan Kroenke and hedge fund manager Steve Cohen who would eventually go on to buy the New York Mets baseball team.

Although Boehly was serving as president of Guggenheim Partners, he was heavily invested in the operation of the Dodgers, helping the club to partner with Time Warner Cable to create their own regional sports network.[41] Rather than sell away the television rights as Frank McCourt had tried to do, Boehly was trying to extract as much value from the Dodgers various revenue sources. The primary reason for this was not to maximize profits from the baseball team but instead was rather to finance the wave of spending the Dodgers were about to embark on.

For decades, the New York Yankees held the title of the biggest spenders in professional baseball, assembling rosters full of pricey superstars. While this meant the team typically did not turn a profit, these financial losses were purposeful in nature. Rather than focus on short-term earnings, the team's infamous owner George Steinbrenner outspent all the other teams to ensure that the Yankees were the most watched team in America, whether fans were doing so because they loved them or hated them. This strategy helped to skyrocket the value of the Yankees, while also making Steinbrenner rich through affiliated assets such as the team's television network.

With the Dodgers, Boehly copied this model established by the Yankees, but did so on steroids. In the first four years of Guggenheim's ownership of the Dodgers, the team spent around $1 billion on player salaries resulting in the league demanding the team cut salaries.[42] Although the team complied to some extent, the Dodgers are consistently one of the top spenders in professional baseball. As such, since Boehly and his consortium took over the Dodgers, the team has made the playoffs in every season, including four National League championships and two World Series titles.

After leaving Guggenheim Partners in 2015, Boehly founded his own holding company, Eldridge Industries that invests in everything from technological innovation to television studios.[43] Having spent time in London, and with an interest in further expanding his collection of professional sport teams, Boehly set focus on joining the exclusive club of Premier League owners. In 2019, Boehly attempted to purchase Chelsea soccer club for the eye-opening sum of $3 billion.[44] This bid was rejected by Russian oligarch Roman Abramovich who owned the club. However, when Russia invaded Ukraine on February 24, 2022, Abramovich and all his assets were quickly sanctioned by the UK government, as Abramovich was shown to have close ties to Russian President Vladimir Putin.[45]

With Chelsea included in the list of sanctions, the club effectively had to shut down all its business. Although the club was allowed to continue playing its scheduled matches, it was no longer able to complete any new financial transactions, including the sales of merchandise and tickets. The only people who were allowed to watch Chelsea in-person for the rest of that season were those who had already purchased tickets. With their commercial activities shut down for the season, and sponsors such as telecommunications firm Three cutting ties with the club,[46] Chelsea were put in a tough financial situation resulting in losses of around $162 million for the 2021/22 season.[47]

Having been put under sanctions, Abramovich released a statement that because of the governmental restrictions he intended to sell Chelsea, as he believed it would be in the best interest of the club and its employees.[48] Boehly wasted no time in responding to this news, forming another ownership consortium with Mark Walter with the intention of purchasing Chelsea. Moreover, Boehly was also able to attract Clearwater Capital, a private equity firm that currently manages more than $80 billion in assets, to the ownership group. In May, Boehly's consortium came to an agreement with Abramovich to pay roughly $5.7 billion to acquire Chelsea FC.[49]

Boehly was named as the chair of Chelsea FC, as well as the interim sporting director allowing Boehly to instill his philosophy on how the club should operate at all levels. Naturally, as he had done with the Dodgers, the first order of business was to entirely revamp the squad, including the purchases of Raheem Sterling, Marc Cucurella, Enzo Fernandez, Mykhailo Mudryk, and many others within the first season. In total, Chelsea brought in twenty new players across the summer and winter transfer windows, spending over $1 billion on their transfer fees.[50] As such, it was of little surprise when Chelsea posted $123 million in losses after their first season. Though this unchecked spending was heavily criticized in the media, Boehly probably didn't even bat an eyelid as he previously had lost $200 million in a season with the Dodgers.

However, despite the spending spree on soccer talent, Chelsea was in shambles on the field. After a rocky start to their domestic and Champions League campaigns, the club fired German manager Thomas Tuchel only a month into the season. Tuchel was promptly replaced by Brighton and Hove Albion manager Graham Potter, who was sacked in April after the club fell into the bottom half of the table. After a four-day stint with Bruno Saltor serving as interim manager, Chelsea hired back former club captain Frank Lampard to serve as the interim for the rest of the season. After spending a billion dollars purchasing players and having four different managers in charge of the club, Chelsea finished in twelfth place, with pundits lampooning how toothless and ineffective the club was in their first season under Boehly's ownership.[51]

Perhaps the biggest impact Boehly has had on professional soccer is the financial strategy he has used in managing Chelsea. Boehly is certainly not the first owner to spend wildly on players to try and build a super team. In fact, Chelsea's previous owner Roman Abramovich was notorious for this practice, having built some of the most successful teams in Premier League history through large cash influxes to the club.[52] Instead, Boehly's impact has been through his manipulation of the financial regulations that govern clubs.

After owners such as Abramovich or City Football Group started to spend large sums of money on player transfers and wages, there was concern that other clubs would try to engage in an arms race with these owners. The problem here is that while City Football Group is backed by the Abu Dhabi royal family and has access to virtually unlimited wealth, most other soccer clubs do not have such wealthy patrons to help stabilize their finances. As such, having clubs with relatively poorer owners engaging in a spending war with these powerful clubs would likely result in significant financial stress, potentially even leading to bankruptcy. Because of this, both UEFA and numerous leagues across Europe have created Financial Fair Play regulations that govern how much clubs are allowed to spend in relation to their revenue.

The Premier League has its own standards called Profit and Sustainability Rules (PSR), which stipulate clubs are only allowed to have £15 million pounds in losses over a three-year period, with an additional £30 million per year allowed if the money comes directly from investments made by the owners.[53] Based on these rules, Chelsea's first year under Boehly should have put them in violation of PSR, as the club had around £90 million in losses in 2022/23. Add to that the £121 million in losses from the previous season because of sanctions, and the massive spending on player transfers and salaries and it seemed obvious that Chelsea was in violation of PSR.[54]

However, this is where Boehly began to use his financial tricks—some may call it deception while others would call it wizardry—to avoid violating PSR. Specifically, Boehly used a commonly accepted accounting practice called amortization to help him reduce the yearly cost of the enormous amount Chelsea was spending on players. How amortization works in soccer is that when a player is purchased and signed to a contract, the value of that contract is split equally amongst the length of the contract. So, if a player costs a team $20 million over four years, then the club will log that cost as $5 million a year for the next four years.

Realizing that he could spread the cost of player purchases over the life of a contract, Chelsea began to sign players to abnormally long deals. Where the typical Premier League contract is usually three to five years in length, when Chelsea paid a record £107 million for midfielder Enzo Fernandez in 2023, they signed him to an eight-and-a-half-year deal.[55] That is, where a typical contract would have Enzo's transfer cost the team somewhere between £21 and £27 million a year, by dividing it over 8.5 years, they effectively cut the yearly cost in half to just under £12 million. By 2024, Chelsea players had a stunning 191 cumulative years remaining in their contracts, compared to the next closest team Tottenham who had just ninety-seven collective years.[56]

What is important to note about this use of amortization is that Boehly did not invent it, nor was he the first one to discover it. Instead, he was the one to weaponize it. This shouldn't be surprising considering his background in the hyper-competitive world of finance where small margins can mean the difference between success and failure. Nevertheless, while the practice was not illegal, other owners and league officials saw it as a form of financial doping. As such, in 2024, Premier League clubs voted to close this loophole by limiting amortization to five years. Indeed, Chelsea were able to strengthen their squad while avoiding PSR charge, while clubs that spent significantly less on players like Leicester City and Everton received point deductions for financial infractions.[57]

After the amortization loophole was closed, Chelsea once again faced potential financial issues as they looked for ways to continue improving their squad while avoiding PSR charges. Unable to spread player costs over a long period of time, Boehly knew that the only way to be able to spend money was for the club to generate more revenue. Of course, this is easier said than done, especially considering clubs like Chelsea have already maximized their sponsorship, gameday (attendance and concessions), merchandise, and television revenues.

Naturally, Boehly found another loophole.

To raise more revenue, Chelsea decided to sell two hotels that the club owned right next to their home ground Stamford Bridge for £76.5 million. The buyers for these hotels? Why none other than Blueco, the team's ownership consortium. The sale of these hotels was critical, as it reduced Chelsea's 2024 losses from £166 million to approximately £90 million, once again helping the club escape scrutiny under the PSR rules.[58] Other clubs were unhappy that Chelsea was allowed to essentially sell their hotel back to themselves, especially as neither the club nor the Premier League could provide an assessment of whether the hotels were actually worth the amount being paid for them.[59]

Even after selling the hotels to themselves, Chelsea still had issues with PSR, as the rules stipulate that a club can only have £105 million in losses over a three-year period. As such, after logging a loss of £90 million in 2024, the club needed an influx of revenue that would make it profitable. The problem was that Chelsea had not been profitable for years, as the growth in their wage bill constantly outpaced any increase in revenues. Unable to make any significant cuts to their expenses, Chelsea was once again needed to sell another asset, but this time they needed something bigger than two hotels.

The "something bigger" was Chelsea Women's Football Club, one of the strongest women's soccer teams in all of Europe. Where the Chelsea men had been pitiful on the pitch, the Chelsea women have won the last six WSL titles and have reached the semifinals of the UWCL three years in a row before being knocked out by Barcelona Feminin. This success coupled with the growing popularity of women's soccer allowed Chelsea to value their women's team at

£200 million when it was sold to Boehly's ownership consortium. Although other owners and the media cried foul, the Premier League once again approved the transaction, allowing Chelsea to report a record profit of £128 million.[60] If we consider this from the opposite direction, without the sale of the women's club, Chelsea would have had £72 million in losses and would have been in violation of PSR rules.

After a disastrous first season under Boehly's ownership, Chelsea have improved, partly due to the platoon of star players they have been able to purchase through manipulating financial regulations. The team finished fourth in 2024/25, qualifying them for the Champions League and providing a much-needed revenue boost. However, even though Boehly has helped Chelsea to dodge PSR regulations, the revenue from selling the women's team was never approved by UEFA. As such, while Chelsea avoided being punished by their league, they likely will receive a hefty financial penalty as this is their first FFP violation.[61]

Some describe Todd Boehly as a mastermind who has used his cunning to make a mockery of poorly constructed financial regulations. I would argue that most finance professors could come up with similar solutions, as amortization and selling of assets are basic concepts that are covered in intro level classes. All of that said, Boehly has stood out precisely because he is the first one who has tested the financial fair play rules with such vigor. Whether you hate him or like him, it is impossible to deny that as an owner Boehly has pushed the limits to restore Chelsea to their former glory. Moreover, he has forced the owners and administrators of the most popular sport league in the world to rethink how they run their soccer clubs. While there is clear animosity toward how Boehly has conducted business, the other owners have shown no interest in further regulating the loopholes that he exploited. Indeed, those owners likely want to use it for themselves in the future to avoid PSR regulations, as Aston Villa and Everton have followed suit in selling their women's clubs back to their ownership to help avoid PSR charges.

Chelsea looks to be in ascendancy under Boehly, and if they can follow the same trajectory as the Boehly's Dodgers, they could reemerge as one of the dominant powers in Europe. Having also been crowned as the 2025 Club World Champions, the club has gained another massive financial boost that should allow them to continue building the squad. And if that doesn't work, Boehly will surely find another asset he can sell back to himself to help balance the books.

John Textor

Until recently, most soccer fans had no idea who John Textor is. Textor, who may have the strangest path to becoming a Premier League owner, is a former freestyle skateboarder who competed as part of the prestigious SIMS Skateboard team in the 1970s.[62] After sustaining a head injury while competing, Textor retired from skateboarding to focus on building a business around his passion for technology.[63] After founding Wyndcrest Partners, Textor set about acquiring numerous businesses in the tech and entertainment industry during the peak of the dot.com bubble in the late 1990s and early 2000s. Textor was especially adept at purchasing struggling companies, building them back up, and taking the gains from these companies and investing them in other struggling companies. In this way, Wyndcrest Partners helped notable internet and tech startups such as Art Technology Group, BabyUniverse, and Virtual Bank.[64]

However, being so heavily invested in tech startups also meant that Textor's business ventures have not always been successful. Textor's most notable failure came after teaming up with legendary film director Michael Bay to purchase Digital Domain in 2006.[65] Digital Domain was created by film director James Cameron to develop the special effects for his blockbuster film *Titanic*. Following the success of *Titanic*, Digital Domain became one of the most in demand special effects companies and won an Academy Award for their digital effects in the 2009 film *The Curious Case of Benjamin Button*, as well as producing the science fiction film *Ender's Game* in 2013. Continuing to push the envelope of technological innovation in entertainment, Digital Domain started experimenting with hologram technology, including developing a hologram of deceased rapper Tupac Shakur to perform at the 2012 Coachella music festival.[66] Despite a sudden boom in creating holograms of deceased musicians, Digital Domain declared bankruptcy just three months after the Tupac performance.

After the collapse of Digital Domain, the State of Florida alleged that Textor had defrauded the government and launched an $82 million lawsuit against him.[67] Textor was eventually cleared of any wrongdoing after it was found that investors had driven the company into insolvency, and the courts ruled that Textor be paid $8.5 million in damages as well as be awarded the rights to the technology from Digital Domain. In perhaps one of the biggest examples of taking lemons and making them into lemonade, Textor took the assets from his failed business and launched a new tech startup called FaceBank which specialized in the development of digital human likenesses.[68]

In 2019, using FaceBank's status as a publicly traded company, Textor began the process of acquiring FuboTV, an over-the-top sport streaming service—one that directly delivers content to customers rather than through an intermediary. In its early days, the company described itself as the "Netflix of soccer," allowing consumers to stream various matches from around the world without having to buy numerous cable subscriptions.[69] At the time, there was a growing demand to watch soccer, and FuboTV was focused on being the major disruptor in this market. As such, after completing a reverse merger with FaceBank,[70] FuboTV became a public company, with its value tripling in its first year to around $6 billion.[71] After FuboTV went public in 2020, Textor resigned from his position as Executive Chairman, choosing to focus on his next big investment project—soccer clubs.

At the beginning of the 2021/22 season, Textor purchased a 40 percent stake in Crystal Palace Football Club for around $118 million. The choice of Crystal Palace perfectly fits with Textor's history of strategically investing in struggling companies. At the time of the acquisition, Crystal Palace never finished in the top half of the Premier League table and had been relegated four times to the second division. In other words, they were the closest thing a perennial Premier League club could be to a distressed asset. A few months later, Textor followed up the investment in Crystal Palace by purchasing 90 percent of Botafogo of the Brazilian top-flight, and 80 percent of RWD Molenbeek (now RWDM Brussels) of the Belgium second division.

In November 2022, Textor's investments in these three clubs were all transferred into the newly formed Eagle Football Holdings. By putting all his teams under a single holding company, Textor joined the likes of City Football

Group, Qatar Sports Investments (QSI), and Red Bull GmbH as multi-club owners. Textor further expanded his investments the following month by increasing Eagle Football's stake in French club Olympique Lyonnais to around 78 percent.[72]

Although Textor had joined the ranks of oil-funded investment groups and multinational corporations in purchasing multiple soccer clubs, he clearly did not agree with how these organizations did business. In an interview given to the BBC in 2024, Textor ripped into the way the soccer industry operates, especially in terms of the types of investment they are willing to allow. Notably, Textor argued that QSI's purchase of PSG, one of Lyon's main rivals in Ligue 1, was illegal and the European Union should never allow countries to purchase soccer clubs because it ruins the fairness within the sport. Taking this a step further, Textor noted that if America was allowed to purchase English second division side Sheffield United and funnel the nation's resources into the club, they would in his words: "kick everyone's ass."[73] Clearly not worried about ingratiating himself with the biggest powers in the industry, Textor also went after City Football Group with the backhanded comment that they had one good team, Manchester City, but were not the best model of multi-club ownership.

But it is now Textor who finds his multi-club ownership model under intense scrutiny at the end of the 2024/25 season. At the beginning of the year, the expectation was that Lyon would challenge for a Champions League spot, and that Crystal Palace would have another season stuck in the middle of the table. Instead, Lyon underperformed and ended up falling into the Europa League, while Crystal Palace qualified for the competition by winning the FA Cup—the club's first major title in 120 years.[74] This immediately caused problems, as UEFA rules stipulate that two clubs with the same owners cannot compete in the same competition.

Previously, multi-club ownership groups managed to get around this issue through either selling one of the teams or changing ownership structures to comply with UEFA integrity guidelines.[75] However, after refusing to put Crystal Palace into a blind trust while they are in the Europa League,[76] Textor instead negotiated the sale of his shares of Palace to New York Jets owner Woody Johnson while also starting the transformation of Eagle Football Holdings into a publicly traded company.[77] This move fits perfectly with Textor's career in the tech industry, where he made a fortune buying undervalued companies, rebuilding them, and then selling them for high profits.

And with this latest move, the question is whether John Textor got involved in soccer because of his interest in the sport, or was it just another part of the entertainment industry with assets that he could flip for profit? In either case, Crystal Palace and its fans have had to suffer as the club was demoted down to the Conference League due to Textor's prioritization of other teams in the Eagle Football Holdings family and the club forgetting to turn in paperwork on time. Because of this, it has come to a point where Textor is now challenging the Glazers as the textbook example of what a bad American owner can do to a club.

The Americans Are Coming

Who is the American soccer owner? It is hard to categorize or stereotype the Americans who own soccer clubs. Whether it be the firebrand John Textor, the visionary Michele Kang, or even Arsenal's notoriously quiet owner Stan Kroenke, there is such a range of personalities and business philosophies that makes it hard to predict how an American owner will behave. That is not to say that supporters and leagues should just be welcoming any American with a few billion dollars in their pocket to be their new owner. As evidenced by the first American owner in the Premier League Malcolm Glazer to more recent entrants like Todd Boehly, there is no guarantee that barrels full of cash will pave the way to success for a club.

And yet one commonality among most of the American soccer owners is that they are trying to build their portfolios through soccer. It is somewhat unknown why Frank McCourt purchased Marseille, but there likely was a redemptive aspect to it. Michele Kang purchased OL Lyonnes and London City Lionesses to further her vision of the growth potential of women's soccer, as well as the impact that women can have on the world. Todd Boehly purchased Chelsea to win at all costs, just like he did with the Los Angeles Dodgers. John Textor has assembled a collection of soccer teams from around the world and now seems ready to start selling them off.

As such, whether it be ego, financial gains, altruistic motives, or simply joining one of the world's most exclusive clubs, American dollars will continue flowing into European soccer clubs. Perhaps the biggest impact Americans have had on the soccer industry, is their business-focused approach. This can be evidenced by how much business jargon is now a part of soccer conversations. Rather than simply talking about whether a team needs to purchase a new center forward, fans are also now worried about how things like amortization, IPOs, and leveraged buy-outs will impact their clubs.

In this manner, American owners have taken away some of the purity that came with being a soccer fan, as they pushed the game further into the hyper-competitive world of business and finance.

And like it or not, there doesn't seem much that can be done to stop them.

3

Soccer's Biggest Mystery
Why Are So Many Women Tearing Their ACL?

A world record 91,648 fans pack into Camp Nou for critical first leg of the Champions League semifinal. Thirty-eight minutes into the match, the opposition defense is split by a pass that is received by the reigning winner of the Ballon d'Or—the top individual award in soccer—who brilliantly smashes the ball home to give Barcelona a resounding 4-0 lead over Real Madrid. There is no comeback—or "remontada" as the Real supporters call it—in the works here. Barca will ease their way back into the Champions League final for the second year in a row.

Two months later, the best player in the world is struck down by injury and is about to go missing for more than a year, and most soccer fans will not even notice. This Barcelona superstar is Alexia Putellas, arguably the greatest woman to ever play soccer. The injury Alexia—her preferred name—suffered was a tear of the anterior cruciate ligament (ACL) in her left knee, a grueling injury that even with successful surgery and rehabilitation has a recovery time of around nine to twelve months for a professional athlete. In some cases, an ACL tear may not just mean the end of a season for a top-level athlete but can even force them into retirement. In 2022, around 160 professional women's soccer players reported suffering a serious ACL injury, and eleven of them were forced to retire.

For Alexia, the fateful day was July 5, 2022. The Spanish national team was training in preparation for the 2022 Women's European Championship. Alexia was in top form, having just led Barcelona to one of the most dominant seasons in history winning all thirty league matches on their way to a domestic treble. Spain was seeking to capture their first European title in women's soccer, and with Alexia at the helm, they were the consensus choice to win the tournament. Then, in an instant, the ACL which stabilizes Alexia's knee joint ruptured. Without her, Spain was unable to play to their full potential and were knocked out in extra-time of the quarterfinals by hosts England.

Alexia's knee injury not only ended Spain's hopes for its first European title but also closed the chapter on one of the most dominant spells in the history of women's soccer. Her performance over the previous eighteen months had been so commanding, that despite only playing for half of the year in 2022 and missing out on the Women's Euros, she still won the Ballon d'Or trophy, making her the first woman to win the award twice.

Unfortunately, Alexia is not an exception when it comes to suffering this injury. In 2022, over 160 professional women's soccer players tore or ruptured their ACL. That number increased to around 175 in 2023 and surged to a record 197 recorded ACL tears in 2024. To put these figures into perspective, when comparing ACL injury rates between male and female professional soccer players, women are approximately six times more likely to suffer this injury.

And this is the core mystery of this story. There are substantially different rates of ACL injuries between men and women who play professional soccer, but the exact reason for this difference is mostly unknown. In a multibillion-dollar industry that values cutting-edge technology, data analytics, tactics, strategy, and most of all, outcomes, everyone has been left scratching their heads. How could players, the biggest financial investment a professional sport team makes, keep getting injured and no one knows why?

Why Is an ACL important?

Before we dive into the potential causes of ACL injuries in women's soccer, it is important for us to first understand what an ACL is, and why it is so important. The ACL is a connective piece between the thigh bone (femur) and the shin (tibia). According to the American Academy of Orthopaedic Surgeons, the ACL works in conjunction with other ligaments to provide stability in the knee and prevents the lower leg from moving too far forward. When you run, and then quickly change direction, whether it be to elude a defender or to avoid a dog on a jogging path, the ACL is what helps to keep your knee stable as your foot plants on the ground. Likewise, when you jump, such as going for a header, when you land the ACL is again what is providing stability and keeping you from collapsing to the ground. This ligament is important for anyone doing even moderate levels of physical activity and is vital for professional soccer players whose livelihood is dependent on knee stability so they can make quick cutting movements.

So how does one injure their ACL? Typically, ACL tears occur because of sudden movements such as changing direction, rapid deceleration, or coming to a complete stop. It is these kinds of dynamic movements, as well as awkward landings after jumping or collisions—such as from a slide tackle—that can cause an ACL tear. You know, just the exact movements that a soccer player will have to make hundreds of times in a match.

There are different levels of ACL injuries that one can suffer, with the most common being either a mild (Grade 1) sprain or a more severe Grade 3 tear. A Grade 3 injury occurs when the ACL tear is complete (rupture) or near-complete. With a Grade 3 tear, the knee is no longer able to stabilize or hold any weight when making dynamic movements. Although an athlete can potentially walk or even do light running with a ruptured ACL, they would be unable to make any sideways movements. Following a completely torn ACL, surgery is recommended for professional soccer players so that they can regain as much stability, strength, and range of movement for their knee. As noted in the case of Alexia Putellas, a Grade 3 tear requires a long recovery period, with the timeline to return to competitive play typically ranging between ten and twelve months.

The Impact of ACL Injuries in Women's Soccer

Because of the long recovery times for ACL tears, it is one of the worst injuries that a professional athlete can experience in terms of the overall impact on their playing career. However, for a women soccer player, this impact can be further complicated by the nature of the industry. In 2017, FIFPro conducted a survey of over 3,000 women's soccer players from around the world to study the state of employment within the game. The report produced several glaring issues, one of which was that the average contract provided to a female soccer player by their club was twelve months in length, approximately the same amount of time it takes to recover from an ACL injury. In essence, there is a very real possibility that a player who suffers a serious ACL tear could find themselves out of a contract by the time they have fully recovered and are ready to play again. Though many teams usually support an athlete through their full rehabilitation, there is no guarantee that an athlete will fully recover from an ACL tear. As such, it is common practice now for teams to sign replacements for players who suffer ACL tears so that they can maintain a competitive roster.

Although top-level clubs like those in the Women's Super League (WSL) in England tend to provide better medical care and longer contracts for their players, the ACL injury crisis is an issue that spans across all levels of women's soccer. Thus, while we are aware of superstar soccer players such as Alexia Putellas, Sam Kerr, and Beth Mead who have all suffered ACL tears and were supported by their respective clubs in their recovery process, there are also clubs in lower divisions and other regions of the world who do not have the wealth and resources of Barcelona, Chelsea, or Arsenal. Because of this, many players who suffer an ACL injury are not just dealing with physical pain and stress but must also cope with the anxiety of losing their job, financial instability, and the end of their career as a soccer player. Even women who play for big clubs may not always get the assistance they need in training, prevention, and recovery from ACL injuries because resources tend to be directed toward the men's team. One only needs to look at a club like Manchester United, which despite perennially being one of the top earning soccer clubs in the world, consistently treats its women's team as second-class citizens. Notably, Manchester United owner Sir Jim Ratcliffe emphasized in an interview that he was focused on the "first team" meaning the men, indicating the women were secondary at best.

From the players' perspective, the endemic of ACL injuries in women's soccer has become a serious matter that has led to growing fear amongst the players. In the spring of 2023, a group of Arsenal players posted a seemingly innocent photo of themselves smiling together in a training room after a loss to Wolfsburg in the Champions League semifinals. In the caption striker, Vivianne Miedema wrote: "At least we will be in the gym together. Ps. ACL group is full now. Please no more … "[1] Sitting on the medical table is defender Laura Weinroither, who was stretchered off the Emirates Stadium pitch a few hours earlier with a torn ACL. The three teammates surrounding her in the photo are superstars of women's soccer—Vivianne Miedema the all-time scoring leader for the WSL and Dutch national team (men's or women's), Beth Mead the all-time assists leader in the WSL, and Leah Williamson, captain of the England national team that won their first ever European title in 2021. All four women in the photo had each torn their ACL within a six-month period.

Beth Mead was the first to go down, rupturing her ACL in a WSL match on November 19, 2022. Less than a month later, Vivianne Miedema tore her ACL in a Champions League match against Lyon. At the time of their injuries, both Mead and Miedema were among the twenty finalists for the Ballon d'Or. In an acceptance speech for the BBC Sports Personality of the Year award, Mead noted that 25 percent of the finalists for the women's Ballon d'Or were currently unable to play because of ACL injuries, and that if such things were happening to Messi and Ronaldo a lot more would be done to figure out the cause of the problem.[2]

Leah Williamson went down with her ACL injury in late April 2023, and was then followed by Weinroither less than two weeks later. The timing of these injuries had widespread ramifications for the players and their national teams. Mead and Williamson's ACL injuries were especially problematic for England, as it meant that the squad would be without their best attacking threat and defensive talisman for the 2023 FIFA Women's World Cup. England who had been considered one of the favorites to win the World Cup ended up losing in the finals 1-0 to Spain. Likewise, the Netherlands also missed the presence of their all-time goal scorer Miedema and were eliminated by Spain in the quarterfinals.

Knowing that Miedema and Mead would likely be out for the first several months of the 2023/24 season, Arsenal signed England striker Alessia Russo to the richest contract in women's professional soccer estimated to be worth around one million pounds a year. Moreover, with both Williamson and Weinroither missing for most of the season, Arsenal also signed two defenders—Amanda Ilestedt (Paris Saint-Germain/Sweden) and Laia Codina (Barcelona/Spain) to help bolster the backline. Even with these reinforcements, Arsenal was missing much of their attacking and defensive prowess and ended up finishing third in the 2023/24 season.

The final layer of this story is the impact these ACL injuries have on the personal lives of players. After picking up her ACL injury, Williamson talked about the mental toll of going from a profession where there is daily pressure to perform, to being put into a training room where no one cares about what she is doing. For Mead and Miedema, their ACL injuries took on a different meaning, as the two players are in a relationship with each other. In an interview that was published by Arsenal, the couple discussed the stress of having to go through recovery together, with Miedema noting it would either end in a break-up or make them stronger[3].

And yet, the story of these Arsenal players is only a snapshot of the large impact that the endemic of ACL injuries has had across women's soccer. Just the absence of four Arsenal players had wide reaching ramifications that even influenced the outcome of major competitions and the labor market. Additionally, from an economic perspective, research has shown that the presence of superstars plays an important role in attracting consumers to sporting events. As such, with many of the stars of the women's game constantly missing, it could be said that the spate of ACL injuries also could hinder the overall popularity of the sport. In this sense, it is fitting to call it the "ACL crisis" as it is not just impacting the health and careers of players but also could be influencing the future of women's soccer.

Anatomy

There are numerous potential causes for the ACL crisis—workload, training regimes, travel, etc. However, the logical starting point is anatomy. The reason for this is there are biological differences between men and women, and thus the question is whether these physical differences can manifest into different rates of ACL tears. An extensive search through databases and academic journals revealed a substantial number of studies focused on ACL injuries. These studies ranged from examining what types of training methods can prevent the occurrence of ACL tears[4] to techniques to prepare an elite soccer player to return from such an injury.[5]

Let's start out with the basics. From an anatomical perspective, the female ACL has a smaller cross-sectional area, about 20 percent smaller than a male's when standardized for body size and height. This means for equally matched men and women of the same height and weight, the muscles around a woman's knee will tend to be smaller. As such, a woman's ACL may not be able to handle as much torque and shear that comes from cutting, jumping, and stopping motions. Indeed, early research using cadaver leg bones concluded that female ACLs are more likely to be strained when pivoting because of having a smaller cross-section.[6]

However, these findings are from studies on the general population, and do not consider elite athletes who have spent their entire lives training their bodies. As such, this raises the question of whether physiological differences have an impact on injury rates in elite women's soccer players. As a physically demanding sport that requires a great deal of running, dynamic movements, kicking the ball—and in some cases opponents—those who play soccer typically develop significant leg strength. And for professionals, their physical strength is at an entirely different level than the rest of us. Numerous studies have found that elite players are able to consistently physically outperform sub-elite soccer players in leg strength, jumping, sprinting, and other core functions.[7] Therefore, it does not make sense to try and draw conclusions about ACL injuries in elite-level athletes based on studies of the general population. Rather, what is needed is research that specifically analyzes women professional soccer players.

And here is where we get to one of the most striking parts of the research being done on examining the cause of ACL injuries in women. There is almost none. To be more precise, before the most recent outbreak of ACL tears in women's soccer, most of the research published on ACL injuries and elite athletes was done specifically on men. Estimates vary, but it is believed that only about 6 percent of the research done on ACL injuries before 2020 studied women in any capacity. There are numerous reasons for why women have been excluded from previous studies, but perhaps the primary reason is because of the difference in resources.

Academic research is often influenced by funding organizations, whether they are grants from nonprofits or industry stakeholders. Thus, the economic reality is that leagues such as the National Football League or Premier League are able to direct the focus of research studies on professional athletes because of the wealth of financial resources they can offer. As such, the massive financial gulf between men's and women's pro sports means that research studies produced from industry partnerships will mostly focus on male subjects. Add in the fact that other researchers will then attempt to replicate these male-focused studies, and it creates a market-driven research system that excludes women from being studied because of a lack of financial resources.

So, what findings do exist that can provide at least some understanding of the role that anatomy plays in the ACL crisis? One emerging line of research has examined the potential impact of menstrual hormones. Notably, medical research has found that ovarian hormones can weaken all soft tissue by affecting their structural integrity.[8] For women, the levels of hormones fluctuate during the menstrual cycle, with the highest levels being during the fourteen-day follicular phase (preovulation) that begins at the start of their period. This means that because of the increased production of ovarian hormones, there is a two-week window during which women may be more prone to knee injuries. However, the most recent studies have only found weak evidence[9] linking hormones to the occurrence of knee injuries.

Despite the limited research findings, the theory that menstrual hormones could be playing a role in the ACL crisis has begun to gain traction with some players. Notably, former England striker Jodie Taylor stated that in addition to managing how much rest players get, teams should also be considering their menstrual cycles to help avoid potential ACL injuries. Based on this, researchers have started clinical trials using contraceptives that lower the levels of hormones linked to ACL tears. However, these trials have only had limited success, with the best results lowering injury rates by about 20 percent, well short of the change needed to explain the drastic number of injuries in women's soccer.

So, what are the main points we can take away regarding the relationship between anatomy and ACL tears in women's soccer players? Basic medical facts highlight that women have 20 percent narrower ACL's than men of the same size, and thus the prevailing logic suggests women are more prone to tearing this ligament. At the same time, there is almost no research on elite female athletes, with recent meta-analysis—a research method where the data from previous studies are combined into a single study to examine if there is a statistical trend across all published studies—of the existing data suggesting a weak relationship at best. Perhaps the major point is how women have been ignored by researchers and the sport industry. It is only now, with the sudden outbreak of injuries, increased media attention, and enhanced research funding that scientists have started rushing to solve the problem.

Overall, there is not enough evidence to conclude that anatomy and physiology alone are responsible for women's soccer players being two to six times more likely to have an ACL tear. But there is a silver lining to all of this. Although we live in a time of medical advances where you can edit your genetic makeup and have surgery to make yourself a few inches taller, there are limits to what can be done to change our physiology. And thus, if the root of the problem is not physiological, it might be in other aspects that can be better controlled like training and workloads, meaning there may be potential solutions to this crisis.

Participation and Training

A common argument for the increased number of ACL injuries suffered by women soccer players is it is a natural consequence of the expansion of the sport. That is, the launch of numerous leagues and competitions over the last several decades means there are more opportunities for women to participate in elite-level sport and thus has caused an increase in ACL injuries. But the reality is that the ACL crisis is not a new phenomenon, it has been around for almost half a century.

In a 2020 publication in the *British Medical Journal (BMJ) Sport & Exercise Medicine*[10] researchers noted that women's sports such as basketball and volleyball had gone through their own version of the ACL crisis in previous decades. Moreover, in the 1980s, the National Collegiate Athletic Association, the governing body of college sport in America, began to collect data on player injuries and published a study led by medical experts reporting that women who played soccer and basketball had significantly higher rates of ACL injuries. This is further evidence that ACL injuries have been a long-standing problem in women's soccer and thus are likely not a result of increased participation opportunities.

Instead, this raises a different issue that could be related to ACL injuries in women's soccer. Even though both soccer and basketball were identified as having higher rates of ACL tears for women more than forty years ago, soccer persists in having issues while basketball has managed to reduce the number of ACL injuries. What exactly happened that led to these sports heading in different directions? The answer partly lies in the training regimes used within these two sports.

As the number of women's basketball players suffering ACL tears started to increase in the 1980s and 1990s, team trainers and doctors started to examine the cause of this issue. What they found was that men and women have physiological differences when they jump, and that this could lead to more lower-body injuries in women. In response to this, women's basketball training programs were entirely redesigned to specifically cater to the female body and reduce the risk of injury. Counter to this, women's soccer has continued to employ the same training programs that men's teams use.

It is clear there is a need for more advanced and specialized training in women's soccer to reduce ACL injury risks. And while some teams have started to make these changes, the reality is that even at the toplevel of the sport, trainers are still copying the drills and conditioning programs that were developed for male soccer players. This brings up another form of inequality faced by women players in that there is typically a significant salary difference for trainers and doctors for the men's and women's teams, even at the same club. As such, the best and most qualified staff are naturally drawn to working for men's teams, meaning that women's teams are not able to hire the most experienced and knowledgeable medical team. This then translates into women's teams repeating the same programs as men's squads, when their staff should be working to develop specific training protocols to help reduce injuries as was done in women's basketball decades before.

But just like anatomy, training alone doesn't seem to be the solution that will entirely solve the ACL crisis. Of the ninety-four ACL tears that were reported in elite women's soccer in the first half of 2024, just over a quarter of them occurred in training. While specialized training certainly could reduce the general incidence of these injuries, the reality is three in every four ACL tears are suffered in a competitive match. Consequently, this draws our attention to the matches themselves, especially as the women's soccer calendar becomes busier with each passing year, and more and more players are being overworked to the point of exhaustion.

Load Management and the Soccer Calendar

Load management is the process of controlling the amount of gametime for an athlete with the goal of reducing the risk of injury and enhancing player and team performance in future games. It is not a new phenomenon but has become a popular buzzword in the last decade, especially amongst those who listen to podcasts about basketball analytics. The concept is simple and obvious. Taking breaks helps someone to avoid becoming tired. But in the high-stakes world of professional sport, load management is a complicated balancing act where teams must consider the potential tradeoffs of not fielding their best players.

Think about a top-level Premier League team who is in the early rounds of the Carabao Cup. Let's assume they have drawn a team from a lower division who they are clearly favored to beat. The club knows that they have a good chance of beating their opponents if they rest some of their star players. At the same time, fans are also aware of this and may be less interested in attending the match, resulting in a loss of revenue. On the other hand, if the club uses its stars, they may be able to sell more tickets but also could place unnecessary workload on key players resulting in injuries or underperformance in other competitions. There is a direct cost to this underperformance, as placement in the league table determines merit payments and potential qualification for European competition that is often worth tens of millions of euros.

From the perspective of players and coaches, the primary motivation for load management is to keep players in top condition. Basic logic dictates that overworked athletes will likely not be able to perform to their best ability and thus could potentially impact the performance of the entire team. In the National Basketball Association (NBA), where the league champion is determined by a playoff series at the end of the season, the best teams will often rest several members of their starting roster once they have clinched a spot in the playoffs. The belief is that by resting players during regular season games that have little importance, the team will be refreshed and deliver peak performance during the playoffs.

In recent years, soccer players have likewise come to see load management as a necessary protection from potential injuries and burnout as more games get inserted into an already packed schedule. Indeed, players and their unions have also argued that the addition of all these matches is "killing"[11] soccer, as it is watering down the product by overworking the stars of the game. On the opposite side of the equation, teams, leagues, and soccer associations such as FIFA and UEFA view load management as an issue from a business perspective. While they will argue they are doing everything they can to protect players and make sure that fans get the best product, the reason that the number of matches has increased for players is the gains in revenue that can be realized from additional matches and competitions.

Load Management in Women's Soccer

What about load management in women's soccer? Somehow the answer is even more complicated than for men's soccer or the NBA. Women's soccer players are ensnared in a system where they must contend with organizations that only a few years ago considered them an afterthought and refused to give them resources but have now awakened to the money-making potential of the sport. Think about how terrible this must feel as a woman soccer player. One season your team and association tell you there is not enough money to pay your salary, that you need to travel economy class for all matches even if you are world champions—famously, the Japanese women's national team flew to the 2011 World Cup which they ended up winning using economy class tickets, whereas the men's team flew even to friendlies in business class—pay for your own kit, and that you are lucky to even get to play the sport. That you should just give away your life for below minimum wage for the love of the game. Then the next season they come back and tell you that you will be going on a massive tour with dozens of extra games around the world, increased media attention, oh … and that you should be thankful to the team and federation for making all of this happen.

Unfortunately, women's soccer players are stuck within a system that only has come to appreciate their skill and contributions to the game once it was recognized they had the ability to generate large amounts of cash. This is not to say that everyone in charge of women's soccer clubs and federations are greedy capitalists whose only pleasure in life derives from squeezing every cent of value from their players, as there are some clubs which have prioritized the women's game. However, soccer federations and clubs that had almost exclusively focused their attention and resources on the success of their men's teams are suddenly racing to find ways to commodify their women's team.

The problem with this is that both national and club teams want to play more matches so they can line their pockets with the sales of additional tickets, merchandise, and increased media rights deals. Rather than negotiate how many more matches players would have to play for their respective clubs and national teams, those in charge basically created a free-for-all over the last six years that has all the respective organizations looking out for their own financial and sporting interests. For a top-level women's soccer player, this means more friendlies and tournaments with their national team and more league and cup matches with their club. Increasing the number of matches not only creates strain on players from the amount of time they spend on the field, but also by requiring more travel while providing less rest and recovery time between matches. As research shows that an ACL can suffer from structural fatigue from overwork,[12] the congested match calendar was creating a perfect storm to increase the number of serious ACL injuries.

Then COVID happened.

The deadly COVID-19 pandemic that caused global lockdowns in 2019-20, also had significant impact on the workload of women's soccer players. To prevent the spread of the pandemic, the 2020 Tokyo Summer Olympic Games were postponed till the summer of 2021. This immediately had major ramifications for European players, as the 2021 European Women's Championship then had to be shifted into 2022. This then meant that for European soccer players, there was the very real potential that they would have to play the Tokyo Olympics (2021), Euros (2022), the 2023 World Cup, the Paris Olympics (2024), and then the 2025 Euros in successive summers. This is important because summers are one of the major rest periods for players, typically allowing them several weeks to recuperate and recover before starting training for their next club season. Moreover, whereas the Olympics are considered a secondary tournament in men's soccer with countries sending their under-23 squad to compete, women's teams send their full squad and view the tournament as the second biggest trophy in soccer. Thus, where an elite European male soccer player might compete in two to three major tournaments in a five-year period, many top women's players are playing on a yearly basis during what should be their main rest period.

And that's just matches for national team duty. Most women's soccer players still must make a living playing with their clubs. Although the number of league matches a professional team takes part in has remained rather consistent over the past few years, clubs also have other obligations such as domestic cups and continental competitions that can quickly fill a player's calendar. Moreover, as women's soccer continues to gain in popularity, many of the top women's clubs have also started doing off-season/pre-season tours of other countries to generate more revenue. For example, Arsenal Women played their final league match of the 2023/24 season on May 18th, and then immediately hopped on a plane to then play a friendly against the A League All Stars six days later in Melbourne, Australia. They then announced a US tour from August 15th through the 26th. For the Arsenal players who also played in the Olympics, this meant only a few weeks' rest before they had to join their national teams in training camp.

But the congestion of fixtures is just the tip of the iceberg in terms of workload issues and their relation to ACL injuries in women's soccer. To really comprehend the scope of how the calendar is impacting injuries in soccer, we first need to understand the concept of overload. Simply put, overload is when a player participates in too many matches or is not given enough time to recover from the stress put on their body in previous matches and training. In essence, overload is a complex equation that considers the amount of time and effort logged during matches, training and travel schedules, previous injuries, and other factors that can affect a player's recovery.

To better understand the extent to which elite players are overloaded, let's consider Barcelona and England midfielder Keira Walsh, who holds the title of the most overworked women's soccer player over the past six seasons. Using FIFPro's workload monitoring platform,[13] data shows Walsh has played 23,617 competitive minutes during this time, with 73 percent (17,363 minutes) spent with her clubs Manchester City and Barcelona and 27 percent with England. Walsh's playing time is the equivalent of having participated in 263 complete ninety-minute matches, or about an average of forty-seven complete matches a year. In 2022/23, she made a career high fifty-seven appearances, which is more than most male professional soccer players average.

Since overload also deals with the amount of rest time a player has between matches, let's also consider Walsh's recovery data. The general recommendation is that professional soccer players have breaks of at least twenty-eight days in the off-season and fourteen days in-season.[14] Throughout her career, Walsh has generally had more than a thirty-day break in the off-season, but only eleven days off during the average season. However, this all changed in 2022/23, where Walsh only had seven days rest during the season, and then eight days of rest in the off-season. The lack of rest can mainly be attributed to England making it to the World Cup finals but also means that within days of losing the final, Walsh had to be back in training with Barcelona. Perhaps more frighting was that fifteen other women's soccer players have had less rest than Walsh.

A final consideration that needs to be made in terms of overload is the amount of travel time that a player is subjected to. Although we often imagine professional athletes living a glamorous life, flying business class around the world to play matches in exciting locations, staying in five-star hotels, it is a grueling lifestyle. Let's consider the flight log of Yui Hasegawa who plays midfield for Japan and Manchester City. Between June 2018 and June 2024, Hasegawa made seventy-nine international trips with either her club or country for a total of 421,000 kilometers, or the equivalent of having flown around the world more than ten times. This means she spent approximately 33,000 minutes in the air, almost double the 18,000 minutes of competitive play that she logged during this time. It should be noted that this data only includes air travel and does not consider domestic travel by bus for her team or her own personal travel for vacation and other matters. Research has shown that flying, especially for extended periods of time, not only hampers recovery in soccer players, but may also increase various health related risks.[15]

Along these lines, the extensive international travel that is a standard part of women's soccer has started to be scrutinized by players and coaches. Emma Hayes, current US women's national team manager, highlighted a pattern that she and many others have started to notice regarding ACL injuries. Specifically, she pointed out that the transition period between international duty and club soccer seemed to be a danger point for women's soccer players.[16] That is, many within the industry were noticing that most ACL injuries come within the ten-day period of when a player leaves their national team to rejoin their club, or vice versa. After suffering her ACL tear, Beth Mead referenced Hayes' theory,[17] stating that her own injury happened right after she had left the England camp and rejoined Arsenal. Mead has been especially adamant that there is a need to fix the women's soccer calendar, especially as the schedule looks to become even busier in the next few years before it is up for renewal in 2026.

We now have more data on player workloads, recovery, and travel than at any point in history, and it shows 30 percent of professional women's soccer players are overloaded. As there is a correlation between the uptick in matches and the number of ACL injuries suffered by elite female players, common sense tells us players are being overworked and thus they are being injured. However, despite all these observations and data, there is no definitive research that has been able to tie overload, recovery times, or travel distance to the increase in ACL injuries in women's soccer players. There are potential connections, but we have yet to find the smoking gun.

After load management became a hot topic in the NBA, the league commissioned a study using ten years of data to examine whether resting players helped reduce injuries. The conclusion from their fifty-seven-page report was that resting players did not reduce the risk of injury.[18] However, independent medical research using the same NBA data found that the more minutes a player was on the court, especially in late season games, the more likely they were to have a season-ending injury.[19] Essentially, while the NBA was publicly arguing that load management had gone too far because it did not actually protect players from injuries,[20] peer-reviewed research was suggesting quite the opposite. The same dynamic is also unfolding in soccer, with leagues and governing bodies trying to squeeze more money out of the game by packing more games into the calendar than ever, while denying the need for load management.

Managing the Crisis

Samantha Kerr is the face of the Australian women's national team, and one of the best natural goal scorers in the world. In January 2024, Kerr ruptured her ACL, ruling her out of the Paris Olympic Games. Although the media widely covered the injury, most ignored the fact that this was her second ACL injury. In 2011, a teenage Kerr exploded onto the soccer scene and earned a starting role at the World Cup for the Matildas—the Australian Women's National Team. Then a torn ACL ruled her out of the 2012 Olympic Games, and after suffering additional lower-body injuries over the next several years, Kerr contemplated retiring from the sport.[21] Fortunately, instead of quitting after her most recent ACL tear, Kerr has worked hard on rehabbing and returned for Chelsea in the 2025/26 season.

And yet, when I look at Kerr's career, and those of all the women who have gone down with ACL tears, I can only think about what has been lost. Kerr should have played in four Olympic Games, not two. Beth Mead and

Leah Williamson could have led England to a World Cup victory the country is so desperate for. Alexia should be a household name, the most dominant soccer player on the planet. Now, every tackle, collision, awkward landing is a moment of fear for these players. The realization is that the next time they go down holding their knee, it could be the last moment they kick a ball.

This raises the critical question, and really the purpose of this chapter, how do we put an end to this? It is impossible to bring an end to all knee injuries in women's soccer. It is a physical sport, and even if you wrapped players in bubblewrap there would inevitably still be injuries. The focus should be on how we can significantly decrease the rate of ACL tears.

Perhaps the best solution may come from a conference room of administrators in a nondescript room somewhere in Europe. For it is in the FIFA headquarters where the next cycle of the global women's soccer calendar is due to be set in 2026. In my mind, there couldn't be a more critical event in women's soccer. It is at this meeting where FIFA executives will not only determine the dates for future competitions like the World Cup, but also the precise timing and number of international friendlies. In turn, this will then influence how leagues and clubs are able to schedule their competitions, training, and pre-season tours. Essentially, if FIFA and professional leagues can cooperate in the development of this calendar, it could mean a system where women's soccer players are given proper time to rest and recuperate.

Unfortunately, to come to such a solution would require FIFA, soccer associations, and professional leagues to all work together. This seems highly unlikely in the confluence of greed that is the profit-driven soccer industry. Those that control the game now see women's soccer as a pie that must be shared, causing the various leagues and associations to all try and carve up the biggest most valuable slice for themselves. At this point, the only way for every league and association to get a bigger piece is to increase the size of the pie, which means packing more games into an already congested schedule. Something which keeps happening every year, putting more and more women's soccer players at risk.

But there is hope. As the injury crisis has continued to grow, players have taken the leading role in calling attention to the problem. Their efforts have brought the issue to the forefront of media discussions, broken decades of disregard from administrators and researchers, and even spurred notoriously slow-moving bureaucratic soccer associations into action. If FIFA and other leagues and associations will not make the changes needed, the players are motivated to empower themselves to continue fighting for the future of their sport. And really, isn't it those who are going through the crisis who should have the biggest say in what should be done? Rather than a middle-aged man in an expensively tailored suit, shouldn't players have a greater say in all of this? As Beth Mead stated in a recent interview: "The people who understand ACL injuries are the players who have gone through it."[22]

From this perspective, the smart thing to do would be to concede more power to the players, to give them a seat at the table to represent their interests in matters of health, rest, and building competition schedules. If a quarter of the stars of the game are constantly on the bench, headed to the operating table, or in recovery rooms, it is not helping to grow the popularity of the game. Sadly, the powers that govern soccer have continued to focus on economic growth within the sport, abandoning a holistic approach that incorporates player well-being and future potential.

Recognizing that bringing about substantive changes to the governance of soccer is a slow and cumbersome process, players have taken it upon themselves to start developing solutions to the ACL crisis. As has been noted throughout this chapter, one of the biggest roadblocks in tacking the number of ACL injuries in the sport has been the lack of research on women's soccer players. Along these lines, players such a Chelsea's Lucy Bronze have played a prominent role in establishing initiatives like *Project ACL* that are focused on accelerating research on women's soccer players.[23] In this way, the players are ensuring that they are being studied by researchers, and that a body of knowledge will be developed to better understand the cause of ACL injuries in women's soccer.

Conclusion

As I write this in the spring of 2025, it is now over two years since Alexia ruptured her ACL. After a long rehabilitation process, she returned to the

Barcelona and Spain squads only to have to undergo another surgery in December 2023 on the same knee.[24] During her three months of recovery, questions began to be raised about Alexia's future with Barcelona and as a professional soccer player,[25] especially with Patri Guijarro emerging as a dominant midfield presence for the club. And yet, despite all these setbacks, Alexia still can change a match in an instant. Coming off the bench in the UWCL final against Lyon, Alexia scored the winner and was hailed as the "Queen of Barcelona" by her teammates.[26]

Alexia was Spain's leading scorer at the Paris Olympics, and yet things have changed considerably from when she was winning the Ballon d'Or. Before the injury, Alexia would start every match, play every minute, and was the dominant presence on the pitch, able to impose her will on a match with such ease it almost seemed scripted. She is still able to do it, albeit in more limited roles as we saw in the UWCL Final and Olympics. No longer Batman, Alexia has become Robin, appearing three-quarters of the way into the film to save the day.

Alexia is now thirty years old, which in soccer terms is often the turning point in a player's career where their bodies begin to cooperate less with the demands of competitive play. Having had two surgeries on the same knee and spent more than 60 percent of the last two years out of the game injured, it is miraculous that she is still so prolific on the pitch. Her limited role could also be a precaution by the medical staff and her coaches hoping to avoid an even more tragic end to her career.

As if the ACL crisis wasn't bad enough as it is, the reality is that any athlete who suffers from ACL tear has an increased chance of suffering a second one. The average career length for a woman soccer player is about five to eight years, meaning a single ACL tear essentially takes away 10 to 20 percent of a player's career. A second tear could cost them half their career, or even worse, end it altogether.

The existing theories and research point toward load management and physiology as being the main contributors to the significant difference in ACL injuries between women and men soccer players. At the same time, there are other factors that may exacerbate this issue further, including women being forced to play and train on artificial turf, boots being designed to the specification of men's feet and not women's, and men having better training staff and facilities. Underneath all of this is a common thread—that women soccer players have generally been forgotten and ignored by their own industry.

As it stands today, despite more resources being directed toward studying the ACL crisis, the injury rate in the sport has continued to grow—almost 200 professional women soccer players tore their ACL's in 2024. There clearly is not some magic pill that will instantly put a stop to these injuries, but instead several factors—anatomy, training, workload, etc.—that should all be considered to try and reduce the incidence of ACL tears. To do this would require even more resources, and the question is whether the major players that control women's soccer—the federations, leagues, and teams—will see this as a worthwhile endeavor.

Hopefully, these profit-driven organizations can break away from their historical treatment of women's soccer as an inferior product and take actions to save the careers of players and continue growing the beautiful game.

4

The Pyramid
What Is Happening in the Lower Tiers of Soccer?

The Premier League is widely considered as the pinnacle of club soccer. Although individual clubs like Barcelona, Real Madrid, and Bayern Munich have more titles and fans than any single English club, as a collective the Premier League is unrivaled. Not only does the Premier League have the highest total match attendance of any soccer league in the world, but it also has the most television viewers, and as such also commands the largest broadcast rights fees for its games. Additionally, with strong commercial and sponsorship revenues, Premier League clubs also pay the highest total salary to players of any soccer league in the world. Notably, where the Premier League pays a collective €2.2 billion a year in salaries, Spain's La Liga is a distant second with a league-wide wage bill of €1.1 billion.

On the field, the Premier League, which had once been eclipsed by Spanish, German, and Italian clubs in previous decades, has flexed its economic muscles to become the dominant power in Europe. While Premier League clubs are not winning the Champions League every year, the league has the highest UEFA coefficient—a weighted statistical measure of team strength across Europe—and qualified a record six teams for the 2025/26 edition of Champions League. Indeed, nine Premier League teams, essentially half the league, will be playing in one of the three European cup competitions in 2025/26, and as such will likely further increase their coefficient and dominate prize money earnings.

However, what most fans tend to forget when we are watching players such as Arsenal's Ben White, Aston Villa's Ollie Watkins, or even Tottenham's James Maddison is that these and many other players came from the lower divisions of English soccer. In essence, the Premier League is only the tip of a massive soccer iceberg, as below it resides thousands of clubs that are organized into a pyramid which serves as the bedrock of the sport. Technically speaking, there are more than twenty tiers of soccer leagues in England, with many of these lower tiers comprised of numerous local "feeder" leagues whose clubs are entirely part-time amateurs.

Things become more serious when one moves up to the seventh division, where some of the clubs are semi-professional, indicating that some players receive a salary from the team, but that being a soccer player is only a part-time job for them. Continuing the climb up the ladder, the fifth division, known as the National League, represents a significant change as most of the clubs in this division are fully professional—that is, their players only job is to play soccer. It is somewhat of a necessity for National League clubs to be professionalized, as one promotion up takes them into the elite territory of the English Football League (EFL).

The EFL is the three tiers of soccer that reside directly below the Premier League and is where most professional soccer players in England ply their trade. The promotion and relegation system has not only made it possible for clubs to be able to move up and down the soccer pyramid but also has meant that there is a decent geographic distribution of clubs across the country. This is critical not only in terms of providing access to watch live soccer, but also in terms of scouting, recruiting, and developing young talented players. Thus, it is not a stretch to say that the lower tiers of English soccer play a critical role in helping to prop up the Premier League as we know it. One can look at any Premier League squad and find players who were trained at smaller regional clubs, and who themselves worked their way up the ladder as they became better players. Even Real Madrid and England superstar Jude Bellingham got his start in the lower tiers of the English pyramid. Though most associate him with his time at Borussia Dortmund, Bellingham started as a child with seventh division Stourbridge F.C. and then spent his youth career with Birmingham City while they were in the second division.

The pyramid system has been critical to the growth and success of the Premier League. However, what may be surprising is that despite serving as a cornerstone of the soccer's success in England and the rest of the world, the lower tiers of English soccer are filled with clubs that are constantly fighting just to survive another season. This is especially true of the fully professional clubs in the pyramid who are faced with the economic reality of having to make enough money to pay wages and remain financially solvent. At the same time, there has also been an increase in investment in lower division clubs, especially as the Premier League has become the playground of billionaires. All of this had led to the lower tiers of the English pyramid having become a sort of wild west of soccer—filled with prospectors, gamblers, sleezy businessmen, and even Hollywood stars all chasing the same dream of promotion to the Premier League. The stark reality is that most of them will fail, and in some cases, will result in disaster for the clubs they own.

So, what really is happening in the lower tiers of English soccer?

To answer this, we examine the success and failure of clubs across the pyramid. Doing so helps us understand whether the existing models of operating clubs are sustainable and also provides a critical glimpse into the future of the sport.

In the Wake of Wrexham

Wrexham Association Football Club is one of the oldest soccer clubs in the world. Located in a small Welsh mining town, Wrexham AFC spent most of their history bouncing between the third, fourth, and fifth tiers of the pyramid. In all honesty, people outside of the UK shouldn't really know the club exists. And yet, when the soccer database site FBref.com published 2022 usage statistics, it was shown that Wrexham was the most viewed club by users in the state of Iowa. Yes, Wrexham, who were in the fifth division at the time, managed to gain more views than the likes of Arsenal, Barcelona, Liverpool, and Chelsea in Iowa.

The culprits in this sudden popularity of a fifth division club in America's farming homeland were Hollywood stars Ryan Reynolds—famous for his role as comic superhero Deadpool—and Rob McElhenney who starred in the hit sitcom *It's Always Sunny in Philadelphia*. In November 2020, Reynolds and McElhenney announced that they had come to an agreement to purchase a majority stake in Wrexham AFC, which was almost unanimously approved by Wrexham supporters.[1] The takeover sparked a significant amount of confusion from soccer fans and pundits around the world, who all wondered why the hell would Hollywood elites spend their money on a floundering fifth division club. Rich foreigners should be investing in Premier League clubs, such as NBA superstar LeBron James who purchased a stake in Liverpool.

What soon became evident was that the purchase by Reynolds and McElhenney was a strategic decision driven by the pair's popularity and power within the media. As the takeover was happening, a docuseries entitled *Welcome to Wrexham* was being filmed for worldwide distribution through major streaming platforms Hulu and Disney+.[2] While it would be unfair to label Wrexham AFC as simply being a media project, especially as Reynolds and McElhenney have provided millions to invest in buying players, the draw of two Hollywood actors trying to run a club in small Welsh mining town proved to be incredibly popular amongst audiences around the world. All the sudden, people in Des Moines, Iowa, and Toowoomba, Queensland were paying attention to a club in the fifth tier of the English pyramid.

Welcome to Wrexham wasn't the only major piece of business done by the club after their Hollywood takeover. They managed to sign a deal with Entertainment Arts, the publisher of the FIFA (now EA FC) soccer video game series, to become the first English non-League (below the EFL) team to feature in the game. Moreover, with such immense media popularity from their famous owners and various media properties, Wrexham AFC was able to sign major sponsorship deals with companies such as TikTok and Expedia. All of this was great for Wrexham fans, who went from being a mediocre fifth division club, to media darlings overnight.

But what about the rest of the fifth division?

By pure coincidence, while Reynolds and McElhenney were negotiating their deal to take over Wrexham, I was in the process of interviewing owners, executives, and staff members of lower division clubs in England so I could better understand the role of their clubs in the pyramid. By the end of the 2021/22 season, the first complete season after the takeover, the conversations I was having made it quite clear there was a mixture of jealousy, anger, and animosity toward Wrexham and their new owners.

Naturally, the biggest sticking point that came up over and over again was money. And it wasn't just the fact that Wrexham was bringing in lots of money, as this was not the first time a National League club had been taken over by wealthy owners. Instead, the problem was the sheer difference in scale of all business operations. One fifth division chairman was adamant about how ridiculous this discrepancy was, as he noted that Wrexham had managed to sign TikTok as their shirt sponsor, a deal which he argued many Premier League teams couldn't even manage to secure. The chairman, in contrast, highlighted that his shirt sponsor was a local butcher. The message was clear as day, he was never going to compete against a club with that level of resources.

Indeed, in the 2021/22 season, Wrexham embarked on an unprecedented campaign of spending on player transfers and salaries. With the goal of gaining promotion to the EFL, Wrexham adopted a strategy of signing notable players from League Two, including Paul Mullin who had just led Cambridge United to promotion with thirty-two goals, as well as Liam McAlinden and Aaron Hayden. Although Wrexham had a large initial investment from its owners and a growing pool of commercial and media revenue, the club was still highly strategic in its signings. Rather than bidding large sums for the best players in League Two, they found the best players whose contracts were coming to an end. As such, they were able to avoid paying transfer fees and instead could offer wages high enough to convince players to join a nonleague side. In turn, this also meant Wrexham could afford to pay a club record £300,000 for the transfer of Ollie Palmer from AFC Wimbledon. In one transfer window, Wrexham AFC transformed itself into one of the best non-League teams in England.

However, despite the massive spending, Wrexham ended up finishing second behind Stockport County and then crashed out of the promotion playoff on a last-minute winner from Grimsby Town's Luke Waterfall.[3] In some sense, the loss was the perfect ending for the first season of *Welcome to Wrexham*, as the always immaculately groomed Reynolds was shown in absolute distress after the loss, showing how much he had come to care about the club. Moreover, it also provided the perfect transition to season two, where Reynolds and McElhenney reaffirm their strategy of investing in the club to start climbing the soccer pyramid.

While Wrexham could afford to spend large sums of money and fail to be promoted to the EFL, most other clubs in the National League aren't afforded such luxury. One shareholder of a club that was in direct competition with Wrexham for promotion to League Two told me that despite having the most successful season in the club's history, they lost over $1 million in trying to field a strong squad. In this sense, falling short of promotion had more dire consequences for a club that was not backed by Hollywood royalty and sponsors who made billions of dollars every year. In the following years, the financial situation at the club—who will go unnamed to protect those who spoke with me—continued to worsen and only avoided bankruptcy after the ownership group received a hefty bailout from family members.

Of course, the very idea of challenging Wrexham seemed foolhardy to begin with. If there was ever a time that the executives of a National League club should have told themselves to take a year off and just shoot for the mid-table, it was in 2022/23. Having already spent heavily the previous season, Wrexham went in search of more talent to guide the team to the EFL, including signing Elliot Lee from third division Charlton Athletic, as well as convincing former Watford and Manchester United goalkeeper Ben Foster to come out of retirement to play for the club. I was never able to confirm this, but one club CEO told me that of all the agent fees paid out by fifth division clubs during this season, over 75 percent of them came from Wrexham. If this were true, it would mean that Wrexham was not just spending more money than any other club, they were likely spending more than the other twenty-one National League teams combined.

So, while *Welcome to Wrexham* portrays the teams as a poor down on their luck club that had barely survived previous financial crises, the reality was they were the Goliath of the National League. And yet, where it seemed the 2022/23 season would be a cake walk for Wrexham based on their spending on player transfers and wages, the league ended up being a lot more difficult than expected. Just a few years before Reynolds and McElhenney acquired Wrexham, Notts County—supposedly the oldest soccer club in the world—were saved from financial troubles when they were purchased by Alexander and Christoffer Reedtz.[4] Although the Reedtz brothers were unable to bring the kind of media attention and revenue that transformed Wrexham into a lower division superpower overnight, they did have their own special resource—Football Radar.[5]

Football Radar is a company that provides statistically driven information on players and match outcomes to be used in betting analysis.[6] As such, the Reedtz brothers followed a similar model used by Brighton and Brentford in the Premier League, who have both managed to excel in player recruitment through their close ties to betting analysis companies. In other words, where Wrexham's strategy was to just buy the best players they could afford, Notts County was using a more "Moneyball" based approach of identifying highly talented players who were undervalued within the market.

As such, the 2022/23 National League season ended up pitting two very different philosophies of how to build a soccer team against one another. Despite a slow start to the season by the first week of October, Notts County had climbed the table and were in second place behind Wrexham.[7] One of the key players in Notts County's rise was newly signed striker Maccaulay Langstaff, who the club had purchased from sixth division Gateshead, and had only a few seasons earlier had been playing in the eleventh tier of English soccer.[8] The recruitment of Langstaff epitomized the club's data driven approach in recruiting undervalued players, and also displayed the importance of the pyramid in developing players. Indeed, Langstaff would not only go on to set club and National League records by tallying forty-two goals in his first season, he even drew the envy of Wrexham's owners who singled him out for praise for his play against their club.[9]

After the first week of April, Wrexham and Notts County were deadlocked in first place with 100 points apiece, with the two clubs set to face each other in the next fixture. Previously, a match featuring the top two teams in the National League was typically a story for the local news or maybe a quick two-minute soundbite on one of the popular soccer podcasts. However, the media attention that Wrexham had drummed up through their owners and television series had labeled the meeting between Wrexham and Notts County as the biggest match in the history of the National League, even drawing attention from *The New York Times*.[10]

Wrexham ended up winning in dramatic fashion after Ben Foster saved an injury time Notts County penalty. Although Notts would continue to hound them in the table, Wrexham finished top of the league with a record 111 points earning them automatic promotion to the EFL. Just like in the Premier League, the team that won the league was not the one making smart analytical decisions, but instead the club that had the deepest pocketbooks. This is not to say that Notts County was a failure, indeed after finishing second in the league, the club managed to win the promotion playoffs and joined Wrexham in League Two. If anything, what Wrexham and Notts County showed was the extraordinary level of effort—whether it be in spending or data analysis— needed to make it into the English Football League.

A Step Up

A new reality faced both Wrexham and Notts County in the EFL. Although only one tier above the National League, the level of professionalization in League Two was at another level. Where Wrexham had easily outspent their competition in the fifth division,[11] they now found clubs like Gillingham and Forest Green had wage budgets within a few hundred thousand pounds of them. Moreover, for Notts County who had the advantage of using data analytics to out recruit National League clubs, they likewise found they had much stiffer competition after being promoted. This was only natural, as League Two had numerous clubs with a long history of playing in the higher echelons of the pyramid, including Bradford City who had previously played in the Premier League and even had qualified for European competition in the past.

However, despite facing fiercer competition on and off the field, it was still evident that Wrexham's media and commercial power was still in a league of its own. Where National League clubs had sponsorship deals with local butchers and grocery stores, League Two clubs were a slight step higher in partnering with local car dealers.¹² Wrexham, on the other hand, inked a deal with United Airlines—literally the largest airline in the world by number of available seat miles—to replace TikTok. Where mostly residents of a local community would be able to recognize the sponsors on most League Two shirts, Wrexham had replaced one of the world's top social media platforms with the world's largest airline.¹³

Another sign of the difference between most League Two clubs and Wrexham could be seen in their pre-season plans. While clubs like Doncaster Rovers were playing against ninth division Armthorpe Welfare in a 2,500-seat stadium, Wrexham flew to Las Vegas for vacation and then kicked off a preseason tour that included matches against Premier League and Major League Soccer clubs. *Welcome to Wrexham* had made the club so popular, that 50,000 fans traveled to the small American college town of Chapel Hill to watch the fourth division club play against Chelsea. And all of this of course meant additional revenue and content for Wrexham to further monetize through their numerous media channels.

At the same time, while Wrexham was outclassing the rest of League Two in terms of media and commercial deals, things were much closer on the pitch. In what was a rude awakening after entirely dominating in their previous season, Wrexham only managed one win from their first five matches in League Two. Notts County, on the other hand, started off hot, winning six of their first nine games. But again, this is where Wrexham showed the difference in how they operated compared to other clubs in League Two. Having lost Paul Mullin to injury during their preseason tour, Wrexham found themselves unable to score goals once league competition started. Where other clubs would have simply waited for Mullin to recover fitness and look to find solutions within their existing squad in the interim, Wrexham went out and signed former Premier League striker Steven Fletcher to a two-year deal.¹⁴

For most League Two clubs, adding a highly experienced and expensive player to an already ballooning wage bill would have been out of the question from a financial perspective. But for Wrexham, it was just another expense that would be covered by the club's ownership or media deals. What is important to note is that for other League Two clubs, signing a player like Fletcher is not just about the short-term financial strain it would put on the club, but also the long-term opportunity cost of taking him on. For many clubs in the EFL, as well as some in the Premier League, the signing of a player is not just about the on-field production they will create for the team. Instead, when teams acquire a player, they are also thinking about the potential resell value in the future.

The process of purchasing talented players, developing them through training and playing experience, and then selling them for a profit to other clubs is one of the critical functions of the soccer pyramid in England. In essence, this movement of players creates a market that allows those who are talented to continue climbing up the rungs of the ladder, while those whose skills are lacking or diminishing will find themselves sliding down to lower tiers. As such, because of the constant buying and selling of soccer players, some teams in the EFL have come to depend on developing and selling talent as a critical source of income. Thus, when Wrexham bought 36-year-old Fletcher who was nearing the end of his career, the signing represented a luxury that did not fit with the economic logic of how most EFL clubs operated.

With their extravagant reinforcements, Wrexham was able to turn their fortunes around, which were further boosted with the return of Mullin from injury. By the end of October, Wrexham had risen to third place in the table, which if they managed to hold this position would guarantee them automatic promotion to League One. However, Wrexham continued to struggle as the season progressed. Curiously, it was not the clubs that had the closest wage budgets that were giving them problems, but instead clubs like Mansfield, Milton Keynes Dons, and especially Stockport County who were challenging for promotion slots.

One problem of solely looking at budgets to determine the strength of clubs in the soccer pyramid is that clubs who have been recently demoted tend to have higher wage bills. The reason for this is that they typically retain some of the more expensive players they purchased while in higher divisions and thus tend to have large payrolls. This was certainly the case when Wrexham entered League Two in 2023/24, as the other large spenders were Forest Green Rovers who had been relegated the previous season, and Gillingham who had been demoted from League One two years earlier. As such, the total wage budgets of clubs in the EFL do not always provide a clear picture of how good a team will be. While Wrexham's spending on players had translated to strong performances on the field, Forest Green Rovers ended up being relegated in two consecutive seasons despite their relatively high spending.

Although *Welcome to Wrexham* portrayed the second half of the 2023/24 League Two season as being particularly stressful for the club, Wrexham still managed to secure automatic promotion to League One by finishing second in the league. This should have been of little surprise, as even though the gap between Wrexham's wage bill and their opponents had shrunk significantly in League Two, they were still the top purchasers of talent. Moreover, as their transfer policy was built around short-term performance rather than future potential, Wrexham's wealth of financial resources was being wielded with the sole purpose of being promoted.

Perhaps the biggest surprise in the 2023/24 League Two season was that Stockport County finished ahead of Wrexham in the table. However, this was not the first time that Stockport had done this. Indeed, when Wrexham had missed out on promotion in their first season under Reynolds and McElhenney's ownership, it was Stockport who had beaten them out to gain automatic promotion to the EFL. However, in that first season, Wrexham was still getting its footing under its North American owners, who had yet to help them realize its full earning potential through media and commercial partnerships. And yet, despite being massively outspent by Wrexham, Stockport County had managed to win the league.

Having beaten out Wrexham twice was a sign that it was not purely luck that had helped Stockport. Rather, was Stockport's success merely a reflection that money alone was not enough to guarantee promotion through the English soccer pyramid? Or was there something else special that had allowed them to win two league titles in a three-year period?

Up and Comers

At face value, there really doesn't seem to be anything special about Stockport County. The club spent almost its entire history floating between various divisions of the EFL, having never made it to the top-flight of English soccer. Stockport gained some notoriety in the 1990s as a giant killer after they knocked

Blackburn Rovers, West Ham United, and Southampton—all Premier League clubs at the time—out of the 1996/97 League Cup.

However, while the Premier League was growing into a massive business empire in the early 2000s, Stockport found itself in financial trouble. After being demoted to the third division in 2001, the club was sold to Brian Kennedy who owned the Sale Sharks—a top-flight rugby union team based in Manchester. However, even after consolidating operations of his rugby and new soccer club into the same stadium, Kennedy was unable to stop Stockport from hemorrhaging cash. After the club posted losses of around $5 million for the 2005 season, Kennedy relinquished control of the club to the Stockport County Supporter's Trust.[15] Under fan ownership, Stockport was able to improve the on-field performance of the club, gaining promotion back into League One in 2008. But it was not the on-field product that was the problem for Stockport.

At the end of the 2008/9 season, Stockport found themselves unable to pay back a six-figure loan as well as a massive tax bill from the British government.[16] Where a rich investor might have been able to step in and bail the club out of financial insolvency, the supporter run club had no such figure to turn to. As such, they were placed under administration meaning that a financial specialist would take control of the club and its business operations to try and rescue the company if they could. After an initial bid from former Manchester City player Jim Melrose was rejected by the EFL, Stockport was eventually sold to a consortium of owners[17] in 2010 who promised to invest heavily to restore the club to its former glory.[18] Despite these promises, Stockport County were relegated from the Football League for the first time in its history.

As a nonleague club, Stockport continued to struggle, dropping down to the sixth division in 2013 before eventually being promoted back to the National League in 2019. Up to this point, there is nothing in Stockport's history or operations that point toward it being a team on the ascendency that would be challenging a Hollywood-backed money club for promotion into the third division. Instead, they fit the definition of an uninspired nonleague team whose focus seems more on day-to-day survival, then trying to rocket up the soccer pyramid.

All of this changed in 2020, when the club was purchased by Mark Stott, founder of Vita Group—a prominent property development company in the UK. Stott, who grew up close to Stockport, made similar promises to those from the previous owners that he would build the club back up. In Stott's case, he really meant it. After purchasing the club, one of the most critical things he did was to clear the entirety of the club's debt.[19] This may seem like a minor thing, but the reality is that debt load is one of the biggest issues that encumber EFL and nonleague soccer clubs. Financial records that clubs are required to publish show that many clubs in the EFL have large operating losses. In other words, these clubs are losing money through their day-to-day operations as a soccer team.

This is one place where the financials of soccer clubs, especially those in the EFL and National League, differ from most ordinary businesses. If a tire company or a marketing firm was continuously losing money from one year to the next, the owners would likely either shut down the business or try to liquidate the company with the goal of trying to recoup as much value as possible. However, not only do many EFL clubs consistently operate in the red, but they do so by design. Just like Ryan Reynolds and Rob McElhenney's ownership of Wrexham, owners of other Football League clubs have the goal of being promoted into higher divisions. As such, these owners believe that spending heavily is a critical part of improving a squad, meaning that yearly losses are an acceptable part of doing business. Along these lines, many owners provide loans to their clubs on a yearly basis to continue subsidizing the purchase of players that the club would not be able to afford.

It is important to note that this practice of borrowing money from a club's owners is not something that is unique to lower division clubs, or even soccer teams in England. Indeed, it is a widely accepted practice across Europe, especially for those clubs who have extremely rich owners. Before the advent of Financial Fair Play (FFP) rules in European soccer, billionaire owners like Roman Abramovich took advantage of the accounting regulations to pump large amounts of their own cash into the club. Although these loans are still treated as debt, that debt is held by the owner of the team. As such, when Abramovich took over Chelsea, he was able to instantly inject hundreds of millions of dollars into player spending, and then simply say the club could pay him back sometime in the future with no little to no interest. When Abramovich was forced to sell Chelsea in 2022, it was found that he had forgiven around £1.6 billion in loans to the club[20]—an average of £80 million a year.

Precisely because of owners like Abramovich, as well as the takeover of clubs by nation-state run investment funds, FFP rules were instituted to limit club spending to income generated from the soccer side of the business. Included in these regulations were the amount owners could loan to their clubs on a yearly basis, as well as the acceptable loses teams were allowed to have. The basic idea behind setting these rules was to limit super-rich clubs from going on spending sprees, and to prevent poorer clubs from going into massive debt to compete with them.

Where financial regulations were instituted into the top tiers of the soccer pyramid—generally the first and second division—leagues and teams further down the ladder were provided a different set of rules that allowed for owners to continue loaning large amounts to their clubs.[21] This meant that Stockport was able to take advantage of the lack of financial rules, and have Mark Stott clear the club's debt and start loaning money to improve the quality of the squad. No longer burdened by financial impediments, and now armed with a relatively well-off owner, Stockport County was quickly transformed into an up-and-coming club—one that demonstrates the power money has to catapult a team up the soccer pyramid.

The (Almost) Big Time

Upon entering League One in 2024, Stockport were faced with an entirely new challenge. Previously in the National League and League Two, they mainly had to deal with Wrexham as the overspending giants that they had to contend with. However, now in the third division, they had to face numerous clubs who were funded by wealthy foreign investors. Beyond Wrexham, the two main culprits were Huddersfield AFC and Birmingham City. Huddersfield, who had been in the Premier League as recently as 2019, had been stricken down by financial issues similar to those that had relegated Stockport into nonLeague soccer. Even with American businessman Kevin Nagle rescuing the club financially in 2023,[22] it was natural that Huddersfield were the second biggest spenders in League One with a yearly wage bill of around £11.5 million. To put this into context, Huddersfield were spending almost a million more pounds than Wrexham were paying for their squad, and almost double Stockport's £6.7 million in payroll.

However, all the clubs in League One were dwarfed by Birmingham City, who spent £16 million on player salaries for the 2024/25 season. Just like Huddersfield, Birmingham City was a former Premier League club that had gone through near bankruptcy and multiple owners over the previous two decades. Under the ownership of Hong Kong real estate magnate Carson Yeung, Birmingham City had previously qualified for the Europa League in 2011.[23] However, with Yeung unwilling to make large investments in the club, the club quickly fell into disarray and languished in the second division. After being convicted of money laundering, Yeung sold Birmingham to another investment group that placed the club on the Hong Kong Stock Exchange[24] leading to fan protests.[25]

Finally, in 2023, the club was sold to Shelby Companies Ltd, who were owned by Knighthead Capital Management—a New York based hedge fund that manages over a billion dollars in assets.[26] Knighthead co-CEO Tom Wagner was named the chairman of Birmingham County, and the club made major headlines when it brought on former NFL superstar Tom Brady as one of their minority partners. Although they were relegated down to League One in the first season after the takeover, fans were positive that the club would bounce back under the new ownership group.[27] Indeed with the wealth of resources that came along with a billion-dollar hedge fund partnered with one of the highest paid athletes in the history of professional sports, the question wasn't whether they could outspend Wrexham, but by how much could they outspend the Hollywood-funded club.

In League One, rather than being overseen by FFP rules, clubs are governed by the EFL's Salary Cost Management Protocol (SCMP) regulations. Although similar to FFP, the SCMP is much more relaxed in terms of spending and owner investments. At the start of the 2024/25 season, League One clubs were allowed to spend 60 percent of all revenue generated on player salaries and transfers.[28] More importantly for the likes of Birmingham and Wrexham, they allowed 100 percent of owner investments to be spent on player transfers and wages. Essentially, this meant that Birmingham could spend as much as Knighthead Capital and Tom Brady were willing to give to the club. As such, with Birmingham City spending around 40 percent more than their nearest competitor (Huddersfield) on player talent, it was a forgone conclusion that the club would run away with the title and be promoted back to the Championship. Indeed, Birmingham City won the League One title by a whopping nineteen points, easily securing their promotion back to the Championship.

Finishing directly behind Birmingham City in the final automatic promotion spot was Wrexham, who had been hounded by Stockport County and Charlton Athletic through most of the season. Effectively, the two clubs with the largest financial backing had dominated the league. While the domination of Birmingham and Wrexham was not just due to their wealth, as clubs like Huddersfield had spent similar amounts only to finish mid-table, money certainly played a role in determining which teams would be promoted to the second division. Moreover, having large investments from owners is not only beneficial in assembling a strong squad of players but also in hiring the most top-level sporting directors and coaches.

Perhaps the most notable and strategic hiring decision that Wrexham made was not in purchasing highly experience players like Paul Mullin and Liam McAlinden but was instead naming Phil Parkinson as manager shortly after the North American takeover. Parkinson, who had previously coached famous clubs such as Bolton Wanderers and Bradford City, had made a name for himself as a promotion specialist. Before his time at Wrexham, Parkinson had led Colchester, Bradford City, and Bolton Wanderers to promotion. Of these, the most impressive may have been the work he did at Colchester, as he helped one of the most underfunded teams in League One to secure automatic promotion to the Championship.[29] Parkinson had worked wonders on a shoestring budget. With Wrexham willing to provide him the financial backing to buy the best players at his level, it was only natural that the club would go on to achieve three straight promotions.

As such, even though money was not the only factor, it was still the major force in Birmingham and Wrexham's ascendance into the Championship, placing both clubs one promotion away from their Premier League dreams.

A Whole New Game

As much as the emergence of Wrexham has done wonders for the popularity of lower division English soccer around the world, there have been concerns over how the club was able to charge its way from obscurity to potentially being a top-flight club in just a few years. And to be clear, although Wrexham was certainly the most visible of the lower league clubs spending large sums of money to race up the pyramid, they were not the only one. Indeed, beyond Birmingham City's mix of superstars and hedge fund owners, four other clubs in League One were owned by billionaires, including Barnsley FC, Wigan Athletic, Wycombe Wanderers, and Leyton Orient. Outside of Wigan, the majority of the owners of all of these "big money" League One clubs were all based outside of the UK. Where Premier League clubs had once been the target for extremely rich investors from around the world, that interest had now started to trickle down the pyramid.

For the EFL, one of the major concerns was the potential imbalance and disruptions that could come from such large influxes of cash into lower soccer leagues. With owners in League One and League Two effectively able to loan as much money to their club as they had available in their checking accounts, it creates the potential for clubs like Wrexham and Birmingham to outspend the rest of their league with little effort. This spending not only leads to rich teams dominating the leagues and controlling most of the promotion slots but also has an impact on the finances of the rest of the league. With wealthy clubs spending wildly on players, it has a knock-on effect across the entire market by raising the price of transfers and wages for other players. And while the super-rich teams can easily afford a few percent hike in prices, it has much more dire consequences for poorer clubs who already are having financial difficulties.

From the perspective of the EFL, the increase in rich foreign investment into lower league soccer is essentially a double-edged sword. While it has the potential to raise the overall profile, interest, and revenues of all clubs in these leagues, it also has presented a changing market dynamic that could threaten the existence of many historic clubs. As such, in the middle of the 2024/25 season, the EFL announced sweeping changes to the SCMP rules that limit the amount of investment from owners that a club can spend on purchasing talent. Specifically, the new regulations restricted League One clubs to only being able to spend 60 percent of any owner investment of over £1 million on player transfer and wages.[30] In other words, if an owner were to invest £10 million into the club, they could only spend £6 million on players, with the remaining amount having to go into other aspects of the club such as stadium improvements, front office staff, equipment, etc. For clubs in League Two, this cap was increased to 50 percent of owner investments over £1 million.

On paper, this seems like a fairly reasonable rule to slow down the spending from owners, and re-direct some of this income into other critical parts of the club. However, these FFP rules are still nowhere as stringent as those which are found in the top-flight of most European soccer leagues where teams are required to only have a set amount of losses and owner investment over a three-year window.[31] Indeed, these rules were put into place because of the massive amounts owners were spending that was happening in the top levels of soccer.

Notably, where it was common for Premier League clubs to report financial losses on a yearly basis, the situation was a lot more dire in the Championship. In the 2012/13 season, only three of the twenty-four teams in the second division reported a profit, with the number increasing to five if profits from player sales were included.[32] Although some clubs were certainly in a tough financial situation, the reality was that many owners of Championship clubs were injecting massive amounts into their teams with the hope of being promoted to the Premier League. Promotion to the Premier League not only meant joining one of the most elite clubs in the world but also had significant payoffs with promotion guaranteeing around £120 million in just television revenues at the time. As such, owners of Championship clubs were willing to loan massive amounts to their clubs on a yearly basis with the belief that promotion to the Premier League would help to clear these debts. However, many of these clubs were overspending to the point that even a significant boost in revenue from being promoted to the Premier League would not be able to clear the debt they had taken on to get there.

Although FFP rules have only had limited success in restricting spending among the top levels of European soccer, they have helped clubs to do a better job of getting their finances in line. Indeed, after the current set of PSR guidelines for the EFL were implemented in 2016/17, only seven clubs entered administration in the following ten years. In comparison, twenty clubs had gone into administration in the previous decade, including eight clubs in 2008 alone.

From this perspective, one could argue that the new SCMP rules that govern League One and League Two may not be restrictive enough in terms of spending. For example, League Two club Walsall is partly owned by Americans who are associated with a capital asset management company that is worth around $12 billion. Even with a 50 percent cap on spending owner investments on players, Walsall could still flood their club with a billion dollars and use half to buy a squad to rival most Premier League teams and use the rest to build a new stadium. As such, the spending regulations in the third and fourth divisions serve more as a tax to deter owners but do not effectively limit their investments or debt loads in any significant way.

However, most critically for clubs like Birmingham City and Wrexham, the difference in financial rules essentially creates a wall for clubs that use large owner investments to gain promotion to the Championship. That is, the move from the third to the second tier of English soccer means that clubs who had been able to simply outspend their competition in the previous years by asking their owner to write big checks suddenly find themselves governed by new rules limiting these investments. While they are still able to receive loans from their owners, they are no longer able to spend as freely as they had in previous leagues. This means that the strategy which many clubs use to fight their way up the soccer pyramid is no longer feasible upon entering the second division.

As such, though the Championship may seem like a gateway to the Premier League, it actually serves as a wall.

The Wall

If Wrexham were to enter the Championship with the same payroll they had in the 2024/25 League One season, they would find themselves moving from being one of the top three spenders in the league to the bottom three. Indeed, in 2024/25, the only Championship sides who spent less than them were Portsmouth and Plymouth who finished sixteenth and twenty-third respectively. Even Birmingham City's outlandish League One spending would merely translate to a top-ten wage bill in the Championship. Leeds United, who won the 2024/25 Championship, spent £36 million on wages, or more than double Birmingham's wage bill, and triple that of Wrexham's.

Indeed, this is a reflection of the massive gap in resources that exists between leagues as one moves up the soccer pyramid. One year, you can find yourself to be the superpower of your league, only to be just another mediocre club after being promoted the following year. While this difference exists throughout the pyramid, it becomes more evident as one climbs the ladder, first moving from nonleague soccer to the EFL, and then eventually to the Championship. In some sense, the Championship can be considered as a mixture of a safeguard, barrier, and finishing school for clubs seeking to gain promotion to the Premier League. That is, it provides clubs that have been promoted from lower divisions with the chance to entirely retool their organization in preparation for top-flight soccer.

Because of the stricter FFP regulations, clubs like Wrexham and Birmingham City will have to find new methods through which to generate revenue to spend on players just to stay competitive within the Championship. Indeed, while clubs are still able to receive owner investments, the limit on these means that teams become a lot more reliant on matchday and commercial revenue to generate the income needed to strengthen a squad. Teams that are unable to do so will find themselves falling behind the rest of the league in terms of financial resources, which typically translates to a lack of quality on the pitch, and subsequent relegation.

From this perspective, even though Birmingham City may have richer owners, the move to the Championship might actually be more advantageous for Wrexham. Indeed, because of Wrexham's entrepreneurial approach to building their media stardom, it has provided the club with additional revenue sources, as well as a popularity that has helped to continuously attract some of the top sponsors in professional sport. For corporations like United Airlines or TikTok, the point of paying large sums of money to a sport team is to get them to see your brand. And while you can see every other Championship club on television, *Welcome to Wrexham* provides a different level of connection and engagement to consumers. As such, the monetization of Wrexham's media products allows them to generate more revenue as they move up the pyramid and continue to remain financially competitive.

However, no matter how successful Wrexham, Birmingham City, and other clubs are within the Championship, the reality is the true wall is the Premier League itself. The 2024/25 season has been a great example of the true separation that exists between the Premier League and the rest of the soccer pyramid. The three teams that were promoted from the Championship—Leicester City, Ipswich Town, and Southampton—also were the three teams that were immediately relegated out of the top-flight. To put into context how bad clubs promoted from the Championship were, the three teams combined were only able to win twelve matches across the entire season. In comparison, sixteenth-place Wolverhampton Wanderers finished the season with twelve wins. Southampton just barely managed to avoid Derby County's record of the least number of points in a Premier League season.

Moreover, this is not just a one-time occurrence. In fact, the exact same thing had happened in the previous season when Luton Town, Burnley, and Sheffield United all earned promotion to the Premier League and were immediately sent back down to the Championship. Even with seventeenth place Nottingham Forest being deducted points for violations of PSR regulations, they still managed to finish six points clear of the drop zone. Much of this is a symptom of the increasing commercialization of soccer, especially in top-flight leagues. Clubs now spend a significant amount of time calculating optimal ticket pricing and negotiating deals with corporations to maximize their revenue. In this sense, it has created an established guard of the Premier League, not just the "big six"—Arsenal, Manchester United, Manchester City, Chelsea, Liverpool, and Tottenham—of former years who dominated the league, but an exclusive club of the same seventeen teams who will have played in the Premier League for three straight seasons from 2024 to 2026. Yes, three new teams get promoted up the pyramid every year, but it is now becoming a regular occurrence that they are sent back to where they came from. As Stuart Scott used to say on Sports Center: "You don't have to go home, but you have to get the heck up out of here."

Foundation

All of this raises the critical question of whether the English soccer pyramid is functioning as intended. At a base level, the promotion and relegation system is considered to be a true meritocracy where the best teams can continue rising, while the weakest are sent down to a level more suitable to them. In this sense, because teams are still able to move up and down tiers of soccer, it can be said that the pyramid is still serving its base function of sorting clubs based on performance. However, the major issue is that now more than ever performance is linked to the financial resources of a club. Yes, teams still need to win games on the field to be promoted, but that is being heavily influenced by the wealth of clubs and their owners. If building commercial strength was the primary objective of the pyramid, then it would definitely be fulfilling its purpose.

Perhaps a more fitting question would be whether the pyramid is sustainable. This is an important question, especially considering that the Premier League itself was formed when the top clubs in England broke away from the EFL because of their unhappiness with the lack of monetization at the top of the soccer pyramid. Indeed, in recent years, many of the top Premier League teams have even considered leaving the pyramid altogether to join the European Super League[33]—a closed competition comprised of the top clubs across Europe. While a mutiny by the top clubs would not destroy the pyramid overnight, there are a concerning number of issues in the current system: overinvestment and unchecked spending in the lower leagues of the EFL, inconsistent financial rules between the various tiers, revenue disparities between leagues and clubs, all of which are leading to competitive imbalance across the entire system.

Though it still serves as the bedrock of the Premier League and English soccer, there are cracks within the pyramid. And despite having evolved into a money-centered system that rewards wealthy investors and their commercial partners, it still plays a central role in the development of many of the best players and clubs in the world. As such, the major concern really shouldn't be for the pyramid itself, which looks to be on solid footing, but instead for the individual clubs that comprise the system. With even the semi-professional levels of the sport turning focus toward monetization and attracting deep-pocketed investors, the disparities between clubs will continue to grow on and off the field. While this may not kill the system, it will lead to many historic clubs sliding down the pyramid, and in some cases, even disappearing.

Although most soccer fans may not care about the fate of a fifth division club playing in small town in the English countryside, these are the clubs that helped to build and maintain the pyramid for over a century. Soccer as we know it would not exist without these clubs.

Their potential demise should not just be seen as a loss for a few thousand local fans, but as a warning sign of the fragility of many clubs that help prop up the soccer pyramid in England.

5

Cristiano in the Desert
Is Saudi Arabia the
Future of Soccer?

One would expect the most expensive signing in soccer history to be conducted with a little more fanfare. A sparking private jet landing and the superstar emerging in a designer suit with sunglasses. Or maybe a promo video of the player entering a stadium full of cheering fans, excited that their relatively unknown club had just managed to sign one of soccer's biggest stars. Instead, what we got was a picture of Cristiano Ronaldo in a black t-shirt holding up an Al-Nassr jersey alongside a club official. Ronaldo was about to be paid $200 million a year to kick a soccer ball around Saudi Arabia, and all we got was a generic photo that seemed more fitting of a youth team signing for a second division French club.

However, the arrival of Cristiano Ronaldo in 2022 was a true watershed moment for Saudi Arabia and its soccer ambitions. Although they had been making major investments in sport, including the acquisition of a majority stake in Newcastle United, none of these purchases had involved bringing a globally recognized superstar to the country for the longterm. And not just any superstar, but arguably the most well-known athlete on the planet, who is the most followed person on Instagram with over 650 million followers.[1]

Many pundits dismissed the signing as simply showing us that everyone had their price, and that Cristiano's number was $200 million to play for a virtually unknown soccer team. However, the signing of Ronaldo instantly transformed the Saudi Pro League from being a competition that was ignored and easily dismissed, to one that was focus of intense global interest. Al-Nassr shirts began to appear in the streets of New York, Tokyo, and Paris, as fans around the world continued to worship one of the game's greatest players.

So how did Cristiano end up in Saudi Arabia, and what does it mean for the future of soccer? We know money played a big role in this process, but behind Cristiano's arrival was also a complex web of geopolitics and economics that now more than ever influences the fates of clubs and the trajectory of player careers.

The Growth of Saudi Soccer

For much of the Western world, the first introduction to Saudi soccer has typically come at the World Cup. For those who are of my age, they may remember Saeed Al-Owairan's amazing solo run against Belgium in the 1994 World Cup. The goal was named one of the top goals in the history of the tournament by FIFA and helped secure Saudi Arabia's advancement to the knockout round in their first ever World Cup. For younger readers, the moment they probably associate with Saudi soccer is their famous win against Argentina in the group stages of the 2022 World Cup. Even Saudi Crown Prince Mohammed bin Salman, often referred to as MBS, admitted the expectation had been to avoid being humiliated by the Messi-led Argentinian squad. Instead, Saudi Arabia became the only team to beat the eventual world champions during the tournament.

My own personal introduction to Saudi soccer came after I moved to Japan in 1992. At the time, Japan was essentially the small fry of Asian soccer, they had never qualified for a World Cup, and their last meaningful achievement had been a bronze medal in the 1968 Olympic soccer tournament. Standing in the way of Japan were the powers of Asia: South Korea, Iran, and of course, Saudi Arabia. And thus, it was to my great surprise that Japan beat the two-time defending champions Saudi Arabia in the winter of 1992 to win their first ever continental title.

Despite this victory, Saudi Arabia continued to stand out as one of Asia's best sides. Japan had been on the verge of making it to their first ever World Cup in 1994, until tragedy struck in the last minute of their final qualifying match. A short corner taken quickly from Iraq to level the match sent Japan tumbling from top of the group to missing out on the World Cup. Instead, Saudi Arabia and South Korea would represent Asia in 1994, leading to a run of four straight World Cup appearances for the Saudi's.

However, Saudi Arabia didn't just wake up one day in the 1980s and decide that it was going to become good at soccer. Like many countries around the world, soccer is believed to have been introduced to Saudi Arabia by British merchants who likely brought the sport to the region sometime in the late 1800s. Following this, soccer within the country was mostly organized in regional leagues, with amateur clubs being formed to represent various areas. Saudi Pro League club Al-Wehda often claims to be the first soccer club within the country, dating their history back to 1916 when they were originally called Al-Hizb. Counter to this, Ittihad Saudi Arabian Club, or Ittihad for short, claim to be the oldest continuously running club having been founded in 1927.[2] Notably, Ittihad, whose name simply means "United" in Arabic, are one of the most storied clubs in Asian soccer, having won thirty domestic trophies, as well as two Asian Champions League titles, and a fourth-place finish in the 2005 Club World Cup.[3]

Overall, it is hard to say exactly which is the oldest club in Saudi Arabia, or which clubs and regions contributed to the growth of the game as there was a lack of record keeping at the time[4]. To put this into context, the Kingdom of Saudi Arabia as we know it didn't even exist until 1932, when the kingdoms of Nejd and Hejaz were officially unified into a single country. In other words, there are Saudi soccer clubs that predate the formation of Saudi Arabia itself.[5]

Although more clubs continued to be established across the Kingdom over the next several decades, soccer continued to be mostly organized at a regional level. All of this changed in the 1950s, when the Saudi government began to push for greater professionalization within the sport. In 1951, a team composed of players selected from a handful of Saudi clubs played a series of friendlies against Egypt, helped to further the case for the need for a proper soccer national team. This eventually led to the creation of the Saudi Arabian Football Federation in 1956, which became the governing body of all soccer in Saudi Arabia, while also establishing the country as an official member of FIFA.

The 1950s were especially critical in the growth of the domestic game within Saudi Arabia. First off, the first two major national tournaments were formed—the Crown Prince's Cup and the King's Cup. The King's Cup, which has undergone numerous transformations, has essentially served as the main domestic cup within Saudi Arabia since its formation. In this, it has played a vital role in pivoting the focus away from regional competitions within the Kingdom and instead placed greater emphasis on national-level soccer competition. The 1950s were also important because it saw the number of clubs within the country expand, most notably with the formation of Al-Nassr and Al-Hilal that were formed in 1955 and 1957, respectively. Not only would these two clubs go on to become giants of Saudi soccer, but they would also play a prominent role in raising the overall standard of soccer in the country and developing future generations of national team members. Of course, to most soccer fans today, Al-Nassr is now famous because of their signing of former Real Madrid superstar and six-time Ballon d'Or winner Cristiano Ronaldo. More on that whole thing later.

The one thing that was lacking at this point in Saudi Arabia was a national soccer league to develop and showcase the best soccer talent within the country. One of the major problems that stood in the way of organizing a nationwide league was in sorting which teams from the various regional leagues would be granted entry into the top division, and which ones would relegated to lower divisions. In order to settle this fairly, Saudi conducted what was called the Categorization League in 1974/75, which placed the top sixteen teams from the regional leagues into two groups of eight. Each group played a round robin format with the top four teams in each group earning the right to play in the new Saudi Premier League—the old name for the Saudi Pro League—that kicked off in 1976.

The Saudi league has continually expanded over time, immediately moving from eight to ten teams after the completion of its inaugural season. By the late 1980s, the league had grown to have twelve teams in the top-flight and continued to grow to the current format of eighteen teams that started from the 2023/24 season. Before 2023, the league's growth was mostly organic, with expansions mostly being driven by soaring interest in the domestic game amongst fans within Saudi Arabia. Indeed, soccer has enjoyed such widespread popularity that five tiers of professional soccer have been established within the Kingdom. As of 2024, there are 182 professional Saudi soccer clubs, with the majority playing in the fifth tier (Fourth Division). In comparison, England has ninety-two men's professional clubs that are organized into four tiers of competition.

Like other leagues in Asia, the Saudi Pro League has adopted rules that limit the number of foreign players that each club is able to sign. This type of regulation has been widely implemented in leagues such as the Qatar Stars League, J-League (Japan), K-League (Korea), and Chinese Super League to ensure that domestic players are provided opportunities to play and grow within their own country. Indeed, similar rules have even been considered in England, where there was once talk of a 6+5 rule that would require teams in the Premier League to field matchday squads that were mainly comprised of English players. After Arsenal became the first Premier League team to field an all-foreign line-up on Valentine's Day, 2005, pundits and fans started to criticize the lack of playing time for English talent. The belief was that if the Premier League continued to purchase foreign talent to replace domestic players, it would erode the quality of the domestic game and hurt the national team.

It is precisely because of this logic, as well as desire to keep costs low, that teams in Asia tend to cap the number of foreigners on a roster, a practice which extends beyond soccer and is even regulated in baseball and basketball. What is notable about the Saudi league, is that the regulations regarding foreign players have shifted over time. For example, in 2005/6, teams were allowed up to six foreigners on their roster, though some clubs such as Al-Tai and Abha chose to sign only two foreigners. The rules were amended in the following year to limit teams to four non-Saudi players, which was eventually changed to a 3+1 rule, where teams were allowed three foreign players from any country and one additional player from a fellow Asian Football Confederation (AFC) country.

From the early 1990s to the mid-2000s, Saudi clubs quickly emerged as the dominant force within the Middle East, with Al-Hilal and Al-Ittihad both winning two AFC Champions League titles. This is especially notable, as clubs from South Korea and Japan won the majority of the titles during this period, with the only other winners from the Middle East region being Al Ain (UAE) and PAS Tehran (Iran). While the league continued to grow, the balance of power in Asian club soccer continued to shift to the East. In addition to the strong support and structure within Japanese and Korean soccer, Chinese clubs started receiving massive investment from major corporations as the country placed increased emphasis on the sport. Indeed, from 2006 to 2018, only two AFC Champions League titles were won by teams outside of East Asia; one by Al-Sadd of Qatar and another by Western Sydney Wanderers of Australia.

However, the Saudi government was about to ensure that this drought of titles would come to an end.

The PIF Soccer Plan

In 2016, Saudi Arabia launched a new national plan called Saudi 2030 Vision that was focused on revitalizing and transforming the country. A major cornerstone of this was the nation's Public Investment Fund (PIF), a strategic wealth fund that controls nearly a trillion dollars in assets. Soccer was included as a part of the 2030 Vision plan as a tool for economic growth, international prestige, and the development of young adults within the Kingdom. Indeed, as the population of Saudi Arabia is just under 37 million, with a large percentage of residents being below the age of thirty-five, promoting healthy lifestyles was considered an important goal for the country.[6]

Although PIF was not directly involved with the operations of the Saudi Pro League at the time, many of the top clubs are owned by prominent businesspeople or families with close ties to the government and the royal family. As such, in order to start boosting the performance and profile of the league, new rules were instituted at the beginning of the 2017/18 season that changed the number of foreign players on a squad from four to six, with a seventh allowed slot for goalkeepers. This was a major turning point as it allowed Saudi clubs, especially those with rich benefactors, to go out and purchase more foreign players to strengthen their squads. Additionally, it also meant that some of the teams were no longer predominantly composed of domestic players, mirroring squad compositions seen in top European clubs. Although this could have potential consequences for the strength of the Saudi national team in the future, being able to sign many foreign players also meant that Saudi clubs now had much more squad depth. And it is squad depth that is especially critical for teams that are trying to compete in both domestic and international competitions within the same season. Indeed, with a splendor of financial resources and a strong squad, Al-Hilal would bring their number of AFC Champions League titles to four, with victories in 2019 and 2022 crowning them as the most successful club in Asian soccer. In just a few years with relatively little investment, Saudi Arabia had managed to reach the pinnacle of Asian club soccer. Just imagine what they could do if they really put their mind and money into the sport.

As the domestic game was starting to boom in Saudi, PIF turned its focus overseas to make its first major investment into soccer. In January 2020, news broke that a consortium led by PIF had submitted a bid to purchase storied Premier League club Newcastle United.[7] Perhaps the biggest roadblock to completing the estimated £300 million purchase was getting approval from the Premier League's Board of Governors and the UK government. Almost every major professional sport league in the world has an extensive rulebook that includes a subsection dictating all the rules of ownership. For the Premier League, one of the major concerns of the purchase of Newcastle by PIF was that it would make the team a government owned club. Leagues tend to discourage having nation-states or even local governments serving as owners of a team because it can cause an array of issues, including questions of fairness when an entire country's resources can be used to financially back an individual club. Even the richest of American owners in the Premier League have net worths of around $10 billion. In comparison, PIF controls ninety times more assets than this. PIF is not just richer than any single owner, they are richer than the entire Premier League combined. And by several times.

To further scrutinize PIF's potential ownership of Newcastle, the Premier League applied what is called the "Owners and Directors test," a rule in the

UK that requires anyone who owns more than 30 percent of a club to undergo a proper assessment of their finances and business connections.[8] These rules had previously been put in place to protect clubs from either being partially or completely sold to unscrupulous, incompetent, or financially unstable investors. For example, Louis Tomlinson of the boy band One Direction once attempted to purchase his boyhood club Doncaster Rovers, but the bid failed when his business partner was unable to pass the Owners and Directors test.[9]

For the Premier League and its clubs, the biggest concern for the Newcastle takeover was that several members of the Saudi government also were board members with PIF, most notably Mohammed bin Salman. With MBS serving both as the Crown Prince of Saudi Arabia and the Director of PIF, it blurred the lines of whether the investment fund was a state actor. As such, there was a legitimate belief that if PIF purchased the team, it would allow government officials to directly influence the operations of the club. To fight against this, several Premier League clubs lobbied against approving the sale, approaching both the league and the UK government arguing that if PIF purchased Newcastle it would essentially be state ownership of a club.[10] At the same time, it was suggested that the Saudi government, including MBS himself, exerted pressure on the UK government to have the sale approved.[11] However, after consistent delays in the process, the PIF-led consortium pulled out of negotiations for the club.

Although Premier League owners were in opposition to PIF's Newcastle takeover plans, fans of the club had greatly supported the move. After years of discontent toward Michael Ashley's ownership and operation of the club, the bid from the PIF consortium had provided Newcastle fans with hope that not only would their club be rescued from mediocrity, but that they would be given a war chest like Chelsea received when they were taken over by Russian oligarch Roman Abramovich which propelled them to a European title. When the Newcastle United Supporters Trust (NUST)—the club's largest independent fan organization—polled it's 14,000 members, 97 percent of them said they were in favor of PIF purchasing the club.[12] In response to the overwhelming local support for the Saudi takeover, UK Prime Minister Boris Johnson called for an explanation into how the Premier League had conducted the Owners and Directors test of PIF.[13]

Notably, the demand for transparency from the public and government ministers was sparked by rumors that the Owners and Directors test had been unfairly influenced by outside forces. In this case, the "outside forces" was beIN Sports, a Qatari-owned sports channel which holds the broadcast rights to the Premier League and many other major sport competitions across the Middle East and North Africa (MENA) region. At the time of the takeover, Saudi Arabia, the UAE, and several other MENA countries had cut diplomatic ties with Qatar and began blockading the country.

When the blockade of Qatar began in 2017, the Saudi's quickly moved to ban beIN Sports and its parent channel Al Jazeera within the Kingdom. Moreover, with the United Arab Emirates hosting the 2019 Asian Cup, the Saudi's got the Asian Football Confederation to extend this ban to the entire tournament and all other matches hosted in Saudi Arabia.[14] The biggest blow to beIN came when their content started to be stolen and repacked for sale within Saudi Arabia by the pirate television station beoutQ.[15] Because beIN held the regional rights to most major international sporting competitions, the piracy of their content was quickly condemned worldwide, and blame was cast on the Saudi government for not immediately cracking down on beoutQ.[16] Although Saudi Arabia shut down beoutQ in 2019, it caused significant financial damages to beIN who sued the pirate television channel for $1 billion.[17]

All of this led to bad blood between beIN Sports and the Saudis, so that when PIF placed their bid for Newcastle United, the CEO of beIN Sports immediately contacted the Premier League asking them to put a stop to the deal.[18] While normally the Premier League wouldn't get involved in regional conflicts and trade disputes, beIN Sports happens to pay the largest international rights fees to broadcast matches of any region in the world. Thus, the Premier League was put into a difficult situation. On one hand, the government was pressuring them to approve the Saudi Public Investment Fund purchase of Newcastle United. On the other hand, team owners and the holders of their biggest international television contract were telling them to kill the deal. And amidst all of this were the calls for transparency regarding the Owners and Directors test of PIF.

On August 14, 2020, the Premier League came out with an official statement that the Owners and Directors test found that there was not a proper separation of powers between PIF and the Saudi government, and thus the takeover bid was not approved. Moreover, Premier League CEO Richard Masters attempted to dodge further criticism by stating that the test was not influenced by any outside parties.[19] Of course, this does not seem to be truly factual based on what we know. Not only was beIN Sports conducting a media campaign to denounce the Saudi purchase of the club,[20] but they also submitted a legal opinion to the Premier League noting that the television piracy conducted by the Saudi's was an illegal act and should automatically disqualify PIF under the Owners and Directors test.[21]

While all of this was happening, it was reported the PIF consortium had approached Newcastle United and the Premier League to re-open talks about purchasing the club. Part of the catalyst for this was the work of Lord Gerry Grimstone, the minister appointed by Boris Johnson to help cut through the bureaucracy that was hindering investment within the UK. Grimstone, who had strong ties with Saudi Arabia because of his previous role as the head of Barclays Bank, approached the Premier League in August 2020 to try and serve as an intermediary between the League and PIF.[22] Grimstone repeatedly contacted Gary Hoffman, Chairman of the Premier League, to pressure him into allowing the deal to come to fruition. In documents obtained by British newspapers, it was found that Grimstone went so far as to ask Hoffman to get the Premier League's barristers (lawyers) on the phone so that he could talk to them directly about finding a "solution" that would allow PIF to purchase the club under league rules and regulations.[23]

Curiously, even while Grimstone was serving as an intermediary between the Premier League and PIF, the UK government continued to deny any influence over the negotiations.[24] Of course, like many things within the Boris Johnson administration, this was clearly a lie. Indeed, Hoffman informed the Premier League owners in a meeting that the UK administration had been pressuring them to approve PIF's purchase of Newcastle.

Even with governmental influence, the Premier League still was not budging on its stance about PIF's acceptability as an owner and director of a club. With the process still stalled, Newcastle United took to the courts to find a legal solution to complete the sale of the club to the Saudi's in September 2020. A hearing with the UK Competition Appeal Tribunal (CAT) was initially scheduled for July 27, 2021. Specifically, CAT is the court that hears and reviews cases that are related to the Competition Act that deals with potential restraints of trade or uncompetitive behavior in the UK.[25] Notably, Newcastle's barristers argued that the Premier League's blocking the sale to PIF was an anti-competitive practice and was thus illegal.[26] Naturally, the Premier League countered by attempting to have the case thrown out of court for having no legal grounds.[27]

Things became heated as July 2021 rolled around. Knowing that Newcastle supporters were angry at the lack of transparency in the Premier League's process, the club released a statement asking for the hearings, which are normally private, to be open to the public.[28] Moreover, two weeks before the start of the hearing, several hundred Newcastle United fans traveled hundreds of miles across the country to hold a protest in front of the Prime Minister's residence at Downing Street demanding accountability from the Premier League.[29] Amidst all the pressure, the courts acquiesced and livestreamed the hearing which took place on September 29, 2021. In the hearing, Newcastle's lawyers alleged that not only had the Premier League blocked the sale but had even threatened to expel the club from the league.[30] Following the hearing, which was watched by over 30,000 people, the judges announced that the case would enter arbitration in January 2022, upon which the matter would finally be settled.

Newcastle finally had its day in court. Now they only had to wait four months before the courts came to a final decision over whether they would be able to sell the club to the PIF consortium.

That day never came.

On October 6, 2021, news reports began to circulate that Saudi Arabia would allow beIN Sports and other Qatari channels to resume broadcasts within the Kingdom. Although the blockade of Qatar had ended earlier in January of the same year, the Saudi government had continued enforcing its ban of these channels. The official reason behind this was stated as continued issues with the virtual monopoly that Qatar held over sport broadcasts in the region. However, it was likely that beIN Sports' interference with PIF's purchase of Newcastle United also played a role in the channel being banned in Saudi Arabia.

On the following day, Newcastle United announced that the PIF-led consortium's bid for the club had been officially accepted by the Premier

League. After an arduous eighteen-month process, the Saudi Public Investment Fund now was the majority owner of Newcastle United, holding an 80 percent share of the club.[31] Blockades, piracy, political intrigue, backroom dealing, courtroom drama, sanctions, all these things that sound like the makings of a fictional spy thriller had come to life in PIF's takeover of Newcastle United. The facts of what really happened behind the scenes to make the deal happen are only known to a handful of people in the world, and none of them seem willing to talk about the details. We do not know who flinched first in this international game of chicken that was worth billions of dollars, but the ending was almost too clean. Did the Premier League ask the Saudis to allow beIN Sports to start broadcasting again in their country? Did the Qatari's demand this as the only acceptable solution to their impeding of this deal? Or did some intermediary, maybe even a UK government official, step in and broker a deal between Saudi Arabia, Qatar, and the Premier League. There is even the possibility that much of these negotiations happened without Premier League officials present or aware of what was really going on.

Nevertheless, Saudi Arabia through PIF had now accomplished one of their major goals. They had taken control of the one of the most storied clubs in the Premier League, the most powerful and well-known soccer league in the world. The big question now was: what was next?

The Stars

On the day the PIF consortium took control of Newcastle United, they immediately named Yasir Al-Rumayyan as the new nonexecutive chairman of the club. Al-Rumayyan is best known for being the Governor of the Public Investment Fund, the person who MBS has personally trusted with guiding the operations of the sovereign wealth fund. In profiles of Al-Rumayyan, he is consistently described as a "close ally" of MBS,[32] who has helped to run many critical aspects of the financial side of the Kingdom since MBS's rise to power. Indeed, after his initial success as managing director of PIF, he was named to the board of Saudi Aramco—the state-owned oil and natural gas company worth close $2 trillion.[33] Saudi Aramco, or Aramco for short, is it itself a juggernaut that is controls the world's second largest oil reserve and is the fourth highest revenue-generating company in the world behind Walmart, Amazon, and China's state-owned State Grid corporation.[34] Critically, Aramco also plays an important strategic role in the global order through the control of its oil reserves, the distribution and rationing of which can severely impact the world economy.[35]

As such, when bin Salman promoted Al-Rumayyan to also head Aramco in 2019, it further solidified his status as one of the most powerful people in Saudi Arabia, as well as in the entire business world. One could say that while Saudi's future vision is being guided by MBS, it is Al-Rumayyan behind the scenes who plays a critical role in helping to make it into reality. For example, when the Saudi Vision 2030 plan called for expanding the national economy through sport, it was likely Al-Rumayyan who pushed for the creation of LIV Golf as he is known as an avid golfer.[36] And with the acquisition of Newcastle United completed, Al-Rumayyan did not rest on his laurels. Instead, working in conjunction with the government, PIF immediately turned to the next stage of their massive soccer project—catching the stars.

Having joined the exclusive club of the Premier League, Saudi Arabia and PIF strategically turned their focus back inwards toward their own domestic league. Although the league had again expanded the foreign player rules—allowing up to eight foreign players on a roster starting in the 2022/23 season—the foreigners coming to the Saudi Pro League were mostly second-rate players and the occasional faded star looking for one last payday. Moreover, for foreign players, the very idea of moving to Saudi Arabia to play soccer was filled with stereotypes of a desert backwater with extreme heat and empty stadiums. Why would you want to live in a hot congested city surrounded by sand when you could go to Japan, America, or heck, even Australia, with their family friendly matches, easygoing lifestyles, and abundant commercial opportunities.

However, even with expanded roster slots for foreigners, Al-Hilal becoming the dominant force in Asian soccer, and even with the high wages, most prominent soccer players did not even consider Saudi Arabia as a career option. Major League Soccer (MLS) may get mocked as being a retirement league for top European players looking to make some cash before they hung up their boots, but at least they were getting the washed-up stars. Where America and Japan were getting the likes of Thierry Henry, Fernando Torres, Wayne Rooney, and Andres Iniesta, the best players the Saudi Pro League had were Talisca, Ever Banega, and Romarinho. While some of these players had short spells playing in top European leagues, they were not household names that would draw tons of fans and sponsors to matches.

The primary problem in drawing star players, even those at the twilight of their careers, was one of competition and money. While Saudi Pro League clubs were offering salaries that were competitive with other leagues in the region, such as the Qatar Stars League (QSL) or the UAE Pro League, they were not providing total compensation packages that were attractive enough to entice players to sign with them. Just consider the case of Messi's signing with MLS. While his salary from the league was generous, it was nothing special compared to what he had previously made playing for Barcelona and PSG. Instead, what truly convinced Messi to play in America was getting a revenue share from Apple TV subscriptions, an ownership stake in Inter Miami CF, and an abundance of commercial deals.[37] In this, MLS wasn't just throwing cash at Messi like many European clubs were attempting to but instead provided him with the unique chance to shape his future after retiring from football.

This is the reality of the contemporary soccer market. To sign a star player, you either need to be a European club competing at the top-level offering a ton of cash, or you need to be offering generational wealth to convince the player to play at a lower level. Indeed, the QSL came to this realization and offered large salaries to entice European stars like Xavi, Raul, and Wesley Sneijder.[38] While these players were of a higher caliber than had typically played in the professional leagues in the Middle East, they still were not of the level that the Saudi Pro League was hoping to attract. What Saudi Arabia wanted was a true star. Someone that would have everyone talking about Saudi soccer, no matter where there lived or how little they knew about soccer outside of the world's top leagues. Only two male players in the world that fit this profile—Lionel Messi and Cristiano Ronaldo. One could argue that France and Real Madrid star Kylian Mbappe could be part of this discussion, but he's still not someone your grandmother is going to ask you about over a holiday dinner. If you want to sign a player who is going to shock the world, to capture everyone's attention there are only two who can truly do so. And precisely because of this, the Saudi set their sights on signing these two players.

However, there was a problem with this plan. Entering the 2022/23 season, both Messi and Ronaldo had one more year left on their contracts with their respective clubs. This meant that the moment the January transfer window opened, there would be fierce competition from clubs around the world to sign both players. In the case of Messi, rumors were already swirling that David Beckham's Inter Miami club, as well as several other European teams were all interested in signing the Argentinian. Likewise, numerous clubs had publicly expressed interest in Ronaldo as his United contract inched closer to ending. Everything was pointing toward one of the biggest bidding wars in soccer history.

But things didn't work out that way.

From Manchester to Riyadh

While there was growing discontent at PSG as the club continued to flounder in major competitions, there was a bigger storm brewing in Manchester. When Cristiano Ronaldo left Manchester United in 2009, the club had just won its third straight title under legendary manager Sir Alex Ferguson, cementing them as one of the greats of English club soccer. Although he had left on somewhat sour terms, he was welcomed back as a hero with online sales of his shirt setting new first day records.[39] But the Man Utd he had returned to was but a shadow of the club he once knew.

Ronaldo arrived at United in 2021 with former teammate and hero of the 98/99 Champions League Final Ole Gunnar Solskjær serving as manager. Though Man Utd had performed relatively well in the 2020/21 season, they fell short in every competition finishing as runners-up in both the Premier League and Carabao Cup. With Cristiano Ronaldo joining the squad, there were hopes that this would help to rejuvenate the club and help them prevent crosstown rivals Man City from winning another league title. However, after a poor start to the season, Solskjær was sacked in November, who was replaced by Michael Carrick, and then Ralf Rangnick. Despite eighteen league goals from Ronaldo, the team continued a run of poor form and ended the season in sixth place. For Ronaldo, this must have come as a real shock, as it was his first season without winning some sort of trophy since 2010, and in the off-season, he asked to be sold to another club so that he could play Champions League soccer. However, because of his age and high wages there were no interested parties.[40]

Rangnick was replaced by Ajax manager Erik Ten Hag, who was widely hailed as one of the best managers in Europe for his exciting tactical soccer, a true disciple of the Dutch "Total Football" style of play.[41] However, this presented a problem for Cristiano Ronaldo. One of the critical components of Ten Hag's system was that all players, including the forwards, were required to press the opponents when they had the ball. For the 37-year-old Ronaldo, who despite being known for his religious dedication to training and caring for his body, this was too much workload for his aging physique to handle. Unable to press to the same level as his younger teammates, Ronaldo did not fit in with Ten Hag's high-paced tactics and was demoted to being a substitute. As one of the superstars of the game, who had won more titles than anyone else at the club, this clearly did not sit well with Ronaldo.

An already tense relationship between Ronaldo and Ten Hag finally boiled over on October 19, 2022. With United leading 2-0 against Tottenham, Ten Hag signaled for Ronaldo to warm up and get ready to come into the game. Ronaldo refused. In response, Ten Hag suspended Ronaldo for the upcoming match against Chelsea but quickly insisted in a press conference that Ronaldo was still a critical part of the team.[42] After serving the suspension, Ronaldo was placed back in the starting line-up for matches against West Ham and Aston Villa. For a few days, things seemed to settle down, with Ronaldo being held out of a rather meaningless third round Carabao Cup match on November 10th because of illness.

Then on November 13th, Cristiano Ronaldo declared open warfare against Ten Hag. In an exclusive interview with Piers Morgan, Ronaldo said that Man Utd had tried to force him out of the club, and that there was zero respect between him and Ten Hag because of everything that has happened. Harkening back to the good old days, Ronaldo said that the club had made no progress since Sir Alex Ferguson had left more than a decade earlier, and that even the training facilities and food were not of the standards expected at a top-level soccer club.[43] Going after Ten Hag was one thing, as many fans had already expressed their discontent with the quality of play, but in attacking the club Cristiano had gone one step too far. On November 22nd, Manchester United came to a mutual agreement with Cristiano Ronaldo to immediately terminate his contract, with the Portuguese star forgoing any payments owed to him by the club.[44]

Cristiano Ronaldo was now unexpectedly a free agent. Let the bidding begin.

For the Saudi Pro League, it was a situation that was almost too good to be true. Al Nassr had been planning to start negotiations with Ronaldo in January with the hopes of signing him to a precontract that would begin in August 2023. Now, not only had the negotiation period started earlier than expected, but he could immediately join whichever club that he signed with. All Al Nassr had to do was convince one of the greatest players in the history of the game to give up European soccer. Indeed, the biggest roadblock for Al Nassr to sign Cristiano Ronaldo seemed to be his insistence on playing in the Champions League. His name had become synonymous with the competition, the common thread throughout most of his career spanning England, Spain, Italy, and then England again. In his last year with United, the very thought of having to play in the lower-tier Europa League had sparked such revulsions that he demanded to leave the club.

For Al Nassr, there was only one way to get Cristiano Ronaldo to come play in Saudi Arabia. They had to make him an offer he couldn't refuse. And indeed, that's precisely what they did. Before joining Al Nassr, an aging Ronaldo was still one of the highest-paid soccer players in the world, falling just behind Kylian Mbappe and Lionel Messi who were both reported to have made over $100 million in 2022.[45] Notably, most of this compensation does not come from wages the players receive from their club, but instead is from commercial deals and sponsorships. Estimates suggest that Ronaldo's wages with Manchester United ranged somewhere between $46 and $60 million a year, with total earnings close to $100 million. In response to this, Al Nassr provided a simple offer to Cristiano. We'll double everything and then add a little bit more on top. In other words, give us two years of your life, and we will set you and your entire family up for life.

On December 30, 2022, Al Nassr officially announced that Cristiano Ronaldo had joined the club, with his total compensation package estimated to be worth around $220 million a year.[46] It was the largest contract in soccer history,[47] and more than double what his biggest rival Messi was making. On the back of this new deal, Ronaldo topped the 2024 *Forbes* list of richest athletes in the world, earning a salary of $200 million and another $60 million from endorsements. To put this into context, his salary was more than double the next closest player, and only golfer Jon Rahm of LIV Golf came close to him in terms of total yearly earnings ($218 million).[48]

Now in Riyadh, wearing the yellow and blue kit of Al Nassr, Ronaldo's form also experienced a resurgence. Despite being limited to sixteen league matches due to joining the club halfway through the season, Ronaldo still notched fourteen goals and ended up in fifth place in the scoring table. More importantly for the Saudi's, his arrival became one of the most talked-about stories in the sport world. Though some news outlets continued to reference various human rights issues in their reporting of Ronaldo's move to Saudi Arabia, more focus was placed on the reasons for his move and how he would perform in his new environment. And as Cristiano continued to score goals, emphasis quickly shifted toward his highlights rather than the transgressions of his hosts. Moreover, fans from around the world were now trying to figure out how they could watch Saudi Pro League matches so they could continue loyally watching Ronaldo's every move.

With the signing of Cristiano Ronaldo considered a massive success from a business and public relations standpoint, the Saudi Public Investment Fund moved to launch the next stage of their strategic plan for global soccer dominance. In early June 2023, it was announced that PIF would be acquiring the four largest clubs in the Saudi Pro League—Al-Hilal, Al-Ittihad, Al-Ahli, and of course, Cristiano Ronaldo's Al-Nassr.[49] Multi-club ownership is not a new thing in soccer, the UAE's City Football Group has been its most extensive practitioner owning over a dozen top-flight clubs around the world including Manchester City (UK), Girona (Spain), Yokohama F Marinos (Japan), New York City FC (America), and Melbourne City FC (Australia).[50] However, having PIF take majority control of the biggest clubs within the league signaled a major shift in policy toward promoting the domestic game. One star wasn't enough—even if it was Cristiano Ronaldo. They wanted to build a whole league of stars.

With their newly found riches and a generous foreign player policy, the powers of the Saudi Pro League embarked on one of soccer's greatest shopping sprees during the summer 2023 transfer window. Imagine being the director of soccer at a club in a mid-tier league, while you dream of signing a few key players who have proven themselves in a top European league, the reality is that come transfer season, you are typically scraping the bottom of the barrel. Then one day, you find out your club has been purchased by a sovereign wealth fund and you are given a blank checkbook and told money is no object, go buy some star players. Are you going to sit back and just do things as normal? Of course not, you are going to go out there and scream "BUY, BUY, BUY!"

And this is precisely what the top four Saudi clubs did. Take the case of Al Ahli, who despite historically being one of the best clubs in Saudi Arabia, had just gained promotion back to the top division in 2023. After getting acquired by PIF, the club's roster was transformed overnight, going from journeymen players like former Reading winger Modou Barrow, to five-time Premier League winner Riyad Mahrez. In addition to Mahrez, Al Ahli purchased Roberto Firmino (Liverpool), Roger Ibanez (Roma), Franck Kessie (Barcelona), Edouard Mendy (Chelsea), Allan Saint-Maxim (Newcastle), Gabri Veiga (Celta), and Merih Demiral (Atalanta). Outside of Veiga, these players were all considered as standout performers in the top European leagues. Now they were all assembled on the roster of a newly promoted Saudi Pro League side and somehow were not even the best team in the league.

In just a few weeks, the economic reality of the Saudi Pro League had shifted drastically. A squad that once had a chance at potentially winning a cup and qualifying for the Asian Champions League now looked woefully inadequate when compared alongside the four new super clubs. Imagine being the sporting director of one the other fourteen clubs in the Saudi Pro League that didn't get a massive cash injection from PIF. Somehow you must compete against rivals whose budgets were already higher than yours and have now increased severalfold, while you are still working with the same resources you had before. Research has consistently shown that teams with higher payrolls tend to win more games, especially in soccer where open markets and less restrictions make it easier for rich clubs to purchase talent.[51]

Facing this, the only solution is to adopt a Moneyball-type approach of buying highly effective players who are undervalued, or to just give up and hope you don't get relegated. Indeed, this is what Al-Taawoun did by mostly purchasing foreign talent who had proven their effectiveness in other Asian leagues and had relatively low asking prices. For example, they purchased Brazilian Mateus Castro from Nagoya Grampus of the J-League for a mere $3 million and picked up his compatriot Flavio Medeiros for $200,000 on loan from Turkish club Trabzonspor. Although Hilal and Al Nassr—the new Galácticos of Asia—ran away with the league title, Al-Taawoun finished in fourth place ahead of Al Ittihad in the table and earned a spot in the Asian Champions League Two, the Asian equivalent of the second tier Europa League.

In addition to having strengthened the quality of the league, and perhaps more importantly for the Saudi regime, the PIF funded improvements helped to draw Saudi soccer toward the heart of the soccer world. The signing of Cristiano Ronaldo at the beginning of 2023 had helped to build awareness of the Saudi Pro League, but the large number of prominent player signings in the summer brought the league into the forefront of soccer conversations.

There were of course mixed reactions to the Saudi's flexing their financial muscles to build up their league. Some pundits and fans said that it was just a fad, a repeat of what the Chinese Super League had done in 2016,[52] only to end up falling back into obscurity a few years later. Others criticized PIF and the Saudi government for overspending on talent and disrupting the transfer market. But what was undeniable was that fans around the world were talking about the league. Because of this growing interest, the Saudi Pro League started to sign broadcast rights deals around the world,[53] including America where fans were demanding to watch some of their favorite players like Kante, Benzema, and of course Ronaldo.[54]

This Chapter Is Over

In the spring of 2025, Cristiano Ronaldo again made global headlines when he posted a photo of himself in an Al Nassr shirt with the caption "This chapter is over."[55] After two-and-a-half years in the Saudi Pro League, speculation was running wild that Ronaldo may leave Saudi Arabia, or even defect to Al Nassr's biggest rivals Al-Hilal. Despite being the highest-paid player in the world, Ronaldo had shown frustration with Al Nassr's performance on the pitch, having completed three seasons of competitions without a single trophy. This included Al Nassr being knocked out of the 2024/25 Asian Champions League Elite semifinals by Kawasaki Frontale of Japan, whose entire squad had a salary that was a tiny fraction of what Ronaldo made by himself.

As such, when Ronaldo declared the chapter was over, many assumed his Saudi sojourn had come to an end. A month later, Cristiano declared "Al Nassr" forever as he signed a new two-year deal with the club.[56] The new contract, which includes a record $211 million a year salary, will keep Ronaldo in Saudi Arabia until 2027, when the Portuguese star turns forty-two.[57] The message was clear—despite Al Nassr failing to win any titles during his time with the club, PIF still valued Ronaldo more than any other player in the world.

Overall, Cristiano Ronaldo's biggest impact on the Saudi Pro League was not his abilities on the field, but rather his legitimization of the PIF's soccer project. Rather than the goals he scored, the credibility he gave to the league opened the doors to waves of prominent players from across the world to ply their trade in Saudi Arabia. The rapid improvement of these clubs allowed Saudi to utterly dominate Asian soccer by placing three PIF clubs into the 2024/25 Asian Champions League semifinals, with Al Ahli winning the title. Moreover, Al-Hilal would go on to gain further respect for the quality of Saudi soccer by drawing with Real Madrid and beating Manchester City at the 2025 Club World Cup.

However, this also represented a major shift in Asian soccer. The grassroots development that had played a critical role in the development of major clubs across the continent was now being overshadowed by PIF's massive spending. In this sense, Cristiano Ronaldo was correct—this chapter was over for Asian soccer. Now clubs across the region face a new economic reality where financial resources are critical for success.

And with Saudi Pro League clubs backed by the wealth of PIF's assets, it looks like the Saudis will reign over Asian soccer for years to come.

6

Expecting Goals
How Are Analytics Changing the Game?

Late in the first half, the ball is laid off to Manchester United midfielder Bruno Fernandes. A West Ham defender rushes to close him down but Fernandes has already picked out his Portuguese teammate Diogo Dalot sprinting into open space. He strikes the ball perfectly with his right foot, landing delicately for Dalot to gather. The West Ham goalkeeper attempts to cut off the pass, but Dalot calmly dinks it past him. It's every player's dream, Dalot has no one between him and the empty goal. He pushes the ball to the edge of the six-yard box, and only a mere twenty feet away from goal strikes the ball with his right foot.

Just over fifteen minutes later, the referee blows his whistle for half-time. Diogo Dalot has amassed an xG—a statistic used to measure the expected number of goals scored—of 1.0. Compared to this the entire West Ham squad has only managed to generate a measly xG of 0.04. In mathematical terms, this metric indicates that Dalot's combined shots should have resulted in a goal, while West Ham's shots would only have created a goal once in every twenty-five attempts. Man United should have been leading at half-time.

Instead, both teams went into the break locked in a scoreless draw.

Newspaper headlines and social media posts immediately lock-in on Dalot's howler. Moments after he had fluffed his shot over the bar and dropped to his knees in disbelief, pundits and fans began to label it as the worse miss of the season. An open net, the goal right in front of you, the ball on your strong foot, and you send it flying over the ad boards far behind the goal. A decade earlier this miss would simply be labeled as a "howler." A terrible mistake that would be replayed a few times on highlight shows such as Match of the Day as Roy Keane moans about having one job to do—put the ball in the net.

But in today's game, missed opportunities are not just mistakes that we shake our heads at and then try to move along to the next game. Instead, they become heavily scrutinized moments that are quantified through data so that teams, media, and even fans can weigh in with objective evidence-based analysis. Moreover, rather than simply fading away from collective memory, every instance of soccer is now logged into databases that likely will be around long after humanity has gone extinct. It's bad enough that you missed an easy shot in front of 50,000 fans howling in a mixture of drunken rage and glee, but now that folly will continue to live on digitally.

Soccer, a sport that for the longest time held contempt toward any discussion of data and statistics, has now become one of the most heavily scrutinized data products in the world. And it is this data that will be the focus of this chapter, as we consider the history and emergence of data analytics in soccer, and how it has shaped the strategies clubs use to score goals and win matches. It is a strange combination when one thinks about it, the mundane process of developing data-driven decisions also plays a crucial role in creating the most exciting moments in the sport. Nevertheless, data analytics now holds critical importance. If you disagree, ask Man Utd manager Erik Ten Hag who was sacked after his team lost to West Ham.

The Data (R)evolution

In the summer of 2003, a few months after the Arsenal squad attacked Ruud van Nistelrooy at the Battle of Old Trafford, American author Michael Lewis published a book that would entirely change the management of sport forever.

The book, *Moneyball: The Art of Winning an Unfair Game*, chronicled the attempts of Billy Beane—General Manager of the Oakland Athletics of Major League Baseball (MLB)—to combat the antiquated approach to evaluating professional baseball players. Faced with the economic reality that his team would never be able to compete with historical powers such as the New York Yankees and Boston Red Sox who had large payrolls, Beane and his staff began using statistical analysis to level the playing field. Notably, the As were able to find several inefficiencies in the market because most teams were reliant on dated statistical measures to evaluate players. As such, even though they lost three of their best players before the 2002 season, the As were able to exploit their analytical advantage to sign highly effective players at a discount price. This strategy was so successful that the As went on a league record 20-game win streak, and finished the season tied with the league leading Yankees with 103 wins. All of this was accomplished on a budget of less than a third of the Yankees.

The publication of the book represents one of the most disruptive moments in the history of professional sport, launching what is commonly referred to as the *Moneyball* Revolution. The revolution was the idea that the way teams were evaluating talent was based on biases and preconceptions that had been, in many cases, built for over a century. In the case of baseball, scouts had been using subjective analysis to determine whether a player had the future potential to be a star player. In the book, Lewis even details some scouts going as far as to argue that a certain player had an unattractive girlfriend which meant that he lacked the confidence needed to be a pro athlete.

Seeking to avoid this type of thought which seems more fitting for an old wives' tale, the As focused on using statistical analysis to provide a more objective way to examine the game. Who cares what a player's girlfriend looks like, how short they are, or that they have a strange batting stance, are they able to produce in a way that will help the team out? In this, the Moneyball Revolution is about using detailed statistical analysis to cut through the bullshit and find out who the best players are. At the same time, it also represented a departure from the traditional approach of using feelings and instincts to manage, instead replacing it with data-driven decision-making.

In response to the success of the As and the widespread popularity of the book, sports executives around the world started to think about how they could adopt a Moneyball approach within their own organizations. Naturally, the first ones to imitate it were other MLB teams, as the publication of the book essentially tuned them into all the different methods and metrics the As were using to identify quality players. Although baseball statistics do not directly translate to other sports, the general philosophy of using data analytics to try and improve player evaluation and recruitment can be applied into any business. As such, this launched a trend in the mid-2000s where teams in various sports began to invest heavily in hiring data scientists, economists, and other such individuals who were trained in statistical analysis. Notably, most teams in the NBA moved quickly to rebuild their scouting departments, replacing or supplementing traditional scouts with nerds, who instead of going out on the road to watch college basketball games in-person, would sit behind a computer and analyze data being produced by thousands of players across the country.

So, what about soccer? Today, the sport is as mired in advanced statistical analysis as any other sport. But in the mid-2000s, beyond being sacrilegious to most fans and the media, the idea of using a Moneyball approach to analyze the beautiful game was too distant, too foreign. Leave it to the Yanks to use a computer to build their sport teams. One of the main problems at the time was that there was no real data to be analyzed in soccer. Where leagues like the MLB and NBA had a long tradition of gathering statistical information detailing every moment of each game, soccer had yet to develop such practices.

The lack of data naturally presented a serious impediment for those trying to implement a data-driven Moneyball approach in soccer. In the mid-2000s, even a casual fan could go online and look up data on player performance from MLB games played in the late 1880s. And not just simple information akin to the number of games played and goals scored as was kept by soccer leagues in England. Instead, one could visit a website such as Baseball Reference,[1] and find that George Gore, an outfielder for the Chicago White Stockings (who confusingly would be renamed the Chicago Cubs), had a Wins Above Replacement (WAR) score of 4.9 in the 1885 season, meaning that he generated almost five more wins for his team than an average player at his position would.

If I were to do the same for the 1886/87 Aston Villa squad on a soccer data site, all I would be able to tell you is that Jimmy Warner played two matches in goal. Fast forwarding over a hundred years later to the 2003/4 season, the only data available was that the goalkeeper at the time, Thomas Sorensen, played in all thirty-eight Premier League matches.[2] Humans had gone to the moon, created the internet, fought two World Wars, and even figured out a way to edit our genetics. And yet, somehow soccer analysis managed to stay rooted in the era of Queen Victoria who reigned from 1837 to 1901.

The lack of data was a problem that plagued all clubs that were trying to modernize their player evaluation systems by introducing statistical analyses. Internally, many clubs had already started collecting performance data from squad members to optimize training, fitness, and recovery. However, clubs lacked information on players who were not part of their team, especially potential prospects who played in other leagues or countries. Although a few clubs were successful in developing a Moneyball-like approach by focusing on scouting undervalued players—Billy Beane noted his admiration for how Arsene Wenger used this technique to make Arsenal successful without spending large sums of money—this method was still reliant on subjective evaluations from scouts and coaches. Using math to determine a player's productivity and value was still an entirely foreign concept.

Thus, while the rest of the sport world was immersed in the data revolution, soccer had stalled like a race car that had run out of gas, competitors zipping by as the driver watches helplessly unable to get his car to move. In this, the only way for soccer to catch up with a world that had already passed it by was by getting fuel to start the car.

And data was the fuel.

Data-Driven Soccer

The answer to the lack of data in soccer came through the introduction of automated data collection systems such as Global Positioning System and video tracking software. With the information produced from these technologies soccer clubs were armed with masses of data which could be used to provide critical insights into player performance, but the primary hindrance from implementing a more analytical strategy was the willingness to break from the traditional approach to running a soccer club. And yet this very obstacle—to battle against the idiosyncratic culture that has dictated a club's operations for many decades—presents an inertia that makes soccer resistant to change. Even if a manager was interested in using innovative statistical methods to try and re-envision their tactics, strategies, and recruitment policies, they still would have to answer to an owner, director of soccer, board members, and supporters group who have grown to value the existing modus operandi. Use quantitative data collected by artificial intelligence to determine which players we should sign? That's not how things are done at this club, we value our traditions.

This is not to say that all clubs are run by stodgy old men gathered around a large oak table stained by decades of spilled coffee and cigar smoke. Soccer is a business after all, and there are always sharks in the water seeking to exploit any opportunity or sign of weakness from others. Today, clubs like Brighton of the Premier League or AZ Alkmaar of the Dutch Eredivisie are often cited as being clubs who do things "the right way," an indication that even if they are not specifically using analytics to evaluate players, they have adopted a sustainable financial strategy toward team building. That is, in a world filled with clubs like Manchester City, Real Madrid, and Chelsea who have each spent over a billion dollars purchasing players over the last five seasons (2020/21 to 2024/25),[3] some clubs have realized, just like the Oakland Athletics, that it is impossible to compete by trying to outspend their opponents. Instead, these clubs have become models of efficiency, using knowledge and expertise to help them identify potential talent that fits within their much lower budgets.

Perhaps the most famous pioneer in terms of using a data-driven approach to soccer is Southampton FC. The club has long had a reputation for developing players, especially from their youth academy, turning them into stars who are then eventually sold on to bigger clubs. Gareth Bale, Virgil Van Dijk, Theo Walcott, Sadio Mane, Luke Shaw, the list of names of players who started at Southampton and went on to play for bigger clubs is almost endless.

In 2009, Southampton was playing in the third tier of English soccer (League One) and was mired by severe financial troubles which led to the club going into administration (bankruptcy). They were quickly rescued by

Swiss-German businessman Markus Liebherr who found that while the youth academy was effective in producing talent, the rest of the organization was a total disaster. Lacking any senior management or leadership, Liebherr hired Swiss-Italian banker Nicola Cortese to take over as the club's new chairman. Together, Liebherr and Cortese coined the term "The Southampton Way," a new strategic direction that would be focused on improving the operations of the entire club.[4] The Southampton Way was really a business model that was predicated on developing or purchasing soccer talent at a low price and then selling them at a high price to richer clubs. Buy low, sell high, precisely the stuff you would expect from a Swiss banker. The profits amassed from these sales would then be re-invested into growing the next class of talent and selling them in the future. Rinse and repeat.

Liebherr would pass away only a year after purchasing the club, and Cortese would depart in early 2014 after differences in opinion with Liebherr's daughter who took over ownership of Southampton.[5] Despite both men's relatively short tenure at the club, their creation of The Southampton Way helped to instill a strategic vision that would help to guide the future direction of the club for years to come. Notably, under Cortese's guidance the club began to develop a more analytical approach toward talent identification and their transfer policies. Indeed, this system of identifying quality players at a low price is reminiscent of the strategy used by Billy Beane and the Athletics. However, where the Athletics' focus was to identify talent in order to compete against richer teams on the field of play, Southampton's attention was more toward balancing their accounting ledgers. A constant churn of promising talent being brought into the club, shaped into Premier League-caliber players, and then sold along to whichever Big Six club (Arsenal, Manchester United, Manchester City, Chelsea, Liverpool, and Tottenham) needed a holding midfielder. It was a Moneyball approach, but in this case, it was entirely focused on profit as the outcome.

That is not to say that Southampton performed poorly on the pitch. In 2010/11, they finished second in League One and were promoted to the Championship, and then pulled off back-to-back promotions to return to the Premier League starting from the 2012/13 season. What would follow would be eleven straight seasons at the pinnacle of English professional soccer before being demoted back down to the Championship in 2023/24. What was striking about Southampton's approach, especially for the first several years after rejoining the Premier League, was how successful the club was within the transfer market. It wasn't the case where they were having a good window here and there, they were constantly "winning" in the transfer market by selling players at a high price and finding suitable replacements at almost no cost. Other clubs in England attempted to emulate this strategy, but none of them could replicate it to the same level.

However, despite the success of the club's data-driven scouting system, things started to unravel within the organization. In the period between 2012 and 2017, Southampton rotated through six different managers, including Mauricio Pochettino who would leave the club for Spurs and eventually take the US national team job, as well as Ronald Koeman who currently serves as the manager for the Netherlands. Perhaps the biggest weakness in Southampton's Black Box Moneyball approach was that while they were able to constantly find strong replacements for departing talent, they had to deal with constant turnover. This problem was then further exacerbated as the club changed hands multiple times, first being sold to Chinese real-estate developer Gao Jisheng,[6] and then to a sport investment firm in 2022. Amidst all this upheaval, Southampton's competitive advantage in identifying talent eroded. Whether this was due to changes in the management philosophy ascribed by new owners, or competitors catching up in their use of data analytics to identify talent, by the late 2010s, the club no longer dominated the transfer market.

Today, most top-flight clubs in the big five European leagues have their own version of Southampton's data system. But just because a club has built an analytics department and hired a bunch of nerds with degrees in economics, data science, and mathematics does not guarantee success. Indeed, in looking at the NBA, while every team in the league has an analytics department, there are some that stand out for their remarkable ability to evaluate player talent, and there are others that are just playing around with numbers. In a poll of current and former league executives, it was noted that teams like Houston Rockets, Boston Celtics, and San Antonio Spurs all stood out for pioneering the use of analytics in the sport.[7] Counter to this, teams like the New York Knicks and Los Angeles Lakers were labeled as being some of the worst teams in sport in their use of data. Notably, despite the Lakers' significant investment in purchasing a camera system that tracks the movement of each player dozens of times each second, their coaching staff shunned these analyses in favor of traditional methods of scouting and evaluation.[8]

Betting on Data

So, who are the leaders of soccer analytics today? There are several clubs worth mentioning, but two prominent ones that deserve mention are Brighton and Hove Albion and Brentford FC. What makes these two clubs so special? Interestingly, the two clubs share a rather similar background, having both played in the third tier of English soccer in the last fifteen years. Moreover, there are also relatively recent entrants to the Premier League, with Brighton earning promotion in 2017, and Brentford having joined in 2021. As the new kids of the block, the early expectations for these two clubs were that they would either be quickly kicked back down to the second division, or they would linger just above the relegation zone in that area of the table that seems eternally reserved for Everton. And while both clubs did indeed have seasons where they barely avoided relegation, they also have exhibited a trajectory of steady improvement throughout their time in the Prem.

Much of the success of these two clubs can be traced back to their owners. Brighton is owned by Tony Bloom, a professional gambler who made his initial fortune playing poker competitively. Widely considered to be a mathematical expert,[9] Bloom then further grew these earnings by first setting up his own private sport betting group, and then through founding the betting company PremierBet. What is notable in all of this is that even before purchasing Brighton, Bloom was already heavily involved in the world of data-driven decision-making. Whether it be his playstyle at the poker table, or the sporting events he bet on, Bloom had built a reputation as a calculating businessman. Thus, with his purchase of a majority stake in Brighton, his boyhood club, it was no surprise that Bloom wasted no time in defusing his own brand of analytics throughout the club.

Under Bloom, it could be argued that Brighton has further refined the application of Moneyball in soccer. Perhaps the biggest weakness of the Oakland Athletics strategy was the relatively small pool of professional baseball players around the world. It meant that when Beane needed to sign players for the As, he was forced to have to fish in the same pond as the biggest teams in the game and hoped they wouldn't notice his moves and try to outbid him. Counter to this, the global nature of soccer meant that there were many ponds from which to seek talent. As such, Brighton developed a strong global scouting network backed by data analytics to find talent in leagues that the big clubs were not paying attention to.[10] With this strategy, Brighton was able to sign numerous star players including Kaoru Mitoma from Japan's J-League, Moises Caicedo from the Ecuadorian Serie A, and Alexi Mac Allister from the Argentinian Primera Division at relatively low cost.

There are similarities between Brighton's Moneyball approach and Southampton's transfer policy—buy low, sell high. Indeed, after receiving large transfer bids for Caicedo and Mac Allister from Chelsea and Liverpool, respectively, Brighton made the decision to sell both players for large profits. One of the most important rules in gambling—and investment—is to take the profit when provided the opportunity for significant returns. But where Brighton departs from Southampton's method is in their planning. Southampton would sell players once they were able to turn a large profit and then use a portion of these profits to try and find a suitable replacement. On the other hand, Brighton's strategy has been to bring in prospective talent well before a key player is sold so that their replacement is ready to go. As such, Brighton does not have to make a panicked purchase to replace key squad members who leave the club and thus is able to maintain a strong roster who are familiar with the team's style of play.

Brentford's owner, Matthew Benham, is a former hedge fund manager who was hired by Tony Bloom to work for Premier Bet in 2001.[11] Like Bloom, Benham was well versed in mathematics,[12] and also built a significant part of his fortune through sport betting. In 2004, Benham was fired from his position at Premier Bet and founded his own company named Smartodds that sold tips to sport gamblers.[13] This split became so acrimonious that Bloom took Benham to court, and the two haven't spoken to each other since. After years of helping cover loans to support his boyhood club of Brentford FC, Benham finally became the full owner of the team in 2012. Even though he has publicly stated his distaste for the term "Moneyball"—as he thinks there is more to building a scientific approach to running a club than statistical analysis—Benham has pushed Brentford toward more data-focused decision-making.

Despite their owner's words, Brentford has a clear strategic advantage over most other clubs when it comes to the implementation of data analytics, as the club has access to the statistical databases and information developed by Smartodds. Other clubs seeking to start their own data-driven approach would have to begin at square one in terms of building a massive database, hiring statistical expertise, and building and refining methods of analysis. Brentford, on the other hand, simply needs to pick up the phone and set up a meeting between analysts at Smartodds and staff at Brentford to get in-depth evaluations of players to add to their own assessments. As such, this helps the coaches and executives to make informed decisions when signing new players. Ironically enough, the one other Premier League club with a similar setup is Brighton, as Tony Bloom has partnered with the data company Starlizard to assist in analyzing prospective players.[14]

Bloom and Behnam share a similar vision and approach of using data analytics to inform decision-making has made them the gold standard of how soccer clubs should be run. It should be noted that for Brighton and Brentford success has come on and off the field. On a limited budget, Brighton managed to compete against some of the richest clubs in the world to qualify for the Europa League, while also posting the highest single-season profit in the history of the Premier League. This model is not just something that other clubs have come to admire but also could possibly represent the future of how soccer clubs are operated as a business. Today, the soccer industry is more segmented than at any time in history. Rich clubs continue to increase their spending yearly and have been kept in check only by financial fair play rules. Meanwhile, smaller clubs are left to flounder near the bottom of the table, battling for a few leftover scraps in the hopes of simply avoiding being relegated.

Together, Brighton and Brentford have developed a clear vision that shows how small clubs can be transformed using data and analytical decision-making. Though their success cannot be entirely attributed to data analytics, it clearly played an instrumental role in bringing the Moneyball Revolution to soccer.

Mathematical Soccer

So then, how are teams like Brighton, Brentford, and even Liverpool using data analytics? Perhaps the most prominent statistical measure now being used in soccer is expected goals (xG). xG can simply be defined as the probability that a shot will become a goal, meaning that its values range from 0—zero percent chance of scoring a goal to 1—100 percent chance of scoring a goal. In reality, there are almost no shots that have either a likelihood of 0 percent or 100 percent of being scored, with most shots falling somewhere in between. So how then is xG calculated? This is where we get into the world of advanced statistics.

From a mathematical perspective, there has been significant debate on how xG should be calculated. Although the goal is to get the same resulting metric of the likelihood of scoring a goal, various analysts and organizations have differed in the factors they believe should be included in an xG calculation, as well as the weight that should be given to each factor. For the purposes of our discussion, we are going to use the definition of xG that was created by Opta,[15] a data company that collects and analyzes masses of data for soccer clubs. Opta's xG models consider four general categories that impact the quality of a shot, with each of these categories often having several variables to account for various factors. The primary piece of information in calculating xG is the location of the shooter. In this, Opta uses tracking camera data to determine the location for each shot taken in a match. Obviously, the closer one is to goal, the higher their xG should be. Additionally, Opta also measures the angle to goal when the shot was taken—a shot straight on should have a higher likelihood to score than one from a wide angle. Indeed, if we consider Dalot's epic miss for Manchester United again, one of the reasons the shot did not have a higher xG was because Dalot was in a wide position, thus making it a more difficult chance to finish.

xG also considers how the ball is shot, was it struck off the foot, or was it headed? Because shots hit with the foot and the head have different power and probability of being scored, the manner in which the ball struck is introduced into the calculation. Beyond information on the player who is shooting, Opta also takes into account the type of pass that led up to the shooting motion. Was it a goal scored from a corner? Was it a through ball that placed the ball perfectly at an attacker's feet, or was it a whipped cross that presented a high degree of difficulty to make contact with? Again, all of these and other potential scenarios that could lead to a player receiving the ball to take a shot are included in the xG model. Finally, the last group of factors is those related to the type of attack and other external factors that could either increase or decrease the chances of scoring. Specifically, they consider whether a player had possession of the ball when building up to the shot, or if the ball fell to them off a rebound. As rebounds are typically unexpected and often fall in unnatural positions, shots taken off rebounds tend to miss more often than ones where a player is in control of the ball. Opta's xG calculation also accounts for defensive positioning, measuring the total number of defenders who were located between the shooter and the goal due to their potential of having obstructed the shot.

To then calculate the xG for an individual shot, Opta weighs each one of these factors based on a database of thousands of previously attempted shots to determine the precise impact each variable has on the likelihood of scoring a goal. Finally, all these values are tabulated together, producing a singular xG measure for a shot. It sounds simple, but to produce the xG for a single shot requires Opta to track all the specific conditions within their formula for every minute of each match they offer coverage for, transfer all this data into numerical form, and then to conduct the calculation. To be honest, this seems more like a project for NASA than something a soccer club should be working on.

The speed at which xG calculations are performed now is also quite incredible. If you are watching a telecast of a Bundesliga match, you will notice that they can provide the xG of any shot within less than a minute. To do this, the Bundesliga has partnered with Amazon Web Services who use artificial intelligence to track the events within a match, and to automatically calculate xG each time a shot is taken. These calculations are then quickly transmitted back to the broadcast team who typically can get this information displayed while replays of the goal are still being shown. This allows fans at home to not only watch the events of the goal, but also to make their own data-driven decisions of how easy or difficult a shot was.

In addition to the xG for each shot, this metric can also be aggregated for a player or team. This then allows for a comparison of the total xG produced for both teams in a match to determine which one was expected to win based on the shots that were taken. There is even an account on the X (formerly Twitter) social media platform named "The xG Philosophy" that is solely dedicated to posting the total xG for teams after the end of a match. For example, after Chelsea and Arsenal drew 1-1 in early November 2024, the account immediately posted after the game: "Chelsea (1.69) 1-1 (1.27) Arsenal." In this, the xG is posted in parentheses to offer a comparison to the actual scoreline, which in this instance seems to be fairly well correlated with the actual number of goals scored by each team.

This then leads us to the most important question. Is xG a reliable measure of offensive productivity in soccer? There are two main factions within this debate. On one side are the xG evangelists who seek to reduce every soccer match into a comparison of the theoretical number of goals that should have been scored, not the actual ones that produced the outcome in the realworld. On the other side are the xG haters, a mixed mob of data analysts who say that xG is not an effective measure of offensive performance and soccer purists who argue that advanced statistics have no place in the game.

Much of the resentment toward xG stems from a lack of understanding of what the metric is measuring statistically. To many, xG is seen as being predictive—that it is measuring what should happen in the future. From this, when a team amasses an xG of 2.3 in a match, it is often understood as predicting that the team should score two goals. In reality, we should think of xG as a descriptive statistic—basically it is a metric that summarizes information from a moment or set of moments. Thus, if we return to the example of a team generating an xG of 2.3, what it essentially means is that adding all the shots together taken by a team would on average produce around two goals. This is a key distinction. The xG generated in a match is not trying to foretell the future but instead is providing a description of the quality of shots taken by a player or team.

Statistically speaking, although the xG of a single shot is useful in providing a subjective measure of a scoring chance, it generally has been not of great use to teams by itself. Yes, it presents information about how good an opportunity a shot was, but outside of that it doesn't reveal how well a team is playing. Just as a matter of pure luck, anyone who is standing on the pitch can be presented with a high xG opportunity. The miss from Dalot illustrates that it is possible for almost anyone to get placed into a high xG situation at some point through the course of a season. In Dalot's case, he likely scored a higher total xG on all his shots in the West Ham match than all the other attacking players. If we were to go off the xG aggregated over this match, the analysis would suggest that Dalot was the best attacker. So, while xG can certainly reveal the individuals who had the greatest attacking opportunity within a match, it does not always hold that a high xG translates to offensive prowess.

It is also the case that teams often easily win a match while producing a lower xG than their opponents. Should we consider a team that has just won a match 3-0 as having underperformed because they scored an xG of 1.6 compared to their opponents 2.9? For those who ascribe great importance to xG, they would view such a match as a travesty, in a just universe it should never be the team that created more attacking opportunities that loses a match. But where xG fails, especially over individual matches, is that the metric is just describing the shots that were taken by both teams. If a team scores three goals in the first half, it is highly likely that in the second half rather than expose themselves by playing open-attacking soccer, they will adopt a more conservative approach focused on possessing the ball and absorbing pressure from their opponents. It is possible that they may not even generate any additional xG in the second half. Counter to this, their opponents will typically try to get back in the game by placing increased focus on scoring a goal. In many cases, these shots will be desperate attempts to grab a goal, shooting from angles, distances, and positions that they normally would never consider. But each one of these shots would add to the team's xG total for the match. Thus, while a team may produce a higher xG, it does not necessarily mean that they exhibited more quality or control over the match. Instead, it may simply represent that they took a lot more shots than their opponent.

A good example of this can be seen from Japan's wins against Germany and Spain in the group stages of the 2022 World Cup. Knowing that the two European powers of the game would dominate possession, Japan embraced a smash-and-grab counterattacking strategy. In the clash against Germany, Japan managed to generate an xG of only 1.4, compared to Germany's xG of 3.3. But Japan's approach showed its willingness to lose these statistical battles in exchange for getting a famous win. Curiously, this match was the fourth in World Cup history where a team with an xG of 2.5 or higher lost a match—all four of these loses came from Germany.[16] This could be pure coincidence or could indicate that the German strategy of offensive production is effective in producing shots on goal but does not necessarily translate to real-world success.

Despite the reservations with xG, it does not mean that it is an entirely useless metric. In fact, I would argue that xG can be beneficial when used in the right conditions. Where xG can be rather meaningless in individual matches, or even over a handful of games, its true benefits start to emerge when analyzing data over longer periods of time. That is, xG can have wild swings over the shortrun, where a team can produce almost nothing one week, and then have the highest xG in the league for the following fixture. This is just part of the natural ebb and flow of top-flight soccer, where the quality of opponents, weather, fixture congestion, and player form can all impact performance. Because xG data can be noisy—a term used to indicate the presence of many abnormal values—over short periods of time, say five to ten matches, it is much more useful to examine xG for longer spells. As such, examining the xG of a player or team over the course of an entire season (or seasons) can thus produce more reliable measures of offensive productivity.

xG Revolution

Perhaps the club that places the most emphasis on using xG as part of their scouting, recruitment, and tactics is Brentford. After the first ten matches of the 2024/25 Premier League season, Brentford has the impressive distinction of having both the best home and worst away record in the league. However, what stood out the most was the club's fearless attacking strategy. Pundits and fans across the league were caught off guard by Brentford's potency going forward, especially as expectations were low after their star striker Ivan Toney completed a high-profile transfer to Al-Ahli of the Saudi Pro League over the summer. Rather than purchase another striker of the same caliber, Brentford adopted a Moneyball approach to replace Toney. In the film adaptation of *Moneyball*, there is a famous scene where the As scouting staff sits around a table trying to find a solution to replace their offensive star player who had likewise left for large sums of money. In the scene, Billy Beane, played by Brad Pitt, attempts to explain that the team doesn't have the money to purchase a straight replacement. As such, they will be developing a new approach to replace players in the "aggregate." In other words, while we cannot afford a player who can do all the things a star player can do by themselves, we can buy a group of players who can achieve similar productivity when combined together.

And it was this strategy that Brentford had adopted in replacing first team members who left to join bigger clubs. I can only imagine club owner Matthew Benham at a table, where the scouts are telling him that there is no player on the market who can replace Toney, and Benham and manager Thomas Frank replying in unison: "but we can replace him in the aggregate." Brentford's strategy draws further parallels with the Oakland As Moneyball approach by searching for inefficiencies in the market by utilizing xG. In analyzing Ivan Toney's productivity, the primary thing that stands out is his scoring abilities. In the 2022/23 Premier League season, Toney emerged as the one of the league's top goal scorers, registering interest from big clubs such as Arsenal. Toney finished the season with twenty goals, a tally that was cut short as he missed several matches as part of an eight-month ban for breaking league gambling rules.

If Brentford were simply to go out with the objective of replacing the twenty goals that Toney produced, they would find themselves having to bid for the likes of Alexander Isak, Ollie Watkins, or Dominic Solanke. The transfer fees for these players were well outside of Brentford's budget, as evidenced by

Solanke being purchased by Tottenham for £65 million in 2024. It is here that Benham saw inefficiency within the market. Big clubs were willing to pay lots of money for highly productive attackers and their method of evaluation was to search for star players with high goal tallies. Although this strategy was effective for elite teams, who could use their large commercial deals to help underwrite expensive contracts, the reality was that most soccer clubs were using similar methods of evaluation. One of the time-honored traditions of the business side of the sport industry is to simply copy what your competition is doing. Maintain the status quo, don't rock the boat, and just be happy that you get to be part of the game.

To Benham, who if we recall came from working in corporate finance, it must have been maddening to see all of this. In Japan, there is a famous phrase: "The nail that sticks out, gets hammered down." This was a good representation of what was happening in soccer—clubs both rich and poor all using the same dated methods of evaluation, fearful to suggest any change that could get them cast out of the sport like a pariah. But for Benham, as well as his former boss Tony Bloom, this madness also represented an immense opportunity. If the soccer industry refused to modernize, then why not use that weakness to their advantage?

Perhaps one of Benham's greatest advantages over most other owners in the sport was that he was able to test his data-driven approach to soccer for many years before actually becoming directly involved in operating a club. Indeed, while first working for Bloom, and then by building his own sport betting company, Benham matured in the competitive world of sport gambling, where the survival of companies is built on rigorously testing and refining mathematical models of team and player performance. When other owners started taking an interest in using data analytics to improve their squads, their efforts were pedestrian compared to the industry Benham had come from. He was molded by a world of soccer analytics, and now he was going to use it to unleash hell on the Premier League.

Knowing all of this, it caught my eye when I read that Brentford was using xG as one of their main tools for evaluating players as well as in-game strategy and tactics. I was skeptical at first. Was this a smokescreen from Benham trying to hide something more sophisticated that Brentford was doing behind the scenes. Perhaps the biggest weakness of the Oakland Athletics Moneyball approach was granting Michael Lewis inside access to the organization, thus allowing him to publish his bestseller which revealed all their strategies and secrets to every other team in their league. Having come from the world of gambling filled with proprietary information that would ruin a company if shared with competitors, it made sense to me that Benham would try and throw others off his scent.

However, the more I researched Brentford's analytical approach, it seemed that xG was legitimately an integral part of the club's strategy. Returning to the example of Ivan Toney, rather than replace the number of goals he produced for the club, it is likely that Brentford's scouting department started thinking about how to replace his xG. Supposedly, the hints for this came from Smartodds, Benham's gambling company, as they had experimented with xG and other metrics as markers of player performance. In the 2022/23 season, Toney had an xG of 18.7, the highest amount he would attain for the club while in the Premier League. This was the fourth highest xG in the league and was only exceeded by Erling Haaland (28.4 for Man City), Mohamed Salah (21.6 for Liverpool), and Harry Kane (21.4 for Spurs). As players with this caliber of xG production would typically cost at least £80 million on the transfer market, it was once again clear that a straight replacement for Toney was clearly untenable for Brentford's financial situation.

The obvious answer to this situation would be for Brentford to adopt a Moneyball approach to try and recreate Toney's xG in the aggregate through purchasing undervalued talent. Despite any prominent signings during their 2024 transfer window, Brentford not only maintained their offensive production from previous seasons but seemed to instantly transform into one of the most dangerous attacks in the Premier League. The club caught the attention of the media when they set a new league record by being the first team to score a goal in the first minute of a match for three games in a row in September. Their opening in these matches was reminiscent of a heavyweight boxer who starts throwing haymakers the moment the bell rings, hoping to kill off their opponent before they even know what has happened.

Of course, just like with the Oakland Athletics, this sudden improvement in performance from a team that had been written off by most immediately drew attention to Brentford. For weeks, manager Thomas Frank was quizzed in postmatch interviews, prematch press conferences, and other media appearances about the secret behind Brentford's attacking renaissance. At first, Frank coyly avoided the question, but eventually revealed that the club had developed a kick-off strategy without giving away too many details.[17] What was emphasized was that the team changed its strategy for each match, but that it was all part of an overall philosophy of playing attacking soccer.

The secret behind this new attacking playstyle started to be revealed in the following months, as the club boldly published an article on their official website bragging about the club's new data-driven strategy.[18] At the core of this was a new approach toward using xG. Where most clubs have used xG to either recruit players or to conduct postmatch evaluations, Brentford was flipping the script by deconstructing xG and using it as a coaching tool. Indeed, one of the things that made Moneyball successful for the Oakland Athletics was the ability to translate data analytics into specific strategies and tactics that were then drilled into their players. In the case of Brentford, emphasis was placed on trying to create opportunities that would result in higher-quality shots as measured by xG. To paraphrase the club's own words, players were coached to take high-quality shots, rather than simply taking a high quantity of shots. It is not just about achieving a high xG, but an xG that is built on as much quality of opportunities as possible. So far, this plan has been a success for Brentford, which led the Premier League in xG per shot through the first four months of the 2024/25 season and has ended up scoring more goals than high-spending clubs like Chelsea and Tottenham.

Conclusion—xG and Beyond

With clubs like Brentford at the forefront of the data revolution in soccer, one of the major questions is whether they can maintain their status as industry leaders. With their secrets released to all their competitors, the Oakland Athletics soon found that other teams were not only copying their methods but were even improving on them. In the film adaptation of *Moneyball*, Billy Beane is offered a large contract to leave Oakland and join the Boston Red

Sox, with the promise of one of the highest payrolls in baseball to build a true championship team. Though Beane turns them down in the perfect romantic Hollywood ending where he decides to keep fighting for the underdog, in the realworld, the Red Sox simply hired someone else who had embraced a data-driven approach to baseball,[19] and subsequently ended their 86-year title drought. In a competitive business environment, the sad reality is that those who are innovative and take the biggest risks in pushing forward an industry are typically not those who reap the greatest rewards. Those gains are usually swept up by those with the most resources.

In the case of soccer, it is only a matter of time before big clubs like Manchester City, Real Madrid, and Barcelona truly embrace the power of data analytics in refining their recruitment process. Imagine what Real could do with their massive budget and a model to identify the players who have the greatest potential to create goals. Rather than simply buy the next biggest superstar on the planet as they did with Kylian Mbappe in 2024, the club could instead take a more analytical approach to finding all the key pieces needed to make the team a success. Instead of purchasing another winger, a position in which they already had some of the world's best talent, Madrid could have used a data-centric approach to try and maximize the club's xG.

For Brentford, the club didn't even wait for the publication of a book to start giving away parts of their analytical strategy to other teams. Maybe the club believes that they have some of these secrets tucked away that will help keep them differentiated from their competition, but it takes a good amount of hubris to think that others cannot imitate and even improve upon their methods. In fact, all it really takes is for another richer club to write a large check to convince members of Brentford's staff to give their two-weeks' notice and start working for a superclub. This is not a Hollywood movie. The only thing keeping others from poaching Brentford's analysts is a noncompete clause that prevents them from working for competitors. Even Southampton, who had built a secretive room and revealed nothing to their competition, was eventually eclipsed by other clubs and slipped back into relative obscurity.

It may seem there is no hope for the smaller daring clubs who have embraced the world of statistics, data science, and Moneyball as a means of survival. Although the picture is grim, especially in the way that the soccer industry is structured to continuously reward those at the top with a greater share of revenue and media attention, it has not deterred some entrepreneurial spirits from pushing the management of soccer clubs to new frontiers. For Tony Bloom, the frontier potentially lies in Scotland, as it has been rumored that he may add Heart of Midlothian FC to his portfolio of clubs. The idea being to take the model that he created at Brighton and apply it in other top-flight leagues where teams may not have paid as much attention to analytics. For others like Brentford, the future is pushing the envelope of data science, seeking every possible edge that can help their clubs to compete against opponents who routinely spend hundreds of millions of Euros in a window without second thought.

And to come full circle, soccer is now the new frontier for Billy Beane. Beane has long had interest in soccer analytics since his time with the Athletics, as the team owners purchased the San Jose Earthquakes of Major League Soccer and had tasked Beane with applying a Moneyball approach to this team as well.[20] Beane left the A's organization before he was able to implement any type of analytical system and instead has now focused his efforts to help the clubs he purchased ownership stakes in—Dutch club AZ Alkmaar and Barnsley of the English third division. Beane has worked closely with AZ general manager Robert Eenhoorn to revolutionize the club's operations, especially in how they instruct scouts to gather data to be used in the evaluation process. Despite AZ having a smaller stadium and less revenue than their Dutch competition,[21] they have become one of the better clubs in the country, consistently qualifying for the group stages of European continental competitions. Now once again eyes are focused on an underdog team associated with Billy Beane that is punching above its weight, with competitors and pundits hailing the club as a model of how a sport team should be run.

Although AZ's strong finishes haven't convinced many clubs to fully convert to data analytics, Beane predicts that day will come soon when Brighton or Brentford mount a direct challenge against the top clubs in the Premier League.[22] And thus, a process that started in the dingy offices of the Oakland

Coliseum to help a poor baseball team win games, has now infiltrated its way across the soccer world and stands poised to re-invent how teams are built and managed.

Will it be successful? Only time can tell, but I would not want to be the one betting against the likes of Bloom, Benham, and Beane.

7

Too Much Soccer

Is Expansion Killing the Sport?

In the summer of 2025, teams from around the world flocked to America during what is traditionally the "off-season" of the soccer calendar. Indeed, there is nothing new about this. Clubs have been coming to America for decades on pre-season tours mainly to boost revenue, but also to play friendly matches against lesser opposition to help prepare for their upcoming seasons. But the summer of 2025 was unlike anything America, or any other country in the world, had ever experienced in terms of the sheer amount of soccer that was being played in the country.

To begin with, FIFA decided that the traditional format of the Club World Cup needed to be expanded. Previously, this somewhat farcical competition attempted to crown the true "World Champion" of soccer by pitting the champions of all six member federations and a host team against one another in a single-elimination knockout cup. Realizing that Americans had an appetite for soccer and were more willing to pay outrageous prices than any other country in the world, FIFA revamped the Club World Cup into a 32-team competition. Where European supporters hold protests and even conduct boycotts over a $5 increase in ticket prices, Americans have been willing to pay hundreds of dollars per seat to get a glimpse of their favorite clubs and players. This new format meant that the Club World Cup had now mushroomed from a seven-match competition to a 63-match tournament that would be played in major cities across America. From a financial perspective, this meant a significant boost in revenue for FIFA and participating clubs, with even the smallest team from Oceania guaranteed $3.58 million just for showing up.[1]

If it was just the expanded 63-match Club World Cup being played in America, it would seem to be a somewhat reasonable number of matches to quench the thirst for international soccer. However, at the exact same time that the Club World Cup was taking place, America was also hosting the Gold Cup—the competition to determine the best national team in CONCACAF. As the Gold Cup is a 31-match competition, this means that close to one hundred international or elite professional matches were played in just over a month. Tack on various preseason tours and friendlies, including the official Premier League Summer Series, as well as the fact that Major League Soccer was in the midst of its competitive season, and it is safe to say that the summer 2025 fixture list in America was bloated beyond control.

FIFA, CONCACAF, and the powers that be will argue that this is a unique situation, that all of this is happening as part of the preparations for America to co-host the expanded 2026 World Cup with Canada and Mexico. But the reality is that this smorgasbord of matches is a symptom of the direction that soccer has been headed in recent decades. With the earning potential of soccer continuing to grow, administrators and club owners persist in their hunt to seek out all avenues through which to make an extra dollar.

And the easiest way to do this is to just keep playing more matches. For years, professional sport teams have operated with the understanding that matches are the core product for them to sell tickets, broadcast rights, concessions, parking, merchandise, and sponsorships. As such, the drive to continuously monetize soccer has created a system of nonstop matches and content, where even in the off-season games are being played to generate revenue. And the American soccer bonanza is just a small sign of things to come. If the Club World Cup is a success, FIFA will likely continue to expand the tournament, and other associations and competitions will attempt to copy the format. Indeed, FIFA has already started discussions to expand the 2029 Club World Cup to a field of forty-eight teams.[2]

There is a lot of soccer coming our way. But will anyone want to watch it?

The Growth of Soccer Broadcasting

Perhaps the biggest transformation in how fans around the world consume soccer has been the ability to watch matches from anywhere in the world to your phone or television. In the early 2000s watching live soccer on television was a terribly cumbersome process requiring you to purchase expensive cable subscription packages just to get one or two channels that carried matches. And even then, you weren't guaranteed to watch your favorite team live, as the networks and leagues decided which matches were going to be broadcast based on the most popular matchups. While this generally worked well for me as an Arsenal fan, and my roommate—unfortunately, a Manchester United fan—if you supported a smaller club like Bolton Wanderers in America in the 2000s, you were likely out of luck most weekends.

The increasing number of broadcasters televising soccer, as well as the emergence of streaming has entirely changed this dynamic. No more sneaking out of work on Tuesdays and Wednesdays to huddle in the back of the local Irish pub to watch Champions League with fellow soccer degenerates. Instead, you can sit in the comfort of your own home, pretend to be working in your cubicle, or even be at your kid's dance recital and have access to pretty much every top soccer league in the world with a few swipes of your finger or click of a remote. And it is not just the top leagues and teams that are streaming games, as more obscure figures ranging from the English fifth division (National League) to third division Fukushima United in Japan now broadcast their matches online.

To better understand the current soccer broadcasting ecosystem, we need to trace back to the growth of television broadcast rights in the sport. Before the formation of the Premier League in 1992, most European soccer leagues had matches on terrestrial television, meaning there was relatively little to no cost for consumers to watch at home. At the same time, this also meant that the broadcast rights fees being paid to leagues and clubs were quite low, especially when compared to the rights deals that major American sport leagues were commanding for their telecasts. Notably, in 1990, the National Football League signed a three-year $900 million television rights deal that made it the richest league in the world.[3]

As such, it was only a matter of time before the top clubs in England broke away from the English Football League, as they desired greater control over handling broadcast and commercial rights deals to enhance their own bottom lines. Indeed, when the Premier League clubs gained their independence, terrestrial broadcaster ITV who had previously paid around £18 million a season for matches, submitted a new bid of £34 million per season[4]. However, they were quickly outbid by Rupert Murdoch's new satellite television company BSkyB who ended up paying £304 million for the rights to the Premier League through 1996.[5] In effect, while this resulted in a major boost in television revenue for Premier League clubs, it also had a significant impact on how soccer was consumed on television. Rather than just tuning into a free over-the-air station, soccer fans in England were now forced to pay for subscriptions and equipment in order to watch matches of their favorite clubs. However, what had an even greater impact was that by having a satellite broadcast partner, it now allowed the Premier League the ability to televise matches anywhere in the world. The NFL may have commanded far more broadcast revenue than the Premier League, but soccer was the world's game and there was clearly interest from fans around the world to watch matches live.

The successful launch of the Premier League, coupled with their massive increase in television rights, set the new model for how top European soccer leagues would operate. What followed was a mass of leagues and broadcasters partnering to not only televise games domestically but to reach important markets throughout the world, especially in Europe, Asia, and North America. The consequence of this was that within a short period of time, soccer fans went from desperately trying to find any match they could watch on television to having a whole menu of options to choose from.

Too Many Matches, Not Enough Attention

From the perspective of top-flight teams and leagues, the rapid growth of soccer broadcasting was generally seen as a good thing, as it meant increased exposure and revenue for the sport. And at a base level, having an array of options to watch soccer would generally seem like a great thing, especially for fans who had dreamed of the day when they could pick and choose which specific matches they could watch. However, as more and more leagues signed new broadcast rights deals, it also fostered intense competition between leagues as they battle to capture the attention of consumers.

This battle for attention can be perfectly encapsulated in the concept of the "attention economy" which was first proposed by Nobel Prize-winning economist Herbert Simon, who theorized that as we evolved into an information rich digital world, it would be attention that would become a scarce resource.[6] Indeed, that is the predicament that soccer leagues, teams, and broadcasters find themselves in today. Every club wants to have fans watching their matches, but due to the limited supply of attention from viewers—who also have the ability to switch between matches with ease—broadcasters must constantly seek ways to prevent fans from jumping to another game.

To try and keep fans from changing the channel, many networks have adopted an "American" style of broadcasting, where in addition to the match itself, additional content including expert analysis, player interviews, tactical discussions, and even comical antics is provided before and after a match. Perhaps the most successful version of this has been Paramount+ Champions League show, which pairs host Kate Scott with former players Thierry Henry, Micah Richards, and Jamie Carragher. Although having two world-class soccer legends in Henry and Carragher, the show has been able to strike a successful balance between detailed tactical analysis from former stars of the game alongside insider stories and comedic segments involving the entire crew. Part of the success of the Champions League show has also been in the ability to turn both the comedy and the tactical analysis into shortform clips that are easily shared on social media and other online platforms to draw more attention to the broadcasts.

Although some purists dismiss the pregame and postgame show format as an over-the-top gimmick that takes away from the importance of the matches themselves, the reality is that leagues and broadcasters are fighting for the attention of consumers. This means rather than returning to the days of stuffy pundits and former hard-nosed coaches arguing about technical details, broadcasts will continue to move further toward entertainment. Indeed, following this ideal, UEFA had American rock band Linkin Park perform a prematch kickoff show before the 2025 Champions League Final. Naturally, having a rock band kick-off one of the most important soccer matches in the world had the traditionalists in the media bemoaning about how this was another money grab from those in charge of soccer, and that they had lost the plot.

They are correct about it being a money grab, but in crying about a rock band postponing a match for ten minutes, the media and the public seem to be missing a bigger existential threat that is facing soccer. For many years, Americans have enjoyed portraying soccer as being a boring, low-scoring sport where men in shorts basically do nothing for two hours. Whether it be *The Simpsons* or legendary sportswriter Mike Royko, soccer has been mocked for lacking any entertainment value. While I disagree with these characterizations, the stark reality is that the demand for soccer broadcasts seems to have peaked and could even be in decline in some cases.

Most of the top European soccer leagues have signed new television rights deals between 2023 and 2025. Although most leagues were able to get record amounts for their broadcast rights, the actual percentage increase for these deals was quite minimal. For example, in Fall 2024, the Bundesliga signed a new deal that would pay them €4.484 billion over four years. On paper, this looks to be an amazing sum of money, but a comparison against the previous deal shows that it is only a 2 percent increase from the league's previous broadcast rights contract. Even the Premier League, the most watched professional sport league in the world, was only able to get a 4 percent increase when it renewed its TV deal in 2023.[7]

As a point of comparison, the National Basketball Association (NBA) had previously been on par with the Premier League in terms of the yearly value of their television contracts in the 2010s, when both leagues earned about

$2.7 billion a year. However, where the Premier League was only able to have a small percentage increase, the NBA signed a new deal in 2025 that increased its yearly television revenue to approximately $6.9 billion.[8] This difference in valuation from networks can be partially be explained by the fact that the NBA has no competitors in terms of selling elite professional basketball games, while there are numerous other leagues competing against the Premier League in terms of broadcasting top-flight European soccer. Considered from another perspective, the stagnation of the Premier League television contract can be seen as a reflection that the market for televised soccer matches has been flooded with content, thus leading to networks being less willing to pay for these games. Indeed, with Premier League viewership down 10 percent in the 2024/25 season, there does not seem to be a big payday in the league's future.[9]

If the Premier League is only able to command a small percentage increase in broadcast rights fees while also having to provide more matches to broadcast than ever before, it also calls into question what is going to happen for the lesser-known leagues across the world. One of the first hints that something could truly go wrong came from Ligue 1, the French first division. In 2019, the league managed to negotiate the second biggest media rights deal for a soccer league in Europe, getting approximately €1.15 billion a year from Mediapro and BeIN Sports to televise matches.[10] However, Spanish-based Mediapro missed the first two guaranteed payments they were due to make to the league in 2020, leading to the contract being terminated.[11] Amazon was brought in to replace Mediapro at a discount price of €250 million a year, but this meant that Ligue 1 was only receiving about half of the television revenue they had forecasted.

Things became even worse in the summer of 2024 when Amazon announced it would not be continuing its broadcast rights deal with Ligue 1. Believing the previous valuation of €1.15 billion was accurate, Ligue 1 attempted to sell its media rights package for €1 billion, but was unable to find any networks willing to pay this amount. Eventually, Ligue 1 settled for a combined €500 million a year deal split between DAZN and BeIN Sports. The financial impact of only receiving half the television revenue that had been projected by the league had major ramifications for several clubs. Lacking the television revenue they had been expecting, Olympique Lyonnais, more commonly referred to as "Lyon," was unable to pay off the debts it had accrued in recent years. Because of this, one of the most historic clubs in France, which even made it to the 2025 Europa League semifinals, were provisionally relegated to the second division unless they were able to clear their debts before the start of the 2025/26 season.[12]

However, this is not even close to the end of the story. Unhappy with the current broadcast rights deal, Ligue 1 clubs voted to end the existing contract with DAZN and BeIN Sports to try and find a new broadcast partner. As such, for the second year in a row, the top-flight of French soccer which includes the likes of reigning Champions League winners Paris Saint-Germain (PSG), is going into the summer break without any idea of who will be broadcasting their matches or how much revenue they will be receiving from it. Although the league and its member clubs clearly feel they should be earning more revenue from their television and streaming rights, they are taking a major risk in attempting to re-enter a market that is oversaturated with soccer content.

At the same time, this is a risk that many clubs in France feel they must take considering that the lack of television revenue over the last five years has put them in a precarious financial situation. Beyond the potential relegation of Lyon, financial issues have also impacted other historic clubs such as Football Club des Girondins de Bordeaux—Bordeaux for short—who were financially devastated by the lack of revenue during the COVID-19 pandemic and then were unable to properly recover due to the shortfall of television revenue. Unable to recover from this spiral, the club went into administration in the summer of 2024, and had its professional license revoked by the French Football Federation. Although there are many factors that played a role in Bordeaux's downfall, the lack of a lucrative broadcast rights deal coupled with poor financial projections of the league's market power likely exacerbated the situation. To put it another way, too much soccer can inundate the broadcast market to the point of destroying even famous clubs.

The example of Ligue 1 also brings up another major issue that is plaguing soccer leagues and competitions. Throughout their attempts to negotiate their broadcast rights deals, Ligue 1 has been insistent on being valued as one of the top two soccer leagues in the world. Although the league has a strong pedigree, much of this has been driven by the performance of PSG, which with the financial backing of its Qatari ownership group has dominated the league for the past decade. At the same time, if the Premier League and Bundesliga are only able to negotiate single-digit percent increases in their broadcast rights fees, it would seem that those in charge of Ligue 1 have been overestimating the popularity and importance of the league within the global soccer marketplace.

In some sense, it also hints at a level of hubris amongst the powers in the soccer industry who seem to be displaying the belief that because broadcast rights deals have been increasing at a rapid pace over the last pace, they should continue to do so. Basic economic principles and numerous historic examples like the Dutch tulip mania or the dot-com bubble highlight the financial disaster that awaits those who believe that markets will continue to grow at a fast pace without ever declining.

Is Anyone Watching?

Even FIFA is not inoculated from this type of behavior. A quick glance at the 2025 Club World Cup shows that the governing body of soccer has likewise overestimated the demand and willingness of fans to pay to watch their new tournament. With the World Cup being one of the biggest sporting events in the world, it seemed that FIFA believed that this level of interest would naturally carry over to their new club competition. However, when FIFA went out to sell the broadcast rights for the tournament, they were faced with an entirely unexpected reply from media companies—silence. While networks are usually attempting to outbid each other to gain the rights to televise the World Cup, these same companies were entirely uninterested in the Club World Cup. This must have been a stunning moment for FIFA and its executives, who have marketed the tournament as being the ultimate showcase of club soccer.

After not finding a media partner to purchase the rights for the Club World Cup, FIFA eventually struck a global deal with DAZN who purchased the global broadcast rights for the entire tournament for $1 billion. After the rights deal was secured, FIFA and DAZN announced that the tournament would be broadcast for free. Several questions emerged from this announcement. Why would DAZN be willing to offer almost twice the amount they paid to broadcast an entire Ligue 1 season to broadcast a relatively obscure one-month tournament? Moreover, why would they be willing to pay Ligue 1 so little for a product that sells subscriptions, but then give FIFA $1 billion for a tournament that they were going to give away to viewers for free?

While DAZN noted it would be broadcasting the tournament for free, the company also stated it would be selling regional television broadcast rights to various countries to generate revenue from the Club World Cup. However, with many major media companies such as the BBC and ITV unwilling to purchase the rights to the tournament, more questions were raised as to why DAZN would be willing to pay $1 billion for a tournament that clearly was not going to provide financial returns to recover this sizable investment.[13] Could DAZN really afford to throw away $1 billion to show one month of club soccer?

Clearly, the answer is no.

No major media corporation would be willing to pay such a large amount to broadcast a minor soccer competition without the guarantee that they would be able to recoup their investment. However, in the case of DAZN, it may be the case that they do not need to generate any revenue from broadcasting the Club World Cup in order to make themselves financially whole. In February 2025, about two months before FIFA announced it had sold the broadcast rights to the Club World Cup to DAZN, Saudi media company Surj Sports acquired a minority stake in DAZN.[14] The price of the minority stake? Exactly $1 billion.

A quick look into Surj Sports shows that they are the sport investment arm of the Saudi Public Investment Fund (PIF), one of the world's richest sovereign wealth funds. While we will not go into too much detail about PIF in this chapter, as it is covered more extensively in other chapters in this book, it is important to note the organization is worth around $900 billion dollars and has been heavily investing in sport properties and competitions in the last decade. Moreover, with Saudi Arabia winning the rights to host the World Cup in 2034, and having previously hosted the Club World Cup in 2023, the country and its wealth fund have special interest in ensuring that FIFA competitions are widely viewed by the public. That is, as the Saudi government has used its investments in sport to help build its soft power by making it more socially and culturally relevant on the global stage, it has vested interest in guaranteeing the success of the Club World Cup. To further illustrate this point, just days before the competition was scheduled to start PIF signed on to be a major sponsor for the 2025 Club World Cup.[15]

Despite all the financial backing that both FIFA and DAZN have received to host the revamped Club World Cup in 2025, there is a best lukewarm interest in the tournament. While DAZN was able to sell regional deals to have the competition televised in America and the UK, both agreements included less than half the matches. Perhaps the biggest sign that the Club World Cup is not something soccer fans are interested in is the rate at which ticket prices for the tournament have declined. The opening match featuring Lionel Messi's Inter Miami against Al-Ahly of Egypt originally had tickets selling for about $350 a seat. The expectation was that Messi's popularity, which has helped to sell out numerous matches since his arrival in Major League Soccer, combined with a tournament featuring the best clubs in the world would result in high consumer demand. Instead, with tens of thousands of unsold seats for the opening match, the organizers quickly dropped ticket prices to $55, or 16 percent of what FIFA expected fans were willing to pay to watch Messi play in the Club World Cup.[16] If the greatest player of all time can't fill a stadium in soccer hungry America, it did not bode well for the rest of the teams playing in the tournament.

Soccer is still the world's most popular sport, but all the trends suggest that the industry may have hit a breaking point where there is just too much of the product being offered to consumers. Just thinking logically about the timing of the Club World Cup, it comes at the end of a long season, where any dedicated soccer fan will probably have watched dozens, if not hundreds of matches involving their favorite club(s) and national teams. Imagine being an Inter Milan fan who has watched their team play almost sixty competitive matches between domestic and continental competitions in the 2024/25 season. After getting destroyed in the Champions League final, the last thing you want to do is to get on a plane and fly to America to watch your squad play Urawa Red Diamonds of Japan in some cup that you have never cared about in your life. You would rather be at the beach getting some sun, or taking a walk around beautiful Lake Como, finally taking a break from the sport you love so that you can rejuvenate for the next season. Instead, FIFA is doing everything in its power to tell you that you should watch even more matches.

The reality is that soccer fans are fatigued. Everywhere one looks, there is just more and more soccer content. A trip to websites such as Livescore.com or Sofascore.com—which both specialize in providing live updates of scores from soccer leagues around the world—shows that on any given day there are dozens of matches being played, many of which can be accessed with a single click of a button. Want to watch second division soccer in Ecuador? They have you covered.

It truly is a first-world problem to complain about there being too much soccer for one to watch, especially when the simple solution is to just change the channel. But for soccer teams, leagues, and competitions, losing the attention of consumers is probably the thing they fear the most. When soccer broadcasts started to become popular in England, the country created a blackout rule that no matches can be shown on television during the Saturday 3 p.m. slot, as this is the primary time when most teams play their matches. The idea behind this was that if fans were able to watch games on television, rather than going to support their local club, they would end up staying at home watching popular teams like Manchester United or Liverpool play instead. As such, by enforcing the blackout rule, it would keep the superpowers of soccer from grabbing all the attention and allow smaller clubs to still attract fans to games.

Archaic as this rule may seem, it has had some success in the continued support of soccer at various levels of the pyramid. However, as streaming technology has made it cheaper and easier than ever to broadcast matches, lower league teams that had been protected by the blackout rule now also find themselves actively trying to televise their matches to fans around the world. Though we often discuss about how free markets are a good thing, allowing consumers access to competitive pricing and various choices of products, the democratization of soccer broadcasting may have opened Pandora's box for the entire industry. While it allows most fans to access their favorite teams no matter how far away they live, it has opened the floodgates to allow almost any team to broadcast their matches, drowning fans in a deluge of content.

At the same time, it is no longer a point where leagues or associations can simply turn around and say that there shouldn't be so many games being broadcast live. The reaction from teams and fans who are told they must limit the number of matches they televise would not only result in severe backlash but would also likely end up in court on charges of anticompetitive practices. As such, maybe we just need to accept the words of The Clash frontman Joe Strummer, who sang: "London is drowning, and I live by the river"[17] and allow the deluge of soccer content to sweep us all away.

To me, the existential threat is not having access to all of this content, but rather that having virtually unlimited access would render the sport meaningless, each match just another relatively meaningless slog through a 70-match season of mediocrity.

Overworked

If you think fans are tired from watching too much soccer, just imagine how the players feel. A few months before the men's 2024 European Championship (Euro 2024) kicked off, French superstar Kylian Mbappe gave an interview in British GQ where he discussed the heavy toll that playing so matches was having on him and players across the world.[18] Mbappe noted that the calendar for players who play for their national team and at top clubs in Europe has ballooned out of control. According to Front Office Sports, Mbappe played fifty-six matches in the 2021/22 season, and sixty-three matches in 2022/23,[19] and is on track to surpass this number with his new club Real Madrid in 2025 which not only had to participate in the usual slate of matches but were also one of the teams competing in the 2025 Club World Cup.

It is important to highlight that this is not an anomaly that is isolated to a few superstar players. Professional soccer players have been playing more matches than their predecessors in the last few decades. Of course, for star players at top clubs like Mbappe, the workload is even heavier as they must juggle a slate of league, domestic, and continental cup matches, as well as consistently take part in duty with their national team. Although national team duty may only add on ten to twenty matches at most in a calendar year, it exacerbates the situation by requiring players to tack on even more travel and playing time during breaks when most other professionals are able to rest and recover.

In the same interview, Mbappe offers an extremely astute observation that the soccer players at the top of the totem pole are now playing almost as many games in a season as NBA players. However, he notes that there is a critical difference between how the NBA and European soccer approach the idea of resting players. He argues that within the NBA, resting a player is so common that load management is taken for granted as being a strategic part of the game. On the other hand, he notes that if he said he was tired and didn't want to play on a Saturday, it would not go over well, especially among fans who support his club. His words are as clear as day—the European soccer calendar has become so bloated it is difficult for players to give great performances in every match and that overworking players leads to a decline in the quality of play.

Unfortunately, in addition to fans being unhappy with players resting, there are also many important figures in the soccer industry who are not sympathetic to the need for load management. Amongst the ranks of those who think players should just suck it up and keep playing are several former players, who often use their media platforms and popularity to criticize star players who are simply trying to recuperate so they can continue to deliver peak performances when it is needed most.

When US national team and AC Milan star Christian Pulisic announced that he would not be participating in the 2025 Gold Cup in order to recover from the long season, he was immediately lambasted by several former national team members including Alexi Lalas and Landon Donovan, both of whom have prominent media roles. If anyone could understand the level of exhaustion that comes from playing professional soccer, it would be those who had previously experienced it themselves. However, rather than empathizing with Pulisic, these statesmen of American soccer targeted him as the perfect scapegoat for criticism, even though several other US national team members who play in Europe also dropped out of the squad because of fatigue. Instead, with a few callous comments, Lalas and Donovan cast Pulisic into the center of a firestorm that had the media and fans questioning whether Pulisic really deserved his nickname of "Captain America."

At the same time, it is ironic that Alexi Lalas and Landon Donovan chose to question Pulisic's commitment. During his career, Lalas' heaviest workload came during his one full season Serie A in 1994/95, where he logged forty matches for his club and national team. Moreover, throughout his entire career Lalas played in only 242 competitive club matches, whereas Pulisic, who is only twenty-six years old, has logged 372 matches, all of which have been with top European clubs. And as for Landon Donovan, he himself complained about being fatigued at the end of the 2012 MLS season, to the point where he took a four-month sabbatical from both his club and national team and subsequently received severe media backlash for the decision. Although Donovan made several attempts to play in Europe, he was never ever to break through into the main squad with Everton, Leverkusen, or Bayern Munich. As such, he played most of his career in Major League Soccer, where he typically played less than thirty matches a season for his club.

Based on this, as loud as Lalas and Donovan can be on the subject, they really shouldn't be the ones talking about whether players are lacking commitment when they themselves never experienced the type of season that Pulisic and other national team members are now going through every year. The soccer industry is entirely different from when Lalas and Donovan were players, with more games being played than ever before as leagues, clubs, and media companies all push for more content that can be broadcast and monetized.

Amidst the vitriol directed at Pulisic for skipping the Gold Cup, it was former US defender Jimmy Conrad who provided the voice of reason. While he noted his disappointment with Pulisic's decision, he also stated that he himself once had to request time off from the national team to rest, and that it takes courage for players to come out and say they are being overworked.[20] And in Pulisic's case, his decision to rest from a tournament that is held every two years, and which the US has won seven times, seems to be the wise choice, especially considering that America is hosting the World Cup in 2026. If you asked Americans which they would prefer, another Gold Cup title or a strong performance from their national team in a World Cup on home soil, most would prefer the latter. Heck, some of them might not even know the Gold Cup is being played this year, as they are probably more focused on the Club World Cup.

It is disappointing that prominent members of the soccer media, including former players and coaches, are not more outspoken about the workload issue. In many cases, as is evidenced by the treatment of Pulisic, rather than discussing how much physical stress players are going through by playing so many matches, they instead make it a personal issue with the player. The player lacks commitment, the players are soft compared to when I play, the players don't have the right mentality, and lack professionalism. All of this could be true, but it doesn't reduce the problem of how packed the soccer calendar is for elite level professionals.

Injury Risk

As the number of matches has continued to increase, player unions and associations, especially FIFPro, have begun to further emphasize the physical toll and other difficulties that are becoming commonplace within soccer. Over the last few years, FIFPro has put a great deal of resources into tracking the workload of top-level professional soccer players from around the world, as well as publicizing the data findings using the hashtag #AtTheLimit to emphasize that many players are at the brink of disaster.

Perhaps the FIFPro story that gained the most traction this year was the plight of Bayern Munich and South Korean defender Kim Min Jae. Throughout the 2024/25 season, Kim was heavily criticized for his ineffective play, including allowing crucial goals in the Champions League and the critical Der Klassiker match against rivals Borussia Dortmund. As the mistakes continued to pile up, the media highlighted that Kim was statistically one of the worst defenders in the top five European leagues,[21] and Bayern fans demanded that a replacement be found for Kim.

Then in April 2025, FIFPro published the story about Kim's workload and injury problems throughout the season. Since the early part of the season, Kim had been suffering from Achilles tendinitis, an injury that is often associated with overwork in elite athletes. Typically, an athlete with this injury will be rested for at a month to allow the Achilles tendon to heal properly. However, as Bayern lost center backs Hiroki Ito and Dayot Upamecano to injury, Kim was forced to continue playing despite this injury. By April 1, 2025, Kim had logged 4,557 minutes across fifty-one appearances, or just under ninety minutes per match on average. Additionally, because South Korea was engaged in World

Cup qualifying throughout the season, he also traveled approximately 74,000 kilometers—the equivalent of flying around the entire world twice—to play in competitive matches.

In publishing the report, FIFPro noted that Kim was on pace to potentially play seventy matches this season due to Bayern's participation in the 2025 Club World Cup. Kim's injury situation became so bad that the South Korean national team, despite struggling in qualifiers for the 2026 World Cup, decided to rest Kim for two critical matches in March against Oman and Jordan. Even though his national team had essentially shut down his season, Bayern manager Vincent Kompany continued to play Kim as the club chased both a Bundesliga and Champions League title. After being eliminated by Inter Milan in mid-April, Kim continued to play league matches until he was finally pulled out of the lineup due to his injury. The irony is that despite having struggled through almost the entire Bundesliga season, Kim was finally rested for the match in which Bayern clinched the title.

The story of Kim Min Jae's 2024/25 season reflects the issues that exist in elite level soccer. Despite having Achilles tendinitis—an injury which increases the risk of a rupture which takes anywhere between six and twelve months to recover from[22]—both Bayern and South Korea continued to risk Kim's health in order to try and win matches. While it is not surprising that professional soccer players are overworked, the fact that one carrying a rather painful injury continued to be used at such a high rate shows how expendable their health is to their teams. The irony here is that while continuing to expose Kim to the risk of injury, Bayern criticized the Canadian national team for playing Alphonso Davies when he was not fully fit. After Davies suffered a season-ending injury on international duty, Bayern released a statement saying that the Canadian national team was not prioritizing the health of players.[23] And yet, at the very same time, the club was not prioritizing the health of Kim Min Jae as it continued force him out week after week on a bad ankle to help Bayern chase titles.

This is the hypocrisy of modern soccer. Although teams spend a significant amount of time emphasizing the health of their players, they continue to treat them as assets that exist only for their own benefit. And what happens when those assets are used up? They just sell them on to the next club. Indeed, that looks to be what is happening with Kim Min Jae, as even though he has traveled with Bayern to the Club World Cup, reports suggest both PSG and several Premier League clubs are interested in purchasing him.

All Risk, No Pay

One of the main arguments being made about playing more matches is that the players will be well compensated for taking on an additional load. For the longest time, the NFL had tried to expand its season from sixteen to eighteen games, with the stipulation that by doing so, it would be able to provide a cut of the additional revenue to increase player salaries. However, because the number of games played is negotiated through a collective bargaining agreement (CBA) between the league and the players, this change had been blocked for years out of concern the season was already too long and two additional games would have a severe impact on player health and performance. Eventually in 2021 a deal was struck to add an additional regular season game to the schedule, allowing owners to boost their revenue through increased ticket sales and broadcast rights fees, with player salaries likewise increasing.

In soccer, there is a similar logic that athletes know the risk of playing the sport, and they are well compensated because of this and the unique skills and popularity they possess. However, as the soccer calendar has continued to expand, are athletes actually being paid for the additional labor and risk they are taking on? According to Premier League wage data from the website Capology.com,[24] the average player salary for the 2024/25 season was just over £2.6 million. This is the lowest average wages have been post-COVID, with the average wage in recent years having been well over £3 million. There are many factors that can contribute to the recent decline in salaries, including the newly imposed Profit & Sustainability Rules. However, as revenue and the number of matches have continued to increase for the Premier League and its clubs, it does call into question whether players are truly being compensated for their increased workload.

Let's consider the newly expanded Champions League to consider the logic of how increased revenue from playing more matches should hypothetically flow down to the players. By expanding the number of games played in the Champions League, UEFA should be able to increase the amount it commands in broadcasting rights due to the addition of more matches. After taking a cut for administrative fees and other expenses, UEFA creates a prize structure that rewards clubs for participation in the tournament, including prize money for winning matches and advancing through the competition. As a sign of how lucrative the Champions League is compared to other cup competitions, despite being knocked out in the group stage of the Champions League, VFB Stuttgart earned €43 million, almost as much as Europa League winners Tottenham, whose total prize money was €45.4 million.

Based on this revenue distribution, as well as the increased match day revenue from ticket, merchandise, and concession sales, clubs should experience a significant boost in revenue from playing in the expanded Champions League. In turn, clubs are then able to decide how to use this additional revenue. Although some of it will certainly be distributed to owners or used to pay off debts, most teams will likely want to use this increased windfall to strengthen their squad. It is at this point where the money should flow to the players, as teams renegotiate contracts to keep key players from leaving, and purchase players to help improve the team in order to continue competing in the Champions League. So, while players may not be directly getting a cut from their participation in the expanded Champions League, the way the soccer labor market works generally means that some of the revenue will reach the players.

While this hypothetical trickling down of revenue from UEFA to clubs and players seems to be fair, there is a problem in that some players who take part in additional matches could be excluded from these financial gains. That is, a club could choose to not negotiate a new deal and thus keep a player on the same salary despite having to play more matches, or they could even sell or cut them in the off-season. And thus, when the argument is made that players know the risks of playing professional soccer and are well compensated for them, this is not always the case. Indeed, from this vantage point, the addition of new competitions and more matches can be seen to have an exploitative angle as well.

Perhaps the most egregious example of this type of exploitation of players not being properly compensated for participating in extra matches comes from the new Club World Cup. One of the main talking points that FIFA kept reiterating about their revamped version of the competition was that in addition to having more teams, there would be a significant increase in prize money. Based on the distribution model, if a top European club won all their matches at the Club World Cup, they could earn around €115 million—prize money equivalent to making the UEFA Champions League semifinal.[25] Even for teams from MLS or the Mexican Liga MX, there is the realistic potential to earn well over €10 million for participating in the competition.

Despite this giant pool of prize money backed by sponsorship deals with organizations like Coca-Cola, Adidas, Qatar Airways, and the Saudi Public Investment Fund,[26] there is already trouble brewing about the lack of revenue being paid out to some of the players participating in the tournament. Two weeks before the tournament kicked off, players from the Seattle Sounders took the field in a league match against Minnesota United wearing shirts that said "CLUB WOLRD CA$H GRAB" written on the front, with a caricature of the Monopoly man wearing a hat that said "MLS" on it.[27]

Because of the unique single-entity structure used by MLS, it means that players in the league all sign contracts with the league rather than individual clubs. Under the current CBA, MLS players are only able to receive 50 percent of the revenue a club earns from outside tournaments. Moreover, the total amount that can be split among players is capped at $1 million per team. As MLS clubs are guaranteed to earn $9.55 million to participate in the Club World Cup, it means that the maximum players can earn is $1 million, and that the remaining $8.5 million would be paid out to the club. Considering that MLS allows clubs to have a roster of thirty players, the most an MLS player could earn from playing in the tournament is just over $33,000. After deducting taxes from this prize money, a player would basically have just enough to purchase a Nissan Sentra.

However, as the MLS CBA stipulates that clubs are capped at paying out $1 million in outside prize money to their entire squad, it raises another potential issue. The Sounders have already participated in the CONCACAF Champions Cup this season and are also due to participate in the Leagues Cup later in the year.[28] As such, this means the prize money that players can earn from the Club World Cup has already been reduced because of the money earned from the Champions Cup, as well as the fact that they will not be able to receive any prize money from the Leagues Cup. So, in the midst of their busy season, the MLS players will have to play extra games which will provide large payouts to their clubs, and yet they will likely receive little to no compensation for the additional workload.

Following the match against Minnesota United, Sounders owner Adrian Hanauer accosted the team for wearing the shirts, as FIFA officials were present at the match as part of the Club World Cup trophy tour.[29] In response to this, MLS made a new offer to the players participating in the tournament that removed the cap on how much could be made, and increased the payout to players to 20 percent of the earned prize money. In response to this, the MLS Players Association (MLSPA) issued a statement highlighting that the new offer was well below the revenue-sharing standards used by clubs in other regions.[30] Five days before the Club World Cup kicked off, the two sides were still locked in heated negotiations over the payouts players should be receiving.

The players knew that too much soccer was being played and had finally taken a stand rightly demanding to be compensated for it.

The Soccer Bubble

It is without a doubt that there are more soccer matches and content today than at any point in history. The administrators and owners who control the sport seem to be hell bent on trying to squeeze as many matches as possible into the calendar, without thinking about how players and consumers will react to this glut of soccer. Where other professional sport leagues are strategically growing their products to maximize fan interest and revenue, soccer has become a free-for-all with all the leagues throwing content at fans like pushy used-car salesmen. This competition between all the different soccer leagues has created an industry that has ballooned out of control.

Now after decades of explosive growth in all dimensions, soccer is now coming to the point where revenue growth driven by fan consumption and viewership is starting to slow. Numerous clubs are already experiencing financial difficulties, and some have even gone out of business, a hundred years of soccer history wiped off the face of the earth because of the unchecked need for growth in the sport. In some sense, it could be said that soccer is in an economic bubble—that the high valuations for broadcast rights and matches led to many leagues speculating they could also achieve similar financial gains as the World Cup or the Premier League. However, as has been shown with Ligue 1 in recent years, many of the leagues overestimated their value in the market, and now prices are beginning to stagnate or decline in some cases.

And somehow the response to this from the main governing bodies and leagues who are in charge of soccer is to keep adding more competitions. Soccer is already being oversupplied to consumers, and the players are paying a physical price by being overworked without any guarantees of extra compensation. In any other industry, this type of behavior would be considered as foolhardy or even negligent. But because soccer is the world's game, the belief seems to be that there is an endless supply of interest that will continue to consume whatever pointless competition FIFA comes up with next.

But there is a danger in this assumption that soccer, especially the traditional ninety-minute 11-on-11 form we are used to watching, will continue to be the magnet that draws fan interest with ease. The sport has already reached a point where big clubs are participating in competitions that most fans don't care about. Now with younger generations of fans shifting their consumption habits more toward highlight packages and soccer video games rather than watching full matches, there is a very real possibility that the soccer bubble could burst in the coming decades.

Although the outcome could mean a reduction in the number of matches and competitions, it would come at a severe financial cost for clubs, leagues, and players.

There is too much soccer. Hopefully it will not permanently ruin the sport we love.

8

Who to Support
Which Clubs Deserve
Our Attention?

As soccer has continued to grow in popularity around the world, I often find myself engaged in discussions with fans who are new to the sport and are trying to pick a club to support. For those of us who started watching soccer in earlier decades, Barcelona, Manchester United, Real Madrid, and Arsenal were popular choices as they were clubs that fans could consistently watch on television anywhere in the world. However, with the expansion of broadcasting and streaming, it has now become the case that choosing a club has become a much more nuanced matter. As such, it is no longer simply choosing the biggest or best club in order to have access to them. Moreover, choosing a Manchester City or Liverpool now seems like a lazy choice and can even lead to new fans being labeled as "glory hunters."

Instead, the decision to pick a club has become a highly detailed process, as the choice not only will have an impact on your mood based on how the team performs but also is treated as a reflection of your psychology, personality, and politics. Alas, picking Manchester City not only positions you as someone who only supports teams that win, but also aligns you with a club that has been charged with 115 financial violations that were allegedly committed in building the superclub that has dominated England for the past decade. We may want our managers and players to have a win at all costs mentality, but do we really want that amongst our friends, neighbors, and coworkers? As such, what many fans who are coming into the game now desire is to pick a fashionable club. Not an established winner who everyone already knows and has legions of fans around the world. Instead, they want one whose stock seems to be on the rise so that in a few years' time they can tell others how they were a supporter of the club before they were good.

You can already see this in action with many of the up-and-coming teams in the Premier League as they attract new fans from around the world. Recently, I met an American who told me how he had chosen to support Brentford because they "do things the right way." What he really meant was that rather than choosing some club funded by a nation-state or billions of dollars in real-estate development, he was picking a club of more modest means that was trying to compete through grassroots development and strategic decision-making. A perfect club for a thoughtful person.

What really struck me about this conversation was his repeated insistence that Brentford do things the right way. And indeed, he has a point. Every year, my colleague and I take American sport business students to England for a week to tour stadiums, meet club executives, and of course to watch a few matches. Of all the clubs that we visit, Brentford is the only one that takes the money we pay them and then donates it to charities and other local community projects. While other clubs do not tell us what they do with the payments we provide them, my guess is that most of them are keeping the money to maximize their revenues. Although my allegiance is with Arsenal on the pitch, I now have a soft spot in my heart for Brentford and their commitment to helping their community.

As more and more fans continue to be drawn in by the excitement and passion of soccer, the reality is that most of them will end up choosing to support the most visible ultra-rich clubs that play in the Champions League. It is just the natural order of how the free market of the soccer industry works. However, this does not mean we should just cast aside the clubs that do things the right way. Whether it simply be the way they run their business, their involvement with community organizations, the sociopolitical stance of their fans, or even attempts to save the environment, there are many clubs that are trying to make the world a better place. And whether we are new to the game or have been following a team for decades, aren't these the clubs that we should support?

I'm not demanding that you burn the $150 shirt you just bought from your favorite club and immediately switch allegiances because another club is trying to reduce its carbon footprint. Indeed, as fans our consumption of the game does have an impact on the success and failure of clubs. As such, it is worth recognizing which clubs are trying to have a positive impact on society, as it shows us the potential benefits that soccer clubs can have on our world.

In the following, we will examine some of the clubs that stand out as trying to do the right thing, as well as one that forgot about the culture of their club. These examples are not just clubs we should consider following, but that the rest of the industry should be paying close attention to.

AFC Wimbledon—Do

AFC Wimbledon may have one of the most unique stories in all of soccer. Wimbledon is a small suburb in the commuter belt just west of London that is famous worldwide for the annual tennis tournament that is hosted there. Originally named Wimbledon FC, the team lingered in the obscurity in the seventh division of English soccer for most of its history. However, after a run of strong performances in the mid-1970s, Wimbledon FC was chosen to replace Workington in the English Football League (EFL), officially making them a professional soccer club.

Just nine years after being named to the EFL, Wimbledon earned promotion to the First Division, the name for the top-flight of English soccer before it was replaced by the Premier League in 1992. Ten years earlier, Wimbledon was in the seventh-tier Southern League, and now had miraculously fought its way to the pinnacle of professional soccer. Incredibly, rather than being a yo-yo team that bounced back and forth between the First and Second Divisions, Wimbledon managed to stay in the top-tier of English soccer for thirteen consecutive seasons, until they were relegated from the Premier League at the end of the 1999/2000 season.

Wimbledon FC's greatest moment came in the 1988 FA Cup, when they shocked the world by beating league champions Liverpool in the final. At the time, Liverpool was the strongest team in England, having won five of the previous eight league titles, and was the heavy favorite to win the double—both league and FA Cup titles in the same season. Despite having only been in the First Division for two seasons, Wimbledon FC showed little fear in facing the team that had dominated European football for the past decade. Indeed, Wimbledon had already built a reputation as a gritty squad that relished in a rough style of play and antics on and off the field. Though the club had some amazing players such as Dennis Wise and John Fashanau,[1] they also had certified lunatics like Vinnie Jones who is more famous for antagonizing and kicking players than kicking a ball. To most of the world, Jones is most notable for playing enforcers in Guy Richie films such as *Snatch* and *Lock, Stock, and Two Smoking Barrels*.

In the prematch program, Fashanau himself delivered a message to Liverpool, stating that while this was supposed to be a showpiece to finish Liverpool's coronation, "the last team they wanted at the party was us."[2] One can only imagine what Liverpool were thinking when they saw Fashanau punch Vinnie Jones in the face during a prematch interview, and then have Vinnie turn to the camera and say "there'll be plenty of that."[3] In what was a hard-fought match, in which Jones would likely have been sent off in today's game for his cynical tackle on Steve McMahon, Wimbledon emerged as victors, with Lawrie Sanchez scoring the deciding goal from a glancing header.

When the whistle blew at full time, John Motson who served as the BBC commentator for the match exclaimed "The Crazy Gang have beaten the Culture Club."[4] And thus, Wimbledon FC's new nickname was born—The Crazy Gang. Despite this success, things were not going well for the club, especially off the field. After the FA Cup victory, club executives announced plans to rebuild the team's home stadium Plough Lane to become compliant with new regulations introduced in the aftermath of the Hillsborough disaster. However, as this redevelopment never came to fruition, Wimbledon FC was forced into a temporary ground sharing deal with nearby Crystal Palace.

Unable to secure a new stadium deal anywhere in the West London region, Wimbledon FC were forced to extend their short-term deal to use Palace's Selhurst Park into subsequent seasons. This resulted in significant anger from supporters who demand their own home ground. Things became even worse when the club's chairman Sam Hammam proposed looking outside of London, even considering Ireland as a potential home for the club. Incapable of finding a solution to Wimbledon FC's plight, Hammam sold off the club to Norwegian investors, as well as allowing Plough Lane to be redeveloped by a supermarket.

Wimbledon FC was effectively homeless.

A solution was offered to Wimbledon by former CBS music executive Pete Winkleman who offered the club a space to build a ground in a large property development he was leading in Milton Keynes.[5] The club initially rejected the offer, partly because of the distance. Milton Keynes is over sixty miles from Wimbledon, a move which would rip the club out of the community it had been part of for over a century. All of this changed when Wimbledon FC's Norwegian owners appointed Charles Koppel as the club's new chairman at the beginning of 2001. Although a successful businessman, Koppel is said to have never attended a match before becoming chairman of the club, and his charge from the ownership group was to solve the club's stadium problem while also enhancing its commercial opportunities.[6] With Wimbledon FC effectively bankrupt, the club's executives began negotiations with Winkleman, and announced on August 2, 2001, their intention to relocate to Milton Keynes.[7]

Naturally, there was an immediate uproar from supporters who demanded that the club should stay in Wimbledon. To American readers, moving a professional sport franchise sixty miles may not seem like a big deal, especially considering how often teams in North America relocate to cities hundreds or even thousands of miles away. However, Wimbledon FC was considered an important part of the community, with fans often walking or making short trips on public transit to attend matches. The very idea that the ownership would allow a team to be moved such a distance was almost unfathomable at the time, especially as clubs typically only move a few kilometers at most in England. For example, when Arsenal decided to build a new stadium, rather than move thirty miles away to a cheaper parcel of land in the suburbs, the club decided to build its new home just a few hundred meters away.

Despite protests from Wimbledon FC fans, the deal to move to Milton Keynes was given approval by both the EFL and the Football Association (FA) in 2002 after an independent commission voted 2-1 in favor of relocation.[8] With the fans now powerless to stop the move, they did the next best thing. In 2002, they started their own club—AFC Wimbledon.

Because Wimbledon FC still held the name of the club, the newly formed team was allowed to use AFC Wimbledon. As such, AFC Wimbledon is considered to be a phoenix club—a team that is reborn from the ashes of the demise of a previous club. AFC Wimbledon began play in the 2002 season in the Combined Counties League, which is the ninth tier of the English soccer pyramid. Despite being seven levels below where Wimbledon FC had been playing, the majority of supporters abandoned Wimbledon FC and changed allegiance to the new club that would be staying in the community. Those supporters who chose the higher tiered club over their new community organization were treated to a harsh welcome at Wimbledon FC's first match of the 2002/3 season, as AFC Wimbledon fans stood outside the gates protesting and yelling "scab" at those who dared enter.

Although AFC Wimbledon were in the ninth tier of English football, they still managed to draw around 3,700 fans per match, while Wimbledon FC was able to get around 3,000 mainly due to traveling supporters for the away teams.[9] Wimbledon FC became such a pariah, they set the record for the lowest match attendance in the second division when only 849 people showed up a late October match against Rotherham United.[10] When questioned about setting the record for lowest attendance, Charles Koppel who was still serving as chairman of the club, audaciously stated that he expected attendance would bounce back to levels from when the club was in the Premier League.

He couldn't have been more wrong.

With the split in the club causing a massive drop in attendance, Wimbledon FC lost a significant portion of its main source of income. The decision to move the club was considered good business that would prevent the club from going into administration and boost future revenues. Instead, they went bankrupt because of it.[11] Moreover, no one wanted to do business with the club because of their newfound status as the most hated soccer team in the country. Several clubs, including Premier League side Tottenham Hotspur had scheduled preseason friendlies with Wimbledon FC, but all ended up canceling after receiving pressure from their own supporter groups.[12]

With the Norwegian owners refusing to provide any more financing to save the club, Pete Winkleman had to step in with a consortium of investors to purchase the club. With Winkelman reluctantly now in control of the club, he quickly finished a temporary stadium deal and got approval for the club to move Milton Keynes in September 2003.[13] Having moved to Milton Keynes, and also being told that their use of Wimbledon's two-headed eagle was illegal, the club was rebranded as Milton Keynes Dons FC, or MK Dons as they are now commonly known. MK Dons also changed their kit colors from blue to white, allowing AFC Wimbledon to appear as the true heir to Wimbledon FC's history and culture.

Part of what makes the AFC Wimbledon story so great is how the club is run from an ownership and business perspective. After having seen what a single owner, or even a group of investors can do to a club, the founders of the phoenix club wanted to ensure that history would not repeat itself. As such, they set up a supporters' ownership group named "The Dons Trust." Notably, The Dons Trust is committed to holding at least 75 percent of the club, meaning that AFC Wimbledon is one of the few teams in professional sport that is truly fan-owned. Although the club had to sell smaller minority stakes to help raise funding for them to purchase Kingsmeadow stadium in the early 2000s, they have generally managed to fulfill their promise of being 75 percent supporter owned.

However, being a supporter-financed club also meant that AFC Wimbledon must run on a tight budget. Despite the limited funding, the club skyrocketed through the tiers of professional football in its early years, including an English football record seventy-eight league matches in a row without a loss between 2003 and the end of 2004.[14] After only seven seasons of existence, AFC Wimbledon had climbed from the ninth tier of English football to fifth tier Conference National, putting them just one promotion away from gaining entry back into the EFL. In their second season in the Conference National, they finished in second, qualifying them for the promotion playoff. After easily dispatching Fleetwood Town in the semifinals, AFC Wimbledon faced Luton Town for the ultimate prize of rejoining the EFL. Wimbledon goalkeeper Seb

Brown would be the hero on this day, keeping Luton Town scoreless for the entire 120 minutes of regulation, and then saving two penalties in the shoot out to confirm Wimbledon's return to professional football.[15]

In just nine years, AFC Wimbledon had gone from a brand-new club started by supporters to replace the one they had lost to gaining entry back into the English Football League. In 2015/16, AFC Wimbledon earned promotion to League One, while MK Dons were relegated down to League One, meaning that Wimbledon had now caught up with the club that had been stolen from them. In 2017/18, both AFC Wimbledon and MK Dons found themselves embroiled in a relegation battle near the end of the season. MK Dons ended up losing all six matches they played in April, while AFC Wimbledon finished their season by scrapping four straight draws to keep them in the safety zone. The impossible had happened, AFC Wimbledon would now be playing at a higher level than MK Dons.

One last piece of unsettled business for AFC Wimbledon was the loss of Plough Lane. After former chairman Sam Hammam had sold the ground to supermarket chain Safeway, the stadium was eventually demolished to build housing. With the former stadium gone, Wimbledon decided to do the next best thing—build their own. And true to form, they raised over £5 million for the new Plough Lane project through crowdfunding and selling bonds to supporters.[16] After a final investment from local businessman Nick Robertson, the club was able to begin construction of their new home just a few hundred meters away from where their original ground had been.

When it is said that AFC Wimbledon has done the improbable, it really should be the fans who get all the credit. When it was announced their beloved team was leaving, it would have been easier for them to just become fans of Crystal Palace or Fulham, or even to just buy a satellite dish and watch matches from home. Instead, they fought for their club's history and identity. In doing so, they showed the entire football industry that a club really is nothing without its fans. To this day, MK Dons are often mockingly referred to as "the franchise" indicating they are not a club with a real tradition and culture. Instead, they are just another outpost, a football version of McDonald's.

At the same time, it needs to be acknowledged that AFC Wimbledon is also an oddity. They are the only club formed in the twenty-first century that has managed to gain promotion into the EFL. And while I would love to see AFC Wimbledon mimic their success of years past and try to battle their way up to the Premier League, the likelihood of that happening is quite small. The reality is that while a club is nothing without its fans, a club is also dependent on having lots of money to be able to compete. In this sense, by ensuring that no single owner can ever take control of and ruin the club again, AFC Wimbledon restricts itself from obtaining the resources it needs to compete at the top level.

AFC Wimbledon is the reflection of what soccer could look like if the fans were in control. And I think that is one of the best reasons we should support them.

Borussia Dortmund—Don't (For Now)

Borussia Dortmund with their bright yellow and black striped kits were for the longest time the club for soccer hipsters. Playing in the German Bundesliga, Dortmund were continually outshone by their richer more powerful rivals Bayern Munich. For much of the 1990s and early 2000s, they were precisely the club that fans with a passing interest in German soccer would buy the kits of, wanting to stand out against a sea of "sheep" who flocked to Bayern. When Dortmund won back-to-back titles in 2010/11 and 2011/12 under future Liverpool manager Jurgen Klopp, there was a glimmer of hope among Bundesliga nerds—myself included—that Bayern's dominance of Germany was coming to an end.

Bayern replied by winning the next eleven league titles in a row, as well as tragically beating Dortmund in the Champions League final in 2012/13.

So why am I saying that you shouldn't support Borussia Dortmund? Isn't it Bayern whose downfall we should all be rooting for? While it would be nice to have more clubs realistically competing for league titles in Germany, the issue here is not about the dominance on the field of play. Rather, it is for the loss of something special that once existed in the club culture. Outside of Germany, the natural assumption among soccer fans is that as the most successful club in the country, they are also the most popular. However, a survey of the German population found that about 52 percent of the country said they had an affinity for Dortmund, compared to the 41 percent who liked Bayern.[17] At the heart of this interest in Borussia Dortmund has been the long-standing culture of the club.

Dortmund is a small city located in west-central Germany with a population of around 600,000, which makes it almost a third of the size of Munich. Historically, Dortmund was known as an industrial town due to the city's prior dependence on the steel and coal industries. Although the collapse of companies in these sectors has helped the city to transform into a modern tech hub, much of the city's politics still derives from its industrial era. As with many regions across the world whose economies are highly dependent on steel or coal, there was a strong pro-labor focus among the workers and residents within the city. Indeed, this led to Dortmund being named the heart of the Social Democratic Party (SDP) in Germany. To further put the city's fiercely democratic ideals into context, the SDP was the only party to vote against the Enabling Act of 1933 which gave Hitler and the Nazi Party total control over the country.[18]

This democratic free spirit has been embodied by Borussia Dortmund supporters and has been a major part of how the club has won the hearts of so many Germans and soccer fans from around the world. Just a quick glance at a match played at Dortmund's home stadium Signal Iduna Park shows the passion and fervor of the club's fans. This is especially highlighted by "The Yellow Wall" the massive southside terrace of the stadium which is the largest stand in European soccer which allows fans to stand during a match. And as massive as The Yellow Wall is, the influence Dortmund supporters have had on the club's identity and direction has been even bigger.

Indeed, Dortmund supporters are one of the most notoriously outspoken and political fanbases in all of soccer. When the club's supporters feel something inappropriate is happening in football, the fans will take the stands with banners and start social media campaigns to protest and raise awareness of these matters. For example, when it was announced that UEFA was going to expand the Champions League to add more teams and games, fans unfurled large banners reading "You don't care about sport. All you care about is money" in the club's next match in European competition.[19]

While UEFA has been a constant target for Dortmund fans who have previously labeled the governing body as the "mafia," even former players and coaches have been singled out by supporters. Notably, when former player Mario Gotze was rumored to be considering a return to Dortmund after having left the club for a pay raise at Bayern, the banners in the stands read: "Milan or Madrid—the main thing is not Dortmund! Piss off Gotze!"[20] Even Jurgen Klopp who managed the club to back-to-back league titles and a Champions League final has not been immune from criticism. When Klopp signed on to serve as the Head of Global Soccer at Red Bull in 2024, fans said that he had destroyed his entire reputation by signing on to work with a corporation that was involved in multi-club ownership and the over-commercialization of soccer.[21]

In this sense, Dortmund has been attractive to soccer fans around the world because the club, especially through its supporters, had acted as the voice of consciousness within the sport. As FIFA, UEFA, and other organizations have been dead set on squeezing every ounce of profit out of football, it was Dortmund who was raising awareness, almost serving as an impromptu regulator focused on all the ways in which owners, leagues, associations, and other stakeholders were ruining the sport for money.

Then Dortmund joined their ranks.

In May 2024, Dortmund announced that Rheinmetall had signed a three-year sponsorship agreement worth about €25 million in total. The deal made Rheinmetall a "Champion Partner" of the club meaning that their signage would appear around the stadium and on advertising boards but would not feature on player kits.[22] There was immediate uproar from the supporters because Rheinmetall, even though a local company, was one of the largest weapons manufacturers in Europe, specializing in building tanks, armored vehicles, as well as artillery ammunition.[23] To Dortmund fans, this must have been one of the biggest betrayals, especially considering the clubs code of ethics includes language about building a society without violence.[24] It is a bit hard to say that you are committed to improving society and eliminating violence when you are taking tens of millions of euros from a massive weapons manufacturer.

The timing of Dortmund's sponsorship was also called into question. With a war between Ukraine and Russia raging just two borders away from Germany, it has been Rheinmetall who has been one of the major arms suppliers for Ukraine. Although Germany and the EU have been supportive of Ukraine defending itself from the Russian invasion, this war had been highly profitable for Rheinmetall.[25] Dortmund's CEO defended the deal, insisting that the military defense was one of the important "cornerstones of democracy" and that this partnership was critical in a war-torn Europe.[26] Despite the manicured corporate language meant to placate fans, Borussia Dortmund members voted overwhelmingly against the sponsorship deal, demanding the club either terminate the deal or not renew it at the end of the three-year contract.

And so, Dortmund, who long were considered one of the strongholds of a socially responsible soccer culture, sold out to an arms manufacturer for a few million euros a year. What makes the deal even more baffling is the fact that Dortmund likely could have found any number of sponsors who were willing to pay the same amount. Instead, they took a few peanuts to help sportswash the image of a company that has sold weapons to the Saudis for their incursions in Yemen, to Israel for their war against Palestine, and many other powers around the world.

No matter your politics, the reality is that Dortmund is now sponsored by a company that makes money from war, death, and violence. This was once the heart of the political movement in Germany that tried to fight back against Hitler's militarization of Germany. It is an utterly disappointing betrayal and destruction of the culture the club and its supporters had built up over decades. For now, the Dortmund shirt in my closet will stay in its place, I hope the club can remember its roots and allow me to wear it again in good conscious.

St. Pauli—Do

For the soccer hipsters struggling to fill the void of having lost Borussia Dortmund to the ranks of sportswashing corporate bureaucracies who care more about profit margins than overlapping left backs or their supporters, I have good news. Germany also happens to be home to the most punk rock club in all of soccer—FC St. Pauli.

Located in Hamburg, FC St. Pauli is what the Germans call a "Kult" club, a team that gains a massive following based on their alternative fan culture, rather than the product on the field.[27] For most of its history, St. Pauli operated as a standard second division football club. That is, they were focused on putting together a competitive team that could keep them comfortably in the second division and occasionally make a hopeful run at trying to gain promotion to the Bundesliga.

Then in the 1980s, the club started to take on a new identity. A critical part of this identity came from the club's stadium being in an area known as Reeperbahn, or more informally the "mile of sin."[28] Located near the Hamburg dockyards, the mile of sin is the city's entertainment district filled with bars, brothels, and nightclubs, and is also where The Beatles got one of their first major breaks.[29] By the 1980s the Reeperbahn had become the center of the German punk rock scene, with bands from across Europe coming to live and perform in the city.

As the influx of punk culture infused a rebellious spirit into this part of Hamburg, it also started to trickle its way into St. Pauli's fan culture. Gone were the days where a bunch of men in coats stood around on gloomy concrete terraces making small talk waiting for players to start kicking a ball. Instead, St. Pauli matches started to take on the identity of the entertainment district around them and started turning into a massive party before, during, and even after matches. A seminal moment in the club's transformation into a "Kult," happened when a punk singer named Doc Mabuse brought a Jolly Roger flag to a match that he had tied to a broomstick.[30] Mabuse, who in fitting with the punk ethos took his name from the villain of a 1930s German novel,[31] is said to have brought the flag as a depiction of St. Pauli being poor downtrodden pirates taking on richer and more powerful clubs.[32] No matter the intentions, the skull and crossbones were quickly adopted by other fans and became one of the main symbols representing the club's newfound subversive identity.[33]

This antiestablishment approach to life taken by St. Pauli fans was not just directed toward society, but also against the soccer industry and its fan culture. At the time, right-wing nationalistic fervor was spreading across Europe and had found its way into soccer through hooliganism. In response to this, St. Pauli became the first club in Germany to ban right-wing signs and symbols from their stadium.[34] Moreover, even though the punk movement was in decline, the club's rebellious nature continued to attract like-minded individuals from other rebellious and marginalized subcultures.

As the forerunner of a fan driven philosophy in German soccer, St. Pauli was the first club to develop a set of guiding principles on how the club would operate and treat its fans. Specifically, in 2009, they published a list of fifteen principles focused on inclusion, respect toward others—including opposing fans and teams, as well as the pledge to require all sponsors and commercial partners to align with the club's social and political stances. Other clubs in Germany quickly followed suit, but as can be evidenced with Borussia Dortmund, many of these principles are often ignored if a sponsor writes a big enough check.

On the other hand, St. Pauli has fiercely guarded its commitments to its fans. Indeed, this has made it hard for the club from a business perspective. In trying to keep pace with its competitors, St. Pauli tried several times to secure a naming rights deal which would bring millions in revenue to help improve the team and stadium. In every instance, these proposals were voted down by the supporters who remain fiercely against corporate partnerships. However, this philosophy has allowed St. Pauli's executives to consider alternative models of how to run their business. Rather than just bringing in the sponsors who provide the most cash, St. Pauli launched a funding campaign that allowed members to help purchase ownership of their stadium. In total, this "football cooperative" raised almost €30 million, allowing St. Pauli to gain majority ownership of their home ground.[35]

One major consequence of St. Pauli's radical—almost anticapitalist—model of running a football club is that the lack of revenue has translated to mediocrity on the field. To quote illustrious German football writer Uli Hesse, who has covered the sport in more depth and nuance than perhaps any other journalist, St. Pauli is the football club that "stands for all the right things ... except for winning."[36] However, even this has changed in recent years. In

2022, St. Pauli fired head coach Timo Schultz and made the radical decision to replace him with his 29-year-old assistant Fabian Hurzeler. The Texas-born Hurzeler proved to be a breath of fresh air for the club, who ended up winning the 2. Bundesliga title in his first season in charge.

Having been promoted to play in the Bundesliga for the 2024/25 season, the expectation was that St. Pauli would repeat history and immediately be relegated back down to the division as they had done in their two previous top-flight campaigns. Any hopes fell even further when Hurzeler was poached by Premier League club Brighton and Hove Albion to be their manager. However, against all odds, the club that does things the right way managed to avoid relegation and guaranteed their first consecutive seasons in the Bundesliga in almost thirty years.

Even with the additional revenue and attention that comes with being in the Bundesliga, St. Pauli has stayed true to their identity. Midway through the 2024/25 season, the club announced it would be shutting down its X (formerly Twitter) social media account, as it believed the platform had become a "hate machine" that was drumming up right-wing sentiments that could influence the German elections.[37] At the end of the same season, St. Pauli again made headlines, this time for the announcement that they would be installing rainbow colored solar panels on their stadium's roof. This move not only helped the club to become more environmentally sustainable, but also chose colors that purposefully showed their support for LGBTQ+ rights.[38]

Many people would call St. Pauli a "woke" club, that is just a bunch of radicals pretending they can change the world. As true as this may be, these rebels have done what so many supporters wish they could do—have their club take a clear-cut stance on social issues while also eschewing the hyper-commercialization of soccer. Even if St. Pauli's politics do not align with your own, how can you not help to cheer for this band of pirates? Though they will continue to lose against super clubs like Bayern Munich and Borussia Dortmund, at least they will do so the right way.

And they will look cool doing it.

Forest Green Rangers—Do

The way in which the soccer industry operates is not good for the earth. Although you will see every major tournament, league, and team all have environmental sustainability initiatives, the reality is that most of these projects only scratch at the surface of the impact that the world's game has on the planet. It is common now to see professional sport teams around the world talk about their recycling programs, or how they are helping raise awareness of the environment and thus they are champions of sustainability. Many of my colleagues disagree with me on this point, and there is a bit of research examining the impact of these programs, but it just like slapping some paint on a crumbling stadium—it may look good, but it doesn't get to the core of the problem.

So, what is the major problem? Whether it be the International Olympic Committee, FIFA, or any other worldwide governing body of a major sport, all of them have published detailed scientific reports about their carbon footprint, generation of waste, and other environmental impacts. In all these studies, it is consistently found that the largest contributor to the carbon footprint of soccer teams and competitions is from travel, especially fan travel. In general, having a team travel a few hours by bus or plane is typically not going to have a major impact on the environment. But when thousands—sometimes even tens of thousands—of fans decide that they are going to follow the team to support them, the amount of pollution that gets generated really starts to add up. Moreover, the pollution produced from vehicles burning fossil fuels is not just having an impact on the warming climate, it also creates compounds which can be dangerous to short and long-term health.

And the list of culprits pretty much spans the entire soccer industry.

Naturally, FIFA is one of the biggest targets, as its main competitions require a significant amount of travel by teams and fans. The 2030 World Cup stands out as potentially being one of the worst polluting sporting events in history, as in addition to having fans fly to the main host nations of Spain, Morocco, and Portugal, three additional matches will be played in South America to mark the 100th anniversary of the tournament.[39] This means, there is the possibility that a team and tens of thousands of fans could fly from somewhere like Canada, down to South America for one match, then have to fly to the main tournament sites in Europe and Africa, and then fly back home. That's a trip that is great to build up airline miles and terrible for the planet. The crazy thing is that all of this comes amidst FIFA's announcement that they will decrease their emissions by 50 percent by 2030 and have zero emissions by 2034.[40] If it sounds like utter nonsense, just remember that FIFA was caught making false claims about the 2022 World Cup in Qatar being carbon neutral.[41] Moreover, as FIFA continues to build its influence by expanding tournaments, such as the new thirty-two team Club World Cup which had tens of thousands of fans flying in from every corner of the globe, the likelihood is that their carbon footprint is actually growing.

However, it is not fair to single out FIFA as a problem. The same issue exists amongst the various member federations and the tournaments they host, such as UEFA's hosting of the Euros, Women's Euro, Champions League, etc., as well as leagues and clubs. The number of men's and women's teams that are hopping on planes to travel around the world and play in meaningless friendlies to earn some extra cash for the club is a major problem. Before, it was just a few major clubs that would visit Asia or North America to play a few matches and sign some autographs. Now everyone is doing it. The 2025 Premier League Summer Series, hosted in America, does feature Manchester United, but also includes West Ham, Everton, and Bournemouth. Is it worth the environmental cost to have a bunch of mid-table clubs give their backup midfielders some playing time in America? Unfortunately, the commercial reasons seem to outweigh any thoughts for the environment and that is why we have even seen lower division clubs like Wrexham travel the world to boost revenues.

With soccer seemingly headed toward playing more matches and requiring more travel in order to continue the growth of the business side of the sport, is anyone even doing anything about this problem? It is evident that FIFA can't be trusted to even tell the truth about their own environmental impact and so having them serve a regulatory role over environmental matters is foolhardy at best. And while some leagues and clubs have taken important steps to reduce their carbon footprint—such as German soccer clubs providing a free train ticket with the purchase of a match ticket—most of the major soccer powers have taken a wait-and-see approach.

But not Forest Green Rovers.

Forest Green Rovers are a fifth-division club that play in southwest England. For most of their history, Rovers have had the typical resume of a lower division soccer club in the UK—bounced around the lower leagues, a few decent FA Trophy runs, no major trophies, and a few rivalries that only locals know about. All of this changed in 2010, 120 years after the club was founded, when hippie turned green energy entrepreneur Dale Vince purchased a majority stake in the club. A staunch environmentalist, Vince founded Ecotricity, a company that specializes in renewable energy such as wind and solar power. Following the success of Ecotricity, Vince continued to expand his portfolio of environmentally friendly business ventures, including building an ecologically friendly airline,[42] Britain's first electric supercar,[43] and a catering company to serve vegan meals in schools.[44] It begs one to ask, what place does a lower division soccer club have in all of this?

As with all his assets, Vince saw Forest Green Rovers as a chance to make a statement about how a soccer club could be run successfully while also prioritizing the environment. In his first season as chairman of the club, Vince entirely banned red meat at the club,[45] including for player meals and in the concession stands during matches. The logic behind this "burger ban"—which included both beef and pork—is that in addition to the health consequences from eating too much meat, the farming and production of beef has the biggest carbon footprint of almost any food.[46] Instead, Vince had the club replace the usual pies and sausages with free-range chicken and sustainably raised fish. This was followed up by developing the first organic soccer pitch,[47] the installation of solar panels to power the stadium,[48] and using electric robots to mow the pitch.[49]

In 2015, Vince announced that the club would become entirely vegan, meaning they would no longer be selling any animal products. This meant that in addition to meat being removed from the menu, the cow's milk that is typically poured into tea would be replaced by soy or other milk substitutes.[50] It was already a brave move to ban red meat in the stadium, especially as foods like burgers and steak pies are almost considered to be part of the match-day tradition for many supporters. However, to go entirely vegan was certain to invite a different level of criticism. If this move had happened today, I imagine soccer fans from around the world would ridicule the move with the typical comments of "Game's gone" or "Utter woke nonsense."

With help from Vince's Ecotricity, Forest Green Rovers moved to only using renewable energy, leading them to be certified by the United Nations in 2018 as the first carbon neutral football club.[51] Under Vince's leadership, Rovers had become the pillar and model of environmental sustainability in football, leading to a curious mix of recognition from both the UK Vegan Society and FIFA.[52] They even attracted attention from Arsenal fullback Hector Bellerin, known for his outspoken stance on social and environmental issues, who agreed to become the second biggest shareholder in the club.[53]

While Forest Green Rovers were becoming rockstars of the sustainability world, winning awards and accolades from across the world, Vince was also in the process of improving the on-field product. It would be considered a major victory for many owners to create a model that reinvents how an entire industry thinks about their operations and impact within less than a decade. However, for Vince, it seems it was also important to demonstrate that becoming environmentally friendly did not come at the expense of how the team played.

At around the same time that Rovers announced that they were becoming a vegan club, Vince gave an interview noting that the club was using data-driven advanced statistics to analyze and recruit players.[54] Backed by a Moneyball-based approach, Rovers finished in second place in the 2015/16 National League season, and just missed out on promotion to the EFL in the playoff final. The following year, Rovers finished third, but this time won the promotion playoff securing entrance into the EFL. Despite a rocky first season in League Two, the club made it to the promotion playoffs in two of its first four seasons. In 2021/22, Rovers—the team from the smallest town to ever have an EFL club—won League Two earning them automatic promotion into the third division.

However, this is where Forest Green Rovers' Cinderella run came to an end. Rovers only lasted one season in League One, as they were clearly outmatched by stronger opposition. To make matters worse, Rovers finished last again in the following season (2023/24), relegating them out of the EFL. Although the club was able to bounce back and secure third place on their return to the National League, their hopes of immediate promotion back into the upper tiers of English football were dashed when they lost in penalties in the promotion playoff semifinal.

Under Dale Vince, Forest Green Rovers have become trailblazers in proving that running a professional soccer club doesn't have to come at the expense of the environment. Critics argue that Rovers can operate as a sustainable and vegan club precisely because they are at the fringes of the EFL. That while small clubs can do this, it would be impossible to make Old Trafford entirely vegan and could result in a riot. However, what Vince has done is to make Forest Green Rovers the laboratory to develop the best practices for making soccer a sustainable sport. No one would dare stop treating the pitch at Anfield with fertilizers and chemicals for fear that it could impact how the team plays. At Rovers, Vince has his groundkeepers start slopping manure on the pitch to see if they could truly make an organic pitch. While there were issues with the stench of the manure at first, the groundskeepers were able to show that pitches could be grown and maintained during the season without chemicals.

Forest Green Rovers lack a lot of the amenities that fans look for when choosing to support a soccer club—they haven't won a lot of trophies, they aren't the most exciting team to watch, and they don't have marketing campaigns and kit launches led by major fashion designers. But that is not the point of their existence. Forest Green Rovers' presence in professional soccer is a benefit to everyone in the sport. Their continuous challenge against the long-standing models of how soccer clubs have been traditionally operated provides a glimpse into the future of the sport. Not just a future of what is possible, but of what may be needed if soccer is to survive as society and our planet continue to change.

Maybe you will not pick Forest Green Rovers as the club you support, but all of us should be cheering for them not to be relegated. They are needed in the sport now more than ever.

What to Look for in a Club

As evidenced in this chapter, there are many reasons why someone might be interested in supporting a club or absolutely refuse to do so. For some, it is simple as figuring out which team is good and then starting to watch their games. For others, it can be a much more complex moral quandary, a decision that reflects our own politics and belief systems. The problem in all of this, as evidenced in the example of Borussia Dortmund, is that in the current landscape of professional soccer, a club's identity and values can be thrown out in an instant just to make a little extra money for a few years. So even if you felt you had made the correct decision in picking a club, all it takes is a chairman deciding to partner with a new sponsor or signing a certain player to bring on feelings of discomfort.

As an Arsenal supporter, I have experienced this dynamic a few times in my decades as a supporter, most recently when the club renewed its sponsorship deal with Rwanda's tourism board. The renewal went forward despite a vocal group of Arsenal supporters demanding an end to the partnership based on allegations that the Rwandan government was funding terrorist groups to conduct military operations in neighboring Democratic Republic of Congo.[55] Although a peace deal was eventually brokered between the two countries, did it really make sense to put the name of a country cited by human rights groups for the execution of civilians[56] on the sleeve of soccer team's uniform? Was it worth the few million dollars? Unfortunately, this is not something that is exclusive to a small handful of clubs but is a growing symptom of how professional sport teams are willing to do business with a host of unsavory characters, corporations, and countries.

And it is for these reasons that we should consider supporting the clubs included in this chapter as examples of what soccer clubs can strive to be.

In an industry that is so dominated by money and winning trophies, these teams have shunned the ambition-driven status quo of profits and goals to seek something more meaningful from their involvement in the sport. For AFC Wimbledon, it was trying to regain something that was taken away by the rich and greedy. For St. Pauli, it was to capture the independent spirit of the community it was based in. And for Forest Green Rovers, it was to try and save the environment. What really stands out amongst these clubs is that they all have forged their own unique path rather than copying from other clubs that have displayed their own independent spirit.

Another important thing about the Wimbledon's and St. Pauli's of the world is that they don't have the usual red flags that standout among soccer clubs. They are not part of a multi-club ownership consortium that seems more interested in collecting clubs as a display of power. They are not owned by an investment group or wealth fund of a super-rich nation-state who treats soccer as a vanity project. And they don't even participate in some of the more "minor" transgressions such as taking large sums of money from gambling companies that have quietly infiltrated all corners of the sport.[57] Indeed, where Wimbledon could have significant boosted their revenue by putting a questionable gambling sponsor on the front of their shirt, they instead partnered with Sports Interactive to raise awareness for War Child—a nonprofit focused on helping children in war-torn countries across the globe.[58]

Throughout this chapter, I have highlighted several reasons why fans should or should not support a soccer club. At the same time, the main point of this discussion isn't to get people to break the bonds and emotional ties they have developed over the years and switch allegiances. Instead, the fundamental idea is that as fans we should become familiar with what our clubs are capable of. That is, we should not just accept the way the sport is operated but instead demand more from our clubs and the executives that run them.

Many fans would agree that they think clubs should stop worrying about the carbon footprint of their chicken burger and instead focus on avoiding relegation. They want to focus on soccer as entertainment, and not a place where social and political issues are arbitrated. However, even for those who don't care if their club's sponsor makes laser-guided missiles because they need to sign a new left back, it should be recognized that clubs like St. Pauli and Forest Green Rovers are not just battling for their own ideologies and politics. Instead, they are engaged in a Don Quixote like struggle against faceless corporations, oil-rich nation-states, and bureaucratic governing bodies whose aim is to squeeze every ounce of profit from soccer fans.

What they are doing may seem futile, but it is not nonsense. They are battling to protect the future of soccer, and whether it be attending a match, buying a T-shirt, or even becoming a member, these clubs truly deserve whatever support we can provide them.

9

The World's Game Who Is Taking Over Soccer?

"The Line" is a proposed megalithic smart city that the Saudi Arabian government is planning to build over the next three decades. Closer to something you would expect in Star Wars, The Line is perhaps the most ambitious and stupid construction project in human history; if completed it would be a single building stretching 170 kilometers with a height around 500 meters (1,600 feet). To put that in perspective, the entire structure would be the thirteenth tallest building in America and would stretch further than the distance between New York and Philadelphia. Excavation has already started on the $500 billion city, with a massive concrete factory and over 100,000 workers helping to start building the foundations of the city.[1]

So, what does any of this have to do with soccer? At the very center of the digital rendering of The Line is a weird looking box that looks like it is formed out of ice and stone. This is Neom Stadium, one of eleven newly proposed stadiums that were included as part of Saudi Arabia's official bid for the 2034 World Cup. The idea that anyone would be able to keep a straightface while proposing a stadium built 350 meters off the ground as part of the World Cup seems laughable. It is already hard enough getting 60,000 people in and out of a stadium built at ground level. Doing it a thousand feet in the sky at the summit of an unbuilt technological pyramid during the most important sporting event in the world is utter madness.

So naturally, not only did the Saudi's propose this, but the bid received rave reviews from FIFA and earned the highest technical score of any World Cup in history.[2] The only criticism that FIFA dared to offer was that because of the highly ambitious nature of the proposed Saudi stadium projects, there was a "medium" level of risk that the venues would not be completed in time for the games. However, FIFA was quick to note that the resources and leadership being provided by Saudi Arabia would "mitigate" any risks. And thus, with all other countries forbidden or declining to host the event, the 2034 World Cup was officially awarded to the Kingdom of Saudi Arabia on December 11, 2024.

In less than a decade, Saudi Arabia has managed to become one of the biggest powers in global soccer. Other countries have dedicated significant time and resources to try and host the World Cup, and most have fallen well short of what the Saudis have accomplished. So, how has Saudi Arabia surpassed other countries such as China, the UAE, and even much of Europe to be one of the most desired hosts for the World Cup? While the answer is obviously money, there are other key factors that need to be considered in Saudi Arabia's ascendancy in the soccer world—and their impact on the future of the game.

The Outcry

Upon being declared as the hosts of the 2034 World Cup, there was immediate backlash from the media over FIFA choosing a country that is accused of numerous human rights violations. Both Human Rights Watch[3] and Amnesty International[4] have produced multiple reports detailing the conditions faced by residents and workers in Saudi Arabia. The main charges against Saudi Arabia have been the repression of free speech, an unfair trial system which can potentially even lead to the death penalty, as well as a lack of rights for workers, women, and other minority groups.[5]

Sadly, this is not something that is out of the ordinary. Similar charges have been brought up against previous World Cup hosts such as Russia, Qatar, and South Africa. In the buildup to their hosting of the 2022 tournament, Qatar was slammed for human rights issues within the country, especially regarding the treatment of migrant workers who were critical in building the stadiums and infrastructure for the World Cup. Although tournament organizers reported thirty-seven worker deaths in projects related to the tournament, British newspaper *The Guardian* found that more than 600 migrant workers had died within Qatar since they were awarded the rights to host the World Cup.[6] Much of the criticism of FIFA's selection of Saudi Arabia stems from the concern of a repeat of these issues, especially as Qatar and Saudi Arabia share similar searing climates that create harsh working conditions. Indeed, before the World Cup rights were awarded to Saudi Arabia, television reports indicated that 21,000 laborers had already died in the country in construction projects, though these claims have been refuted by the government[7].

To be fair, it is not just a select group of authoritarian countries who have hosted the World Cup that have been noted for human rights issues. Even America, which will co-host the 2026 World Cup, has numerous charges being leveled against it, including discrimination against minority groups, issues in the criminal rights system, as well as the unlawful killing of citizens.[8] So why is the Saudi hosting of the World Cup so contentious and scrutinized when compared to others? There are numerous reasons, but much of it can be traced to the killing of *Washington Post* reporter Jamal Khashoggi, who was murdered and dismembered in the Saudi consulate in Istanbul.[9] Although Saudi courts tried and convicted the individuals responsible for the killing, US intelligence contended that the killing had been ordered by Crown Prince Mohammed bin Salman.[10] While the international response was mostly limited to sanctions imposed by the US,[11] the extensive media cover of the event dealt a severe blow to the Saudi's international reputation.

There are many other major criticisms for the Saudi government, including the lack of rights for women within the country and severe prison sentences for posting anti-government messages on social media. However, Khashoggi's murder was a watershed moment for Saudi Arabia, an irrevocable stain that played a central role in how the rest of the world, especially those living in the

West, has come to brand Saudi Arabia and its people. As such, the Kingdom was at a point of no return. Like Caesar crossing the Rubicon, or John Wick after the Russian mobsters killed his puppy, there was no turning back, no place for amends. For Saudi Arabia, the only path was forward, to bury their transgression through the passage of time and the erosion of collective memory.

The Economic Rebrand

In 2018, Saudi Arabia was at an economic crossroads. Despite amassing significant wealth through the production of oil, there was concern over dwindling oil reserves and potential future economic decline.[12] The country had just experienced two years of significant decline in Gross Domestic Product (GDP) due to falling oil prices, which had resulted in skyrocketing national debt. To combat this, the government launched a new national plan entitled "Saudi Vision 2030" that was aimed at building and diversifying the country's economy, while also transforming the sociocultural landscape of Saudi Arabia. In this, the goal was not just to stabilize the economy, but to position Saudi Arabia as an influential player in the future global order.

However, the backlash from the killing of Khashoggi, which happened two years after the announcement of Saudi Vision 2030, presented a major roadblock for Saudi Arabia's plans. In the immediate aftermath of the murder, there were reports of a mass exodus of foreign investment across the entire region.[13] For instance, English business mogul Richard Branson had been hired by the Saudi government to direct the development of several new resorts along the Red Sea to draw more foreign tourists to the country. After Khashoggi's murder, Branson quickly withdrew from this position and suspended his negotiations to help build Saudi into a space tourism hub.[14] Although companies from around the world announced that they were ending business ties with Saudi Arabia, behind the scenes, foreign investment continued to pour into the country, doubling to $3.5 billion in 2018,[15] and growing another 30 percent in 2019.[16] If anything, despite the international condemnation of the killing of

Jamal Khashoggi, it was business as usual within the Kingdom. Just as Michael Corleone said in *The Godfather*: "It's not personal, it's strictly business."

And yet, the biggest obstacle facing the Saudi's was in revitalizing their reputation on the global stage. While it was clear that companies were still willing to do business with Saudi Arabia, most were either being illusive or even outright secretive of any official ties with the country. Saudi Arabia was simultaneously one of the most alluring places to do business and a pariah that had been excommunicated from mainstream society. As such, with their economic vision well on track, the Saudi government shifted focus on rehabilitating its global image.

The architect behind this project was Mohammed bin Salman, Crown Prince of Saudi Arabia, who is often referred to by his initials MBS. MBS, the seventh son of Salman bin Abdulaziz Al Saud, King of Saudi Arabia, has rapidly ascended to power, first becoming heir apparent to the throne when he was named Crown Prince in 2017, and then becoming de facto ruler of the country as he took over Prime Minister duties from his aging father in 2022. Although all these positions carry tremendous power, it is perhaps his role as chairman of the Saudi Public Investment Fund that has provided him with the greatest ability to expand Saudi Arabia's sphere of influence.

The Public Investment Fund, or PIF for short, is the nation's sovereign wealth fund that was founded in 1971 by King Faisal bin Abdulaziz Al Saud to provide a new source of funding for projects that were deemed of great national importance.[17] For the next several decades, the PIF was primarily used to invest in businesses operated by Saudi nationals that had strong ties with the royal family.[18] In this, PIF provided a vehicle through which to reinvest the revenue the state generated from oil production into conglomerates and private businesses to help grow the Saudi economy.

The strategic focus of PIF began to shift in the 2010s, as neighboring Gulf countries began to use their own sovereign wealth funds to invest in foreign corporations. Notably, the investments were not carried out just to diversify the financial portfolios of these countries but also were conducted to increase their sphere of influence. For example, the United Arab Emirates (UAE) and Qatar both made significant investments in western financial institutions, with UAE purchasing a $7 billion stake in CitiGroup[19] and Qatar acquiring a

6 percent share of Credit Suisse.[20] Although these transactions were described as a way to provide top-notch banking services to wealthy clients in the Middle East,[21] they also further entrenched the role of Gulf states in the global financial system. Indeed, following the Qatar Investment Authority's major stake in Credit Suisse, PIF followed suit buying a 9.9 percent stake in the Swiss bank.[22]

Under the guidance of MBS, PIF has undertaken a wide-range of investments with various strategic goals. I have met numerous people, who for various reasons have said that they would never do business with Saudi Arabia or companies affiliated with the country. This is easier said than done, as PIF has invested in companies that are a common part of our everyday lives. If you were to truly boycott Saudi-owned companies, you would no longer be able to fly with many airlines as PIF has a stake in Boeing who make a large percentage of the commercial aircraft around the world. Oh, that Uber you took to get to the airport? PIF invested $2.7 billion in the company. Want to go buy tickets to watch Taylor Swift? No, the Saudis do not have an investment in the pop superstar herself, but they did previously own 5.7 percent of Live Nation which promotes and sells tickets to concerts.[23] Whether it is using Facebook, watching the newest Star Wars television series, or even playing video games, you are likely consuming products that are partially owned by the Saudi Public Investment Fund.

Even though all these purchases are a matter of public record, most consumers are not aware of the associations these companies have with Saudi Arabia. That is, while the financial media is constantly reporting on the new investments being made by PIF, these matters are typically not of concern to most people. As such, while the general public is blissfully unaware of it, most of us are consuming a variety of goods and services that are partly owned by the Saudis. Although the Saudi sovereign wealth fund isn't the largest in the world—that distinction goes to Norway's Government Pension Fund Global[24]—it is unique in several ways. Most prominently, where most other sovereign wealth funds are consistently funded by income from oil production, the Saudi government typically doesn't provide cash subsidies to PIF. Instead, the expectation for PIF, much like a hedge fund on Wall Street, is that it will need to survive on its own through making smart calculated investments.[25]

As such, PIF's portfolio now approaches one trillion dollars in assets, and thus is a critical part of the Saudi Vision 2030. Not only does the fund provide additional financial resources that align with the Saudi government's strategic vision, but it also allows PIF to wield significant influence over many vital business sectors. And it is here where the Saudi's have used the fund to help repair their global image and become culturally relevant. Notably, Crown Prince Mohammed bin Salman, who is in his late 30s, has been critical in guiding PIF toward investment in the cultural Zeitgeist of the new millennium. Where his elder predecessors emphasized building power through accumulating capital, MBS has redirected the fund's focus toward acquisitions that will help Saudi Arabia connect with younger generations.

This was accomplished through the investment in cultural "products" that were believed to be a core component of youth culture. One of the main targets for PIF was the video game and esports industry, as they believed that using this media would provide a convenient way to connect with a wide-range of individuals across the world. Along these lines, PIF purchased shares of Electronic Arts, makers of EA FC (formerly FIFA), the world's bestselling sport video game, and other video game companies including Take-Two Interactive, Activision Blizzard, Capcom, and Nintendo. Additionally, PIF also bought companies that specialized in making games for phones and other mobile devices, as well as the Electronic Sports League Gaming, one of the top companies for producing and hosting esports events. All these purchases were re-organized under the umbrella of a new company called Savvy Games that would be headquartered in Saudi Arabia. These investments not only provided Saudi with a strong foothold in the video game industry but also allowed it to produce and create the Esports World Cup in 2024, billing it as the top competitive video game competition in the world.

In addition to video games, MBS has also led Saudi Arabia into developing other cultural products aimed at youth. As the Crown Prince himself is noted as a fan of Japanese animation (anime) such as One Piece, he has collaborated with Japanese studios to start producing new anime within Saudi Arabia. Additionally, in Spring 2024, Saudi Arabia announced the construction of the official Dragon Ball Theme Park,[26] billing it as the only attraction in the world dedicated to Dragon Ball—one of the most famous manga and anime series of all time. The aim in all of this is clear, appealing to younger generations using popular cultural products with the hope of building a stronger image of Saudi Arabia.

Overall, spending a few billion dollars on these projects may seem inconsequential compared to the trillion-dollar value of PIF. However, considering the historically low public opinion of Saudi Arabia after the Khashoggi murder,[27] the government likely saw these investments not just to boost their image in the short-term, but also to influence the attitudes of younger audiences around the world. While these investments may not cause a major shift in perceptions of Saudi Arabia today, they could result in future generations having greater affinity with the Saudi's. And all of this is just through video games and cartoons.

Sportwashing?

Realizing the influence that could be wielded through cultural products, Saudi Arabia quickly understood there was an even better vehicle through which to reach people around the world: sport. Although Saudi Arabia has had a vibrant sporting culture, with a professional soccer league that has just celebrated its fiftieth anniversary, outside of Asia little was known about this history. Rather than begin by promoting its own pro league, which would have been difficult considering the intense competition for viewers that already exists in European soccer, the Saudi's started their foray into global sport with a markedly different approach—professional wrestling.

Even before the announcement of the 2030 Vision Plan or MBS's ascent to power, professional wrestling had already established a strong relationship with the country. Due to the transient nature of the sport, professional wrestlers have been coming to Saudi Arabia since the 1980s to perform live shows.[28] In 2014, World Wrestling Entertainment (WWE)—the most popular professional wrestling promotion in the world—started hosting untelevised house shows in the country.[29] As demand for these events continued to skyrocket, WWE launched a weekly Arabic language recap of previously televised events that was broadcast across the Middle East.[30] Up to this point, the growth of professional wrestling in Saudi Arabia was driven more by the WWE's plans for expanding its brand throughout the region. However, this dynamic changed in 2018, when the WWE signed an official agreement with the Saudi Ministry of Sport to host an event—named the "Greatest Royal Rumble"—that would be televised worldwide.[31]

Perhaps the most critical part of this contract was that the WWE also agreed to enter a ten-year partnership directly in support of the Saudi 2030 Vision plan. This was a critical step for the Saudis, as it was one of their first official partnerships with a prominent Western sport organization. This meant that the Saudi's would be able to attach their name to a popular sport brand and have the executives and athletes from the WWE to help serve as ambassadors for the country. Indeed, in the buildup to the Greatest Royal Rumble, questions were directed at WWE in terms of human rights issues within the country, especially as women wrestlers were not allowed to participate in the event.[32] Responding to this, Triple H, the executive in charge of talent and himself a former wrestler, noted that it was not the place of WWE to question the culture of another country but that they were negotiating future events with women wrestlers in the country.[33]

For the Saudi's this was exactly the type of partnership that they had been seeking. Now instead of government officials responding to criticisms of the treatment of women and other minorities, it was renowned Western sport figures who were talking about these points. To further highlight the progress that was being made, MBS helped to institute new laws within the country before the event that would allow Saudi women to attend the event if they were accompanied by a male guardian.[34] In this manner, the partnership with WWE allowed the Saudi's to take control of the narrative and even present themselves as becoming more progressive as they instituted reforms that were demanded by critics.

This use of sport by Saudi Arabia to cloak various social and political issues is commonly referred to by the term sportswashing. Generally, sportswashing is considered a negative term, where countries or corporations will use sport to either build goodwill amongst the public, or deflect attention away from certain transgressions. In this sense, while sportswashing is generally discussed within the media in a negative light, the Saudi's have almost shown indifference when being accused of conducting sportswashing.

In an interview with Fox News, MBS was questioned about his country's use of sportswashing to cover up various issues.[35] In response to this, MBS answered that he doesn't care about the accusations of sportswashing, and in fact almost embraced the term. He noted that sport already accounted for 1 percent of the Saudi GDP, and that his goal was to continue using sport to grow the national economy and their international reputation.[36] His message in his first interview conducted fully in English was clear to the entire world: our sportswashing policy is clearly working so why would we stop now? Indeed, rather than dial back their focus on sport investments, PIF has continued to move forward in purchasing ownership stakes in various sport enterprises.

Despite the massive worldwide popularity of professional wrestling, it mainly reaches niche markets primarily composed of young males. Thus, on the back of the successful partnership with WWE, PIF started to move forward with acquisitions that would help to expand the Saudi sphere of influence into other demographic segments. One such venture was LIV Golf,[37] a new global professional golf tour that was designed to directly compete against the Professional Golfers' Association of America (PGA) Tour, the biggest golf competition on the planet. The launch of the LIV Golf League in 2022 caused a massive stir within the golf world, as many top-level golfers quit the PGA tour in favor of the guaranteed money that was offered by LIV just to participate in their events.[38] Because PGA rules forbid players from playing for rival professional golf competitions, several players officially resigned their membership with the PGA to play in the more lucrative LIV competitions that were being funded by the Public Investment Fund.[39]

The choice of golf as a sport to further the Saudi profile amongst global audiences is a curious one. As a niche sport with a wealthy demographic, there is often a level of power and prestige that is attached to the sport, with many world leaders and captains of industry playing golf in their free time.[40] It is reported that LIV had approached Tiger Woods, the most iconic and commercially successful golfer in history with a $500 million offer to join their competition, but that he ultimately declined.[41] Despite the massive payouts, LIV has been unable to draw the biggest stars of golf and has been relegated to being a second-tier competition, essentially the Carabao Cup of professional golf.

To this point, Saudi investments in sport have been driven by the dual goals of economic expansion and improving its image. In this, the approach of financing niche sport competitions has its merits, as it allows for a greater level of control over these organizations. At the same time, because of the relatively limited audiences for professional wrestling and golf, it does restrict the level of influence the Saudi's can exercise through sport. However, considered from another perspective, starting with niche sports can also be considered as an important stepping stone in moving into more mainstream sports. That is, by working with relatively smaller sport organizations, it afforded PIF and the Saudi government the opportunity to test what type of financial and social returns they receive without the much larger investment needed to get involved with a major sport competition. If it ends up being a mess, they can wash their hands of it and just shrug it off as a minor loss, a rounding error in the greater scheme of PIF's total assets. On the other hand, if things were to go well, then PIF can simply continue to scale up its sport investments, targeting leagues and competitions with larger audiences, influence, and impact on a global scale.

Thus, it is only natural that soccer became one of the main targets for Saudi investment. As the sport with the largest audience, most professional leagues, the greatest number of participants, and the widest reach around the world, soccer is the perfect cultural vehicle to further the Saudi agenda. And with the World Cup as the pinnacle of the game, it was only a matter of time before the Kingdom of Saudi Arabia set its focus on the crown jewel of the sport.

The World

First, through the purchase of Newcastle, and then through investment in their domestic soccer league, Saudi Arabia had successfully used soccer as a tool to build their soft power—the ability to persuade and influence the perceptions of others through policy and cultural products.[42] In this, soccer represented probably the most powerful cultural good that the Saudi's could effectively control with their financial might, without seeming to be overly coercive. Indeed, because the soccer industry is dominated by oligarchs, hedge funds, business magnates, and other sovereign wealth funds, any initial concern over PIF's investment in the sport was always likely to fade away as the next power struggle to take over a club unfolded.

In this, Manchester United presented the Saudi's with another gift on Christmas Eve of 2023, when the Glazer family announced they had sold a 25 percent stake of the club to billionaire Sir Jim Ratcliffe that included full sporting control.[43] In an instant, PIF, Saudi Arabia, and MBS were all forgotten as the media descended on the much-maligned club, pundits providing in-depth commentary on whether Sir Jim would be able to bring United back to their glory days. And while they still couldn't fully escape the taint that came from the murder of Jamal Khashoggi, soccer provided to be an effective tool in persuading other nations that it was acceptable to do business with Saudi Arabia again.

But normalizing relations and doing business with other countries was not the entirety of the Crown Prince's ambitions for his Kingdom. In a yearly event in Riyadh that hosts some of the most important figures in business, technology, and politics, often called Davos in the Desert,[44] MBS has talked about how he envisions that the Middle East could become the "new Europe."[45] That is, with Saudi Arabia as the nexus, his hope is to turn the entire region into a thriving economic power that will have a more central role in global commerce and politics. Soccer alone cannot accomplish the grand endeavor of transforming an entire region's economy. However, the sport can be used as a showcase to promote a country's national project, as has been done with Russia and Qatar hosting the World Cup in recent years. As soccer is still mostly dominated by Europe, especially off the pitch where European administrators and businesspeople control much of the world's game, it should be of little surprise that Saudi Arabia coveted a place within this hierarchy.

One problem with the purchase of Premier League club Newcastle United was that at the end of the day, they played most of their matches thousands of miles away from Saudi Arabia. Even with control of a famous European club, PIF was limited in the ways in which it could further connect this asset with the ambitions of the Saudi royal family. Yes, the club could visit the Kingdom on preseason tours and even wear a green third kit—the color of the Saudi flag—but these were all minor actions that ultimately had minimal impact on how the rest of the world perceived the country. That is, whether you are a Premier League fan living in Tanzania or Oakland, California, your primary concern is typically not the close ties between Newcastle's ownership and the Saudi government, but how your defense is going to stop Newcastle striker Alexander Isak from scoring goals. In essence, the Saudi regime—both its positives and negatives—is not something that is keeping most soccer fans up late at night. I know when I'm up at 2 a.m., my brain is thinking about whether Arsenal will ever buy a world-class striker, not the transgressions of foreign powers.

All of this presented a critical question for the Saudi's; how does one truly build power through soccer? Saudi Arabia is not the first and will not be the last nation that has found itself trying to use its extreme wealth to build up its reputation through the world's game. Most recently, Qatar and China have both attempted to infuse themselves within the sport to varying degrees of success. While the case of Qatar can be seen as a great success in the use of their political and economic resources to be the first Middle Eastern country to host the World Cup, there are questions about the long-term effects of the 2022 tournament. It is reported that Qatar spent approximately $220 billion to host the tournament,[46] which is almost equivalent to the country's yearly GDP which was $221 billion in 2024.[47] Qatar is rich, but to essentially spend the country's entire economic productivity for a whole year to host a three-week sport tournament is just too excessive. Despite these costs, Qatar seems prepared to do it all over again as they are currently bidding to host the 2036 Summer Olympic Games.[48]

China, on the other hand, pioneered an approach of mass investment in both domestic and international soccer that was more analogous to what the Saudi's would eventually execute. Notably, the Chinese government encouraged large corporations and billionaires to pour their wealth into the purchase of soccer clubs across Europe, sponsoring major competitions such as the World Cup and Champions League, as well as building the domestic game. This flow of capital, which began in 2014, moved China to the forefront of the soccer industry, spreading fear across the industry that China would take all the best players for their own league and their corporations were to buy and ruin your local club.[49] Then in 2020, China reversed course and pressured owners to divest from their clubs and repatriate their wealth back home. Overnight, China lost all the capital and credibility that it had built up in the soccer community, its domestic league and strongest clubs disintegrated, and the national team trudged further into mediocrity.

Saudi Arabia, whose soccer ambitions were just starting to take off at the time of the Chinese divestment in the sport, clearly observed the consequences of pulling money out of soccer. Not only was Chinese soccer cast back to the periphery of the industry, but they were mocked and used as a cautionary tale of what happens when you sold the soul of soccer to outsiders. From this, the Saudi's and PIF clearly knew that they were going to meet significant resistance in their plans to heavily invest in soccer. American owners were already hated by Premier League fans; one didn't need much of an imagination to guess what they would say about investors from the Middle East. But perhaps the biggest lesson that China taught to Saudi Arabia was what happened when you stopped partway through a large-scale takeover. China had poured billions into soccer, and by withdrawing had nothing to show for it. No financial gains and no power within the sport.

Saudi Arabia would not be repeating this mistake. Their goal was not a smash-and-grab attempt to gain some slight relevance in the soccer world. No, the Saudi approach one that was focused on becoming omnipresent within soccer. Thus, after taking over Newcastle United, buying the world's most famous (and expensive) athlete in Cristiano Ronaldo, and rebuilding their domestic league, there was one clear target left for the Kingdom of Saudi Arabia—the World Cup.

Buying the World (Cup)

The official bidding for the 2034 World Cup opened on October 4, 2023. If simply buying a major European club and boosting the quality of your domestic league was all it took to get the World Cup, then Saudi Arabia would be waiting in a long line behind China, the UAE, Thailand, Greece, and many other countries. In other words, general investment in soccer is not enough to get you into the good graces of FIFA. Indeed, this is FIFA we are talking about, the governing body who were charged by the US government with wire fraud, racketeering, and money laundering.[50] And even if one ignores the alleged corruption, it seems highly unlikely that FIFA would allow a country to host the World Cup without ensuring they would be heavily profiting from it as well.

This was the final piece of the puzzle for the soccer vision Crown Prince Mohammed bin Salman had laid out for his Kingdom. The World Cup was practically there for the taking, all that remained was sending money to the right parties in a somewhat legitimate manner. At one point in time, it would have been relatively easy to accomplish this. All you had to do was show up with envelopes full of cash to hand out to FIFA delegates for their votes, as was done by former FIFA Vice President Jack Warner.[51] However, after a US Federal probe uncovered evidence of bribery and vote buying schemes by both Russia and Qatar for their respective bids,[52] FIFA quickly moved to implement new rules and ethical standards. This tends to happen when several members of your executive committee are arrested in an early morning raid by Zurich police and are the main news story worldwide.[53]

Under Infantino, who was distancing himself from the image of his disgraced predecessor Sepp Blatter, the signal was that FIFA would only partake in legitimate business. No more buying off delegates with envelopes filled with $40,000. But for Saudi Arabia, this was not really a problem. If FIFA wanted to do legitimate business, the Kingdom was happy to participate, and to do so MBS once again turned to his financier Yasir Al-Rumayyan. The only question was how much it would cost Saudi Arabia to curry favor with FIFA and Infantino.

For Saudi Arabia, which was now dealing with a postcorruption FIFA, the path forward to the World Cup was going to be through the mountain of monetary resources it could mobilize. Although they could have used their sovereign wealth fund, Al-Rumayyan turned to the other financial giant that he controlled, Saudi Aramco. While PIF was busy making headlines with their soccer investments, Aramco was stealthily becoming a household name through its strategic partnerships in sport. Notably, Aramco has become the largest corporate sponsor in the sport world, having spent more than $1.3 billion to become an official partner and have its name posted on everything from trackside signage in Formula 1 racing to ad boards in International Cricket Council test matches.[54] Most fans probably have no idea who Aramco is when they see the advertisements, but the name has become ubiquitous across many sports.

On April 26th, 2024, half a year before the announcement of who would host the 2034 World Cup, FIFA announced Aramco as a new official sponsor. The deal is estimated to be worth $100 million a year[55] and has a potential lifetime value of $1 billion if it carries through to the 2034 World Cup.[56] Naturally, the partnership was highly criticized. Both media and fans questioned the legitimacy of this deal, as taking payments from a state-owned corporation from a county that is bidding for the World Cup seems fishy. And it was not the first time FIFA had made such a deal. Previously, they had done sponsorship deals with Russia's Gazprom and state-owned Qatar Airways for each country's respective World Cups.[57] Though it could be argued that these are legitimate sponsorships being activated precisely when these countries are at the center of global attention, the reality is they seem a bit like a payoff. Thanks for the World Cup, here have some of our advertising budget.

Amidst all this, we need to question FIFA's role in this entire affair. FIFA was never going to intervene in the purchase of Newcastle United or the Saudi Pro League's investment in star players. But there was still an expectation that as the governing body of soccer, FIFA would not just sell the game away so quickly to the next regime waving cash at them. Unfortunately, FIFA's bidding process in recent years has basically become an auction, with the person waving the most money getting what they want.

And that's the thing, when it came to awarding the rights for the 2034 World Cup, FIFA didn't even try to put on the charade of having a fair and objective process. Instead, they cleverly used their own host selection policies to fix it so that Saudi Arabia could be the only winner of the 2034 vote. This policy was first implemented in 2000, after a German newspaper jokingly faxed several FIFA executive committee members a cuckoo clock and a side of ham if they voted for Germany to host the 2006 games.[58] One member was so stressed by this hoax bribe that he abstained from the vote, which resulted in the games being awarded to Germany instead of South Africa as had been expected. In the aftermath, FIFA's executive committee quickly moved to institute a rotational policy, where each continent would take turns to host the World Cup.

This policy led to South Africa becoming the first African nation to host the tournament in 2010, albeit with some bribery to ensure they beat Morocco in the voting. However, this policy was scrapped in 2007 after the 2014 World Cup had been awarded to Brazil and replaced with a new rule stating that any country could bid for the World Cup as long their continent had not hosted the previous two tournaments.[59] Saudi Arabia had been on track to host in 2030, but when Qatar won the rights to the 2022 tournament, it immediately eliminated them from contention. And here is where FIFA's masterstroke ensured Saudi Arabia would host in 2034. With the US, Canada, and Mexico hosting 2026, North America was immediately eliminated from hosting again till 2038. This meant that whoever wasn't selected for the 2030 bid, would then end up as competition against Saudi Arabia. And indeed, there were three strong joint bids, one coming from Uruguay and Argentina, another from the British Isles, and a final from Spain, Portugal, and Morocco. This was a major problem for FIFA.

If Uruguay and Argentina won, it would mean that Saudi Arabia would have to compete against the British Isles, Spain, Portugal, and Morocco, plus any other potential contenders from Asia or Africa. This would be a nightmare for FIFA. Choosing Saudi Arabia over the home of soccer—England—or Spain and Portugal would result in a media firestorm where FIFA would once again be branded as a corrupt organization that was folding to the will of rich and powerful dictators. There would probably even be demands for government inquiries across the UK and Europe demanding greater accountability and transparency from FIFA in the host selection process. But like any great bureaucracy, FIFA found a perfect solution. A technicality, the ultimate weapon of an administrator, that would eliminate all competition for the Saudis.

On October 4, 2023, Gianni Infantino stepped to a podium with six flags arrayed behind him. He started speaking about the world divided in conflict and how FIFA and soccer—yes, he put FIFA ahead of soccer—were a unifying force in these times.[60] And thus, he was announcing a special celebration of the world's game for the 2030 World Cup. The games would be co-hosted by Spain, Portugal, and Morocco. For the Saudi's this meant that they no longer had England as competition for 2034, only South America stood in the way. And now for Infantino's magnum opus. As a special celebration of the 100th anniversary of the original World Cup held in Uruguay, the 2030 World Cup would include three celebratory matches hosted in Argentina, Uruguay, and Paraguay.

At first, most people didn't know what to make of this announcement. The initial outcry was that for an organization that had pledged to improve its carbon footprint, the plan to have teams and fans flying back and forth across the ocean just for a few games was an ecological disaster.[61] But then people started to realize, FIFA had eliminated Europe, South America, and Africa from contention for hosting the 2034 tournament in one fell swoop. Now the only thing that stood in the way of Saudi Arabia was a competing bid from another country in either the Asian or Oceania soccer confederations. But the deck was already stacked against potential contenders.

Notably, the main competition within Asia was coming from Australia and New Zealand who had just hosted the 2023 Women's World Cup, and Indonesia who had approached Australia about teaming up to submit a joint bid.[62] The concern for Australia was that they still lacked enough stadiums, and that there would be a significant cost to either renovate or build new stadiums to meet FIFA's standards. This really didn't matter, because their hopes of submitting a bid were practically ambushed. After Infantino's announcement on October 4, 2023, of Europe, Africa, and South America co-hosting the World Cup, FIFA opened the bidding for the 2034 tournament with a deadline that all bids be submitted by October 31st.[63] Minutes later, MBS announced that Saudi Arabia would be bidding for the rights to host the 2034 World Cup.[64] Nothing strange about that, just a global leader perfectly timing his announcement in sync with Infantino's speech.

Before Australia could even catch its breath, Sheikh Salman bin Ibrahim Al Khalifa, President of the Asian Football Confederation and a member of the Bahrain royal family announced his support for the bid the following day.[65] Then on October 9, Saudi Arabia delivered the coup de grâce. In a letter delivered to FIFA, the Saudi Arabian Football Federation officially announced its intent to bid for the 2034 World Cup,[66] and included pledges of support from over 100 FIFA member associations. Indonesia pulled out of negotiations with Australia a week later to also announce its support for the Saudi bid. The Australian bid was dead in the water. The Saudi's stood uncontested, the only remaining candidate to host the 2034 World Cup.

As Saudi's selection as the hosts of the 2034 World Cup was a forgone conclusion, the official announcement was quite anticlimactic. Rather than the usual room full of delegates waiting anxiously in the hope of hearing FIFA President Gianni Infantino say their country's name, the FIFA Congress was held through a video call. Effectively, the voting and announcement of the world's most popular sporting event was conducted via a glorified Zoom call, the perfect neutered representation of a forgone conclusion.

The Saudi's and MBS had been given the World Cup, and the worst part is that outside of the Norwegian Football Federation (NFF) as the lone dissenting voice that questioned the bidding process,[67] no one even tried to stand in their way. It was an unprecedented moment in the history of international soccer, for the first time ever there was only a single bid to host an upcoming World Cup. This was not a sign that the countries were becoming less interested in hosting the event, as has been the case for several recent Olympic Games.[68] Rather, as NFF President Lise Kalveness hinted,[69] something was amiss as the 2030 and 2034 hosts were predecided without a proper vote.

2034 and Beyond

Just like the ending of *The Godfather*, when Mafia leaders come to kiss Michael Corleone's ring after he eliminated all the other mob bosses, countries were lining up to pay their respects to Saudi Arabia, bowing their heads to pledge loyalty and obedience. Saudi Arabia had won. They now controlled a club in the world's most watched sport league, one of the best players in soccer history played in their domestic league, and now they will host the most coveted sport competition on the planet.

How is the common soccer fan supposed to think about all of this? The Saudi regime has used violence and brutality to silence those who dare speak out against it, and now FIFA has given them the World Cup. Unfortunately, this is nothing new. The Argentinian junta—military dictatorship—was executing political prisoners by hurling them out of airplanes,[70] and FIFA still allowed them to host the 1978 World Cup. Russia invaded Ukraine and annexed the Crimean Peninsula in 2014, and of course FIFA allowed them to have the 2018 World Cup saying it would bring peace to the region.[71] Naturally, less than four years later, Russia invaded Ukraine again, sparking a conflict that continues to this day.

I don't want to say that we should just ignore the transgressions of the Saudis, or the sins of any country that has hosted the World Cup, but can we really blame them for wanting to host the World Cup? It is one of the biggest tools for sportswashing in the world, and if other countries have used it to bleach out their crimes, why shouldn't they? And really, this all points toward a bigger issue within FIFA itself.[72]

Having weathered a major corruption scandal, FIFA seems as determined as ever to control the world's game on its own terms. When women soccer players protested the Aramco sponsorship deal because of the treatment of women in Saudi Arabia, there was silence from FIFA.[73] Likewise, complaints about human rights issues and oppression of speech are left mostly ignored. For FIFA, the focus is on the World Cup, and the games must go on.

And that leaves most of us who pay attention to such things in a sticky situation. One part of me feels that I should be boycotting certain events, that as consumers we should use our economic power to show FIFA, the broadcasters, and sponsors that we will not ignore these issues. The other part of me loves soccer so much and wants to watch every minute of the World Cup no matter where it is hosted. And as I noted earlier in the chapter, it is almost impossible to not consume goods and services that do not have some link with Saudi Arabia and other countries that some of us may want to avoid supporting. It may sound like a bit of a weak excuse to watch soccer guilt free, but it is also the reality of the contemporary business world.

In my mind, it feels like FIFA is the real guilty party in all of this. They have the ability to say no, they could demand more from host nations and show themselves as a true leader in the soccer industry. Indeed, FIFA had the opportunity after their major corruption scandal to reform themselves into a pillar of the international sport community. Instead, they have become a bureaucratic engine of monetization focused on extracting as much wealth from the sport that we all love. Social issues now are seemingly ignored, and rules can be changed if it brings the right financial benefits to FIFA and its rich and powerful allies.[74]

If there is any consolation from any of this, it is that even before the 2034 tournament kicks off, FIFA will already be looking for their next big payday. Just look at Qatar who spent $220 billion to the host the World Cup. After the 2022 tournament ended FIFA remorselessly struck a deal with their biggest rivals Saudi Arabia. If anything, the lesson in this is that when dealing with FIFA, you can buy your way into power and just as easily be replaced by someone with an even bigger checkbook. It's the natural order of how FIFA operates.

So here we are. Saudi Arabia has bought their way to prominence in the soccer industry, but are they really poised to become the rulers of the game? While it is possible, it will require them to continue heavily investing in the sport, including growing their portfolio of top European clubs, purchasing talented players to strengthen their domestic league, and of course lots of sponsorship spending. And I am not sure if all of this is really compatible with the vision that MBS has set out. While sport will continue to be an important cultural tool for his Kingdom, the sport industry is just not lucrative enough to be an economic cornerstone of a powerful country.

Even hosting the World Cup only provides a temporary boost. While host nations do tend to perform slightly better during the World Cup because of home field advantage,[75] it does not guarantee sustained long-term success in the sport at the club or international level. Just look at Qatar, South Africa, Russia, and Mexico. Not only did none of these countries become soccer superpowers after hosting the tournament, but most of them sank back into irrelevance within the sport. And thus, for Saudi Arabia, the question now should not be how do we become a soccer power, but instead should be how do we avoid losing everything that we have built up?

And there is a final point in this whole saga that everyone seems to have missed. With Europe, Africa, and South America hosting 2030, and Saudi Arabia representing Asia in 2034, by FIFA regulations the only confederations that can bid on the 2038 World Cup are North America and Oceania. So, the real winners of the power play by FIFA and Saudi Arabia might be the US, which will host the 2026 World Cup and is now frontrunners to host the 2038 games. Two World Cups in twelve years is unprecedented and could be a massive victory for the expansion of American soccer. It almost makes one forget the Saudi World Cup is even going to happen.

As such, it should be of little surprise that Gianni Infantino was in attendance at Donald Trump's presidential inauguration in January, 2025.[76] Under the Trump administration there has been an unprecedented crackdown on immigration and enforcement of travel bans against citizens of multiple countries—including Iran who have qualified for the 2026 World Cup—all of which has garnered severe criticism from human rights organizations[77] and the media.[78] However, rather than distance themselves from these issues, FIFA has instead forged stronger ties with Trump and the US government including opening new administrative offices in Trump Tower in New York City.[79]

FIFA has seemingly sold away the world's game to the highest bidder, with American and Saudi interests poised the dominate the World Cup and much of the soccer industry for the foreseeable future. The only thing that could potentially interrupt these plans is FIFA's own greed and predilection to constantly be prowling for the next power willing to offer obscene amounts of money for access to the sport.

Unfortunately, this renders fans rather powerless. It may be the most popular sport, but thanks to FIFA, soccer may not be the world's game anymore.

Acknowledgments

There are numerous people who played an instrumental role in helping this book come to fruition. Whether it be providing moral support, engaging in discussions about soccer, giving feedback and thoughts about my writing, I am grateful for all the encouragement and support.

To my wife Grace and son Hiromi, I am eternally thankful for their love and reminding me about the bigger picture in life.

To the Board Room: Hilmir, Ben W, Rep, CMG, M—Director of Football Operations, Whisky, Jasper, Colin, and Eddie, I would like to thank all of you for cheering me on, even if some of you cheer for Spurs, Liverpool, or United.

To everyone at the NBAFT podcast, Kevin, John, and Martin, thanks for allowing me to rant about EA on your podcast.

To Ehren Foley of the University of South Carolina Press whose wisdom and advice helped fulfill the dream of writing this book.

To Christen Karniski and everyone at Bloomsbury who played a role in the publication process, thank you for your kindness and patience.

To my family and friends, especially my uncle, aunt, and great-grandmother who opened their house to me when I was finishing this book, thank you for everything and for tolerating my obsession with Arsenal.

And to all the soccer fans out there. Thank you for loving the game so much.

Notes

Introduction

1. Charlotte Coates, "Premier League TV Viewing Figures Down 10% on Sky Sports Last Season," *BBC Sport*, https://www.bbc.com/sport/football/articles/cwyj7506y5jo (accessed June 11, 2025).

Chapter 1

1. Matt Craig, "Billion-Dollar Ballers: These Athletes—Tiger Woods, LeBron James, Federer, Messi, Ronaldo, Mayweather—Have Earned More Than $1 Billion Apiece," *Forbes*, June 12, 2022, https://www.forbes.com/sites/mattcraig/2022/06/12/billion-dollar-ballers-these-athletes-tiger-woods-lebron-james-federer-messi-ronaldo-mayweather-have-earned-more-than-1-billion-apiece (accessed June 11, 2025).

2. Michael Butler, "Golden Goal: Claude Makélélé for Chelsea v. Tottenham Hotspur" (2006), *The Guardian*, https://www.theguardian.com/football/blog/2017/jan/04/golden-goal-claude-makelele-chelsea-tottenham-2006 (accessed September 17, 2025).

3. Grant Wahl, *The Beckham Experiment* (New York: Three Rivers Press, 2010), 42.

4. "More than 700 media members and 5,000 fans packed into the LA Galaxy's home stadium to welcome David Beckham to Major League Soccer," *The New York Times*, July 10, 2023. https://www.nytimes.com/athletic/4674349/2023/07/10/messi-miami-beckham-money (accessed June 12, 2025).

5. Simon Evans, "Soccer-Beckham talking to MLS about owning a new team," *Yahoo Sports*, May 17, 2013, https://archive.ph/20130625023602/http://sports.yahoo.com/news/soccer-beckham-talking-mls-owning-team-193804208.html (accessed June 12, 2025).

6   Sid Lowe, "Lionel Messi: how Argentinian teenager signed for Barcelona on a serviette," *The Guardian*, October 15, 2014, https://www.theguardian.com/football/blog/2014/oct/15/lionel-messi-barcelona-decade (accessed June 12, 2025).

7   "Giuly remembers the first time saw Messi kill his team-mates," *Sport English*, http://www.sport-english.com/en/news/barca/giuly-remembers-the-first-time-saw-messi-kill-his-team-mates-5378823 (accessed June12, 2025).

8   Balagué, G. (2013). *Messi: The must-read biography of the World Cup champion*. Hachette UK.

9   Sam Marsden, "A history of Lionel Messi's nine deals at Barcelona as he signs to 2021," *ESPN*, https://www.espn.com/soccer/story/_/id/37458495/a-history-lionel-messi-nine-deals-barcelona-signs-2021 (accessed June 12, 2025).

10 "Lionel Messi signs new Barcelona deal," *ESPN*, https://www.espn.com/soccer/story/_/id/37361394/lionel-messi-signs-new-barcelona-contract-club-confirm (accessed June 12, 2025).

11 "Lionel Messi has Barcelona contract for life—Josep Maria Bartomeu," *ESPN*, https://www.espn.com/soccer/story/_/id/37488022/lionel-messi-barcelona-contract-life-president-josep-maria-bartomeu (accessed June 12, 2025).

12 "Lionel Messi officially agrees to new Barcelona contract until 2021," *ESPN*, https://www.espn.com/soccer/story/_/id/37526011/lionel-messi-officially-agrees-new-barcelona-contract-2021 (accessed June 12, 2025).

13 Gabriel Fernandez, "Lionel Messi-Barcelona contract details: $674 million earnings leaked by Spanish paper in bombshell report," *CBS Sports*, https://www.cbssports.com/soccer/news/lionel-messi-barcelona-contract-details-674-million-earnings-leaked-by-spanish-paper-in-bombshell-report (accessed June 12, 2025).

14 Roger Gonzalez, "Barcelona presidential elect ions set for March 7 with big financial challenges ahead at Camp Nou," *CBS Sports*, https://www.cbssports.com/soccer/news/barcelona-presidential-elections-set-for-march-7-with-big-financial-challenges-ahead-at-camp-nou (accessed June 12, 2025).

15 Sam Marsedn and Moises Llorens, "How bad are Barcelona's finances, and how can they be fixed?" *ESPN*, https://www.espn.com/soccer/story/_/id/39956504/barcelona-finances-laporta-laliga-palanca-assets-transfers (accessed June 12, 2025).

16 Sam Marsedn and Moises Llorens, "How bad are Barcelona's finances, and how can they be fixed?" *ESPN*, https://www.espn.com/soccer/story/_/id/39956504/barcelona-finances-laporta-laliga-palanca-assets-transfers (accessed June 12, 2025).

17 "FC Barcelona becomes the first sports club in the world to surpass the $1 billion mark in revenues," *FC Barcelona*, July 16, 2018, https://www.fcbarcelona.com/en/news/876430/fc-barcelona-becomes-the-first-sports-club-in-the-world-to-surpass-the-1-billion-mark-in-revenues (accessed June 12, 2025).

18 "Lionel Messi: Barcelona forward agrees contract extension with 50 per cent pay cut," *Sky Sports*, July 14, 2021, https://www.skysports.com/football/news/11833/12355747/lionel-messi-barcelona-forward-agrees-contract-extension-with-50-per-cent-pay-cut (accessed June 12, 2025).

19 "Leo Messi not staying at FC Barcelona," *FC Barcelona*, August 5, 2021, https://www.fcbarcelona.com/en/football/first-team/news/2207655/leo-messi-not-staying-at-fc-barcelona (accessed June 12, 2025).

20 Joe Prince-Wright, "Cristiano Ronaldo signs $200 million-per-year deal with Al Nassr; report says Newcastle loan possible," *NBC Sports*, https://www.nbcsports.com/soccer/news/cristiano-ronaldo-signs-200-million-per-year-deal-with-al-nassr-report (accessed June 12, 2025).

21 Paul Mueller, "Here's why Lionel Messi's Inter Miami contract will change the way the world's best athletes are paid," *Fast Company*, https://www.fastcompany.com/91030230/breaking-down-lionel-messi-inter-miami-contract (accessed June 12, 2025).

22 Kurt Badenhausen, "Messi's Miami Contract: $50M-$60M a Year Before Adidas, Apple Money," *Sportico*, https://www.sportico.com/personalities/athletes/2023/messis-miami-contract-50m-60m-annually-before-adidas-apple-money-1234726627 (accessed June 12, 2025).

23 Mueller, "Here's why Lionel Messi's Inter Miami contract will change the way the world's best athletes are paid."

24 Kurt Badenhausen, "Messi's Miami Contract: $50M-$60M a Year Before Adidas, Apple Money," *Sportico*, https://www.sportico.com/personalities/athletes/2023/messis-miami-contract-50m-60m-annually-before-adidas-apple-money-1234726627 (accessed June 12, 2025).

25 Shwetha Surendran, "What Messi's MLS, Apple, Adidas deal means for everyone else," *ESPN*, https://www.espn.com/soccer/story/_/id/37975000/lionel-messi-mls-apple-adidas-inter-miami (accessed June 12, 2025).

26 Kurt Badenhausen, "Messi career earnings to reach $1.6B with Miami MLS deal," *Sportico*, https://www.sportico.com/personalities/athletes/2023/lionel-messi-career-earnings-billion-mls-1234730823 (accessed June 12, 2025).

27 Matt Scott, "Beckham drives Madrid to top of money league," *The Guardian*, February 16, 2006, https://www.theguardian.com/football/2006/feb/16/newsstory.sport (accessed June 12, 2025).

28 Nisanth V. Easwar "What are the Barcelona 'economic levers'? Financial term & transfer business explained," *Goal*, https://www.goal.com/en-qa/news/what-barcelona-economic-levers-financial-term-transfer-business-explained/blt95d2a1f87b095208 (accessed June 12, 2025).

Chapter 2

1. "Forbes Lists: Most Valuable Soccer Teams," *Forbes*, https://www.forbes.com/forbes/2005/0418/138tab.html (accessed June 16, 2025).

2. David Bond, "Manchester United owners hit by debt payment rise," *BBC Sport*, http://news.bbc.co.uk/sport1/hi/football/teams/m/man_utd/8931026.stm (accessed June 16, 2025).

3. Wesley Stephenson, "How the Glazer family cost Manchester United £1.2bn," *BBC Sport*, https://www.bbc.com/sport/football/articles/cd9lwdegxvxo (accessed June 16, 2025).

4. "McCourt far from blue," *Boston.com*, June 12, 2004, https://web.archive.org/web/20050527035241/http://www.boston.com/sports/baseball/redsox/articles/2004/06/12/mccourt_far_from_blue (accessed June 16, 2025).

5. "Vote will be taken today," *ESPN*, https://www.espn.com/mlb/news/story?id=1719414 (accessed June 16, 2025).

6. Bill Shaikin, "Frank McCourt might keep Dodger Stadium parking lots," *Los Angeles Times*, January 18, 2012, https://www.latimes.com/sports/la-xpm-2012-jan-18-la-sp-dodgers-mccourt-sale-20120119-story.html (accessed June 16, 2025).

7. Bill Shaikin, "Frank and Jamie McCourt reach settlement involving Dodgers," *Los Angeles Times*, October 17, 2011, https://www.latimes.com/sports/la-xpm-2011-oct-17-la-sp-1017-mccourt-divorce-settlement-20111017-story.html (accessed June 16, 2025).

8. Bill Shaikin, "Steve Soboroff defends Dodgers owner: 'We need more people like Frank McCourt,'" *Los Angeles Times*, April 21, 2011, https://www.latimes.com/sports/la-xpm-2011-apr-21-la-sp-0422-dodgers-web-20110422-story.html (accessed June 16, 2025).

9. Kelly Phillips Erb, "From L.A. Dodgers to Alleged Tax Dodgers: The McCourt Saga Continues," *Forbes*, May 31, 2012, https://www.forbes.com/sites/kellyphillipserb/2012/05/31/from-l-a-dodgers-to-alleged-tax-dodgers-the-mccourt-saga-continues (accessed June 16, 2025).

10. Jerome Pugmire, "American businessman McCourt buying French club Marseille," *AP News*, https://apnews.com/american-businessman-mccourt-buying-french-club-marseille-1462100108984d8b82f5767e241c4b62 (accessed June 16, 2025).

11. "Marseille: Frank McCourt promises £180m investment after buying Ligue 1 club," *BBC Sport*, https://www.bbc.com/sport/football/37685865 (accessed June 16, 2025).

12. Kim McCauley, "Could Dimitri Payet's signing turn Olympique Marseille around? Frank McCourt's history suggests otherwise," *SB Nation*, January 30, 2017, https://www.sbnation.com/soccer/2017/1/30/14286072/dimitri-payet-marseille-transfer-ownership-frank-mccourt (accessed June 16, 2025).

13. Bobby McMahon, "Marseille Has Lost More Than €200M Since Frank McCourt Bought The Team in 2016," *Forbes*, April 2, 2020, https://www.forbes.com/sites/bobbymcmahon/2020/04/02/marseille-has-lost-more-than-200m-since-frank-mccourt-bought-the-team-in-2016 (accessed June 16, 2025).

14. "Marseille fined €3m for breach of FFP settlement, will keep Champions League spot," *ESPN*, https://www.espn.co.uk/football/story/_/id/37584346/marseille-fined-3m-breach-ffp-settlement-keep-champions-league-spot (accessed June 16, 2025).

15. Luke Entwistle, "The lure of Champions League money has turned Ligue 1 clubs into gamblers," *The Guardian*, May 12, 2025, https://www.theguardian.com/football/2025/may/12/champions-league-money-ligue-1-clubs-gamblers-marseille-lyon-europe (accessed June 16, 2025).

16. "Women's football boss Michele Kang: 'I want the next generation to compete on an equal playing field,'" *Financial Times*, https://www.ft.com/content/b7bb32ea-44ef-49cb-bf72-b78f6cffb1be (accessed June 16, 2025).

17. "Women's football boss Michele Kang: 'I want the next generation to compete on an equal playing field,'" *Financial Times*, https://www.ft.com/content/b7bb32ea-44ef-49cb-bf72-b78f6cffb1be (accessed June 16, 2025).

18. Meg Lineham, "How Michele Kang become one of the biggest investors in women's soccer," *The New York Times*, November 22, 2024, https://www.nytimes.com/athletic/5940050/2024/11/22/michele-kang-womens-soccer-investment (accessed June 16, 2025).

19. "Northrop Grumman Names Michele Kang Vice President, Health & Science Solutions," *Northrop Grumman*, https://web.archive.org/web/20240201031749/https://news.northropgrumman.com/news/releases/photo-release-northrop-grumman-names-michele-kang-vice-president-health-science-solutions (accessed June 16, 2025).

20. "Chief Officer Award Finalist Michele Kang: 'Dream Big, Expect Obstacles And Succeed Anyway,'" *Washington Exec*, May 2021, https://washingtonexec.com/2021/05/chief-officer-award-finalist-michele-kang-dream-big-expect-obstacles-and-succeed-anyway (accessed June 16, 2025).

21. Justin Birnbaum, "Inside Michele Kang's plan to reinvent women's soccer: 'Not some corporate DEI project,'" *Forbes*, June 2, 2025, https://www.forbes.com/sites/justinbirnbaum/2025/06/02/michele-kang-washington-spirit-nwsl-future-of-womens-soccer (accessed June 16, 2025).

22. "Senator Daschle joins the Cognosante Board of Directors," *Globe Newswire*, October 16, 2014, https://www.globenewswire.com/news-release/2014/10/16/673842/26050/en/Senator-Daschle-joins-the-Cognosante-Board-of-Directors.html (accessed June 16, 2025).

23. "Y. Michele Kang Joins Washington Spirit Ownership Group," *Washington Spirit*, December 29, 2020, https://washingtonspirit.com/blog/2020/12/29/y-michele-kang-joins-washington-spirit-ownership-group (accessed June 16, 2025).

24 Jason Anderson, "Y. Michele Kang joins Washington Spirit ownership group," *Black and Red United*, December 29, 2020, https://www.blackandredunited.com/washington-spirit-womens-soccer/2020/12/29/22205105/washington-spirit-ownership-y-michele-kang-nwsl-2020 (accessed June 16, 2025).

25 Molly Hensley-Clancy and Steven Goff, "Co-owners of NWSL's Spirit fight for control after abuse allegations against coach," *The Washington Post*, August 30, 2021, https://www.washingtonpost.com/sports/2021/08/30/washington-spirit-owners-steve-baldwin (accessed June 16, 2025).

26 Molly Hensley-Clancy, "'He made me hate soccer': Players say they left NWSL's Spirit over coach's verbal abuse," *The Washington Post*, August 11, 2021, https://www.washingtonpost.com/sports/2021/08/11/richie-burke-nwsl-spirit-verbal-abuse (accessed June 16, 2025).

27 "Investigation Into NWSL Finds Systemic Emotional Abuse, Sexual Misconduct," *Sports Illustrated*, October 3, 2022, https://www.si.com/soccer/2022/10/03/nwsl-investigation-emotional-abuse-sexual-misconduct (accessed June 16, 2025).

28 Molly Hensley-Clancy, "Women describe 'old boys' club' culture at Washington Spirit as NWSL probes franchise," *The Washington Post*, September 22, 2021, https://www.washingtonpost.com/sports/2021/09/22/washington-spirit-workplace-women-nwsl/ (accessed June 16, 2025).

29 Cydney Grannan, "Washington Spirit Coach Richie Burke Fired Following Harassment Investigation," *DCist*, September 28, 2021, https://dcist.com/story/21/09/28/washington-spirit-coach-richie-burke-fired-after-harassment-investigation (accessed June 16, 2025).

30 MLSist, Twitter post, https://x.com/MLSist/status/1442462189722427393 (accessed June 16, 2025).

31 Sunshine Sully, Twitter post, https://x.com/sunshine_sully/status/1445536942385360901 (accessed June 16, 2025).

32 Emily Caron and Eben Novy-Williams, "NWSL's D.C. Spirit Sale: 'Coup, Lies' Baldwin Says in Letter," *Sportico*, https://www.sportico.com/business/sales/2022/washington-spirit-sale-steve-baldwin-letter-michele-kang-1234659270 (accessed June 16, 2025).

33 Steven Goff, "Washington Spirit investors increase pressure on Steve Baldwin to sell to Y. Michele Kang," *The Washington Post*, December 27, 2021, https://www.washingtonpost.com/sports/2021/12/27/washington-spirit-steve-baldwin-michele-kang (accessed June 16, 2025).

34 Emily Caron and Eben Novy-Williams, "NWSL's D.C. Spirit Sale: 'Coup, Lies' Baldwin Says in Letter," *Sportico*, https://www.sportico.com/business/sales/2022/washington-spirit-sale-steve-baldwin-letter-michele-kang-1234659270 (accessed June 16, 2025).

35 Elliot C. Williams, "After Months of Friction, Michele Kang Becomes Controlling Owner of Washington Spirit," *NPR*, February 9, 2022, https://web.archive.org/web/20230516232339/https://www.npr.org/local/305/2022/02/09/1079521602/after-months-of-friction-michele-kang-becomes-controlling-owner-of-washington-spirit (accessed June 16, 2025).

36 "Washington Spirit owner Kang to take over Lyon," *Sports Business Journal*, May 16, 2023, https://www.sportsbusinessjournal.com/Daily/Closing-Bell/2023/05/16/michele-kang-washington-spirit-to-take-over-lyon (accessed June 16, 2025).

37 "Michele Kang Announces Launch of Kynisca Sports International Ltd," *Washington Spirit*, July 27, 2024, https://washingtonspirit.com/blog/2024/07/27/michele-kang-announces-launch-of-kynisca-sports-international-ltd/ (accessed June 16, 2025).

38 Scott Austin, "Who are the new Dodgers owners?" *The Wall Street Journal*, https://www.wsj.com/articles/SB10001424052702303404704577309850685211084 (accessed June 16, 2025).

39 Jamie Johnson, "The real Todd Boehly: High-school wrestler turned ruthless winner who puts his money where his mouth is," *The Telegraph*, June 24, 2022, https://www.telegraph.co.uk/football/2022/06/24/real-todd-boehly-high-school-wrestler-turned-ruthless-winner (accessed June 16, 2025).

40 "Guggenheim Securities Transactions," *Guggenheim Securities*, https://www.guggenheimsecurities.com/capabilities/transactions (accessed June 16, 2025).

41 Adam Wells, "Dodgers Announce New TV Network: SportsNet LA, Starting in 2014 Season," *Bleacher Report*, January 28, 2013, https://bleacherreport.com/articles/1504723-dodgers-announce-new-tv-network-sportsnet-la-starting-in-2014-season (accessed June 16, 2025).

42 Bill Shaikin, "After $1 billion in player spending, Dodgers under MLB mandate to cut debt," *Los Angeles Times*, November 26, 2016, https://www.latimes.com/sports/dodgers/la-sp-dodgers-debt-payroll-20161126-story.html (accessed June 16, 2025).

43 Erik Schatzker, "From CLOs to 'Ozark,' Ex-Guggenheim President Builds an Empire," *Bloomberg*, September 9, 2019, https://www.bloomberg.com/news/articles/2019-09-09/from-clos-to-ozark-ex-guggenheim-president-builds-an-empire?embedded-checkout=true (accessed June 16, 2025).

44 Erwin Caston, "LA Dodgers owner Todd Boehly makes a monstrous $3B takeover bid for Chelsea," *Sportskeeda*, https://www.sportskeeda.com/football/la-dodgers-owner-todd-boehly-makes-a-monstrous-3b-takeover-bid-for-chelsea (accessed June 16, 2025).

45 Aubrey Allegretti and Jasper Jolly, "UK imposes sanctions on Roman Abramovich over clear links to Putin," *The Guardian*, March 10, 2022, https://www.theguardian.com/world/2022/mar/10/uk-imposes-sanctions-on-roman-abramovich-over-clear-links-to-putin (accessed June 16, 2025).

46 "Chelsea shirt sponsor Three to resume marketing activity after sanctions against club lifted," *BBC Sport*, https://www.bbc.com/sport/football/61824493 (accessed June 16, 2025).

47 "Chelsea claim Roman Abramovich sanctions a factor in £121m losses," *The Guardian*, March 27, 2023, https://www.theguardian.com/football/2023/mar/27/chelsea-claim-abramovich-sanctions-a-factor-in-121m-losses-for-last-season (accessed June 16, 2025).

48 Jacob Steinberg, "Abramovich's Chelsea sale statement: his words under the microscope," *The Guardian*, March 3, 2022, https://www.theguardian.com/football/2022/mar/03/roman-abramovich-chelsea-sale-statement-words-under-the-microscope (accessed June 16, 2025).

49 "Consortium led by Todd Boehly and Clearlake Capital completes acquisition of Chelsea Football Club," *Chelsea FC*, May 30, 2022, https://www.chelseafc.com/en/news/2022/05/30/consortium-led-by-todd-boehly-and-clearlake-capital-completes-ac (accessed June 16, 2025).

50 "Chelsea spent £747m on transfers in 2022–23 season," *BBC Sport*, https://www.bbc.com/sport/football/68805247 (accessed June 16, 2025).

51 Jacob Steinberg, "Regrets, big bucks and a toy car: inside year one of the Boehly era at Chelsea," *The Guardian*, May 30, 2023, https://www.theguardian.com/football/2023/may/30/chelsea-inside-year-one-of-the-todd-boehly-era (accessed June 16, 2025).

52 Simon Johnson and Liam Twomey, "That was the Roman Abramovich era: big money signings, furious rivalry, unprecedented success," *The New York Times*, May 23, 2022, https://www.nytimes.com/athletic/3325947/2022/05/23/that-was-the-roman-abramovich-era-big-money-signings-furious-rivalry-unprecedented-success (accessed June 16, 2025).

53 Ron Walker, "Premier League financial fair play rules explained: What restrictions are there on clubs spending what they want?" *Sky Sports*, https://www.skysports.com/football/news/11095/13041990/premier-league-financial-fair-play-rules-explained-what-restrictions-are-there-on-clubs-spending-what-they-want (accessed June 16, 2025).

54 "Chelsea record revenue but £90.1m losses raise PSR concerns," *One Football*, https://onefootball.com/en/news/chelsea-record-revenue-but-901m-losses-raise-psr-concerns-39165924 (accessed June 16, 2025).

55 "Enzo Fernandez transfer news: Chelsea complete British record £107m fee for Benfica midfielder," *BBC Sport*, https://www.bbc.com/sport/football/64463077 (accessed June 16, 2025).

56 Steven Chicken, "This insane Chelsea contract statistic will shock you, especially if you're a Star Trek fan," *FourFourTwo*, https://www.fourfourtwo.com/news/this-insane-chelsea-contract-statistic-will-shock-you-especially-if-youre-a-star-trek-fan (accessed June 16, 2025).

57 Sean Kearns, "Premier League clubs avoid 2023–24 PSR charges," *BBC Sport*, https://www.bbc.com/sport/football/articles/cx2y7l0dk02o (accessed June 16, 2025).

58 Jacob Steinberg, "Chelsea's £76.5m hotel deals raise questions over PSR compliance," *The Guardian*, April 19, 2024, https://www.theguardian.com/football/2024/apr/19/chelseas-765m-hotel-deals-raise-questions-over-psr-compliance (accessed June 16, 2025).

59 Jacob Steinberg, "Chelsea's £76.5m hotel deals raise questions over PSR compliance," *The Guardian*, April 19, 2024, https://www.theguardian.com/football/2024/apr/19/chelseas-765m-hotel-deals-raise-questions-over-psr-compliance (accessed June 16, 2025).

60 Jacob Steinberg, "Chelsea report £128.4m profit after selling women's side to themselves," *The Guardian*, March 31, 2025, https://www.theguardian.com/football/2025/mar/31/premier-league-psr-chelsea-sell-women-team-loophole (accessed June 16, 2025).

61 Dom Smith, "Chelsea to be hit by UEFA punishment after financial rules breach," *Evening Standard*, https://www.standard.co.uk/sport/football/chelsea-fc-uefa-fine-financial-rules-breach-b1231181.html (accessed June 16, 2025).

62 "Indo Board History," *Indo Board*, https://indoboard.com/pages/history (accessed June 16, 2025).

63 "JOHN TEXTOR: Master of Surreality," *YouTube*, https://www.youtube.com/watch?v=LxyaaXUXxL8 (accessed June 16, 2025).

64 Mark Del Franco, "BabyUniverse Merging with eToys Direct," *Multichannel Merchant*, https://multichannelmerchant.com/marketing/babyuniverse-merging-with-etoys-direct (accessed June 16, 2025).

65 Ben Fritz, "Digital Domain Docks with Bay," *Variety*, https://variety.com/2006/film/markets-festivals/digital-domain-docks-with-bay-1200336402 (accessed June 16, 2025).

66 David Rowell, "The Spectacular, Strange Rise of Music Holograms," *The Washington Post*, October 30, 2019, https://www.washingtonpost.com/magazine/2019/10/30/dead-musicians-are-taking-stage-again-hologram-form-is-this-kind-encore-we-really-want/ (accessed June 16, 2025).

67 Richard Verrier, "Florida accuses former Digital Domain Media officers of fraud," *Los Angeles Times*, July 25, 2014, https://www.latimes.com/entertainment/envelope/cotown/la-et-ct-digital-domain-lawsuit-20140725-story.html (accessed June 16, 2025).

68 "FaceBank Introduction," *FaceBank*, https://www.facebank.com/introduction (accessed June 16, 2025).

69 Jared Newman, "The little live-TV streaming service that could," *Fast Company*, https://www.fastcompany.com/90212669/live-tv-streaming-services-fubotv (accessed June 16, 2025).

70 Krystal Hu, "FuboTV to merge with FaceBank; sources say values FuboTV at $700 million," *Reuters*, https://www.reuters.com/article/us-facebank-group-m-a-fubotv-idUSKBN21A3OI (accessed June 16, 2025).

71 Rick Munarriz, "This Was the Top-Performing IPO in 2020," *The Motley Fool*, December 28, 2020, https://www.fool.com/investing/2020/12/28/this-was-the-top-performing-ipo-in-2020/ (accessed June 16, 2025).

72 "US investor John Textor completes Lyon takeover," *Financial Times*, https://www.ft.com/content/2fcdf81d-2abb-4ece-8ede-2a9775a09c35 (accessed June 16, 2025).

73 Alex Howell, "Crystal Palace co-owner John Textor Q&A: Parish, fan protests, Hodgson, Glasner," *BBC Sport*, https://www.bbc.com/sport/football/68437892 (accessed June 16, 2025).

74 Ed Aarons, "Crystal Palace's FA Cup triumph left their fans in tears—I was among them," *The Guardian*, May 18, 2025, https://www.theguardian.com/football/2025/may/18/crystal-palace-fa-cup-final-victory-wembley-fans (accessed June 16, 2025).

75 "The CFCB decides on multi-club ownership cases for the 2024 UEFA club competitions," *UEFA*, https://www.uefa.com/news-media/news/028f-1b4ba6fcea09-078845f25cbf-1000-the-cfcb-decides-on-multi-club-ownership-cases-for-the-2024-/ (accessed June 16, 2025).

76 Matt Hughes, "Crystal Palace's Europa League place in doubt after Uefa rejects owners' blind trust move," *The Guardian*, June 5, 2025, https://www.theguardian.com/football/2025/jun/05/crystal-palace-europe-place-uefa-rejects-owners-blind-trust-move (accessed June 16, 2025).

77 Matt Hughes, "John Textor provides another twist in Crystal Palace ownership saga," *The Guardian*, June 15, 2025, https://www.theguardian.com/football/2025/jun/15/john-textor-twist-crystal-palace-ownership-saga-eagle-football-ipo (accessed June 16, 2025).

Chapter 3

1 Vivianne Miedema (@viviannemiedema), "Instagram Post," *Instagram*, April 28, 2023, https://www.instagram.com/p/Cr0SMvKIM8D (accessed July 11, 2025).

2 Josh Halliday, "SPOTY winner Beth Mead calls for more research into women's ACL injuries," *The Guardian*, December 22, 2022, https://www.theguardian.com/football/2022/dec/22/spoty-winner-beth-mead-calls-for-more-research-into-womens-acl-injuries (accessed July 11, 2025).

3 "Step by Step. Episode one. Football was my happy place," *YouTube*, posted by "Arsenal," April 28, 2023, https://www.youtube.com/watch?v=vxHrH2nCqR8 (accessed July 11, 2025).

4 Crossley K. M., Patterson B. E., Culvenor A. G., Bruder, A. M., Mosler, A. B., Mentiplay, B. F., "Making football safer for women: a systematic review and meta-

analysis of injury prevention programmes in 11,773 female football (soccer) players," *British Journal of Sports Medicine* 54, no. 18 (2020): 1089-99, https://bjsm.bmj.com/content/54/18/1089 (accessed July 11, 2025).

5   Taberner, M., van Dyk, N., Allen T., Jain, N., Richter, C., Drust, B., Betancur, E., and Cohen, D. D., "Return to sport and performance after anterior cruciate ligament reconstruction in elite female football players," *BMJ Open Sport & Exercise Medicine* 6, no. 1 (2020): e000843, https://bmjopensem.bmj.com/content/6/1/e000843 (accessed July 11, 2025).

6   Lipps, D. B., Oh, Y. K., Ashton-Miller, J. A., and Wojtys, E. M., "Morphologic characteristics help explain the gender difference in peak anterior cruciate ligament strain during a simulated pivot landing," *The American Journal of Sports Medicine* 40, no. 1 (2012): 32-40, https://www.ncbi.nlm.nih.gov/pmc/articles/PMC4800982 (accessed July 11, 2025).

7   Manson, S. A., Brughelli, M., and Harris N. K., "Physiological characteristics of international female soccer players," *Journal of Strength and Conditioning Research* 28, no. 2 (2014): 308-18, https://journals.lww.com/nsca-jscr/fulltext/2014/02000/physiological_characteristics_of_international.3.aspx (accessed July 11, 2025).

8   Parsons, J. L., Coen, S. E., and Bekker, S, "Anterior cruciate ligament injury: towards a gendered environmental approach," *BMJ Open Sport & Exercise Medicine* 7, no. 4 (2021): e001170, https://bmjopensem.bmj.com/content/bmjosem/7/4/e001170.full.pdf (accessed July 11, 2025).

9   Herzberg, S. D., Motu'apuaka, M. L., Lambert, W., Fu, R., Brady, J., and Guise, J.-M., "The Effect of Menstrual Cycle and Contraceptives on ACL Injuries and Laxity: A Systematic Review and Meta-analysis," *Orthopaedic Journal of Sports Medicine* 5, no. 7 (2017): 2325967117718781, https://journals.sagepub.com/doi/full/10.1177/2325967117718781 (accessed July 11, 2025).

10 Bahr, R., Clarsen, B., and Ekstrand, J., "Why we should focus on the burden of injuries and illnesses, not just their incidence," *BMJ Open Sport & Exercise Medicine* 6, no. 1 (2020): e000778, https://bmjopensem.bmj.com/content/bmjosem/6/1/e000778.full.pdf (accessed July 11, 2025).

11 "Football schedule is not just a health risk but is 'killing the product', says PFA," *BBC Sport*, February 29, 2024, https://www.bbc.com/sport/football/68423241 (accessed July 11, 2025).

12 Chen, J., Kim, J., Shao, W., Schlecht, S. H., Baek, S. Y., Jones, A. K., Ahn, T., Ashton-Miller, J. A., Banaszek Holl, M. M., and Wojtys, E. M., "New perspectives on ACL injury: On the role of repetitive sub-maximal knee loading in causing ACL fatigue failure," *Journal of Orthopaedic Research* 34, no. 12 (2016): 2059-68, https://journals.sagepub.com/doi/abs/10.1177/0363546519854450 (accessed July 11, 2025).

13 "Player Workload Monitoring Women's Football," *FIFPRO*, https://fifpro.org/en/women-s-player-workload-monitoring-platform (accessed July 11, 2025).

14 "2023 FIFA Women's World Cup Workload Journey Report," *FIFPRO*, 2023, https://fifpro.org/media/xcweuugu/pwm_fwwc_report_2023_twopage.pdf (accessed July 11, 2025).

15 "How does travel fatigue and jet lag affect footballers?" *FIFPRO*, https://www.fifpro.org/en/supporting-players/health-and-performance/drake-football-study/how-does-travel-fatigue-and-jet-lag-affect-footballers (accessed July 11, 2025).

16 "'We're seeing a tsunami of ACL injuries in women's football,'" *BBC Sport*, September 28, 2023, https://www.bbc.com/sport/football/66958486 (accessed July 11, 2025).

17 Emma Sanders, "Beth Mead: Arsenal and England forward to work with Fifa on ACL injuries," *BBC Sport*, February 23, 2024, https://www.bbc.com/sport/football/68362284 (accessed July 11, 2025).

18 David Aldridge, "Diving deep into data, the NBA, formally, says its numbers don't back load management," *The New York Times*, January 12, 2024, https://www.nytimes.com/athletic/5196221/2024/01/12/nba-load-management-report/ (accessed July 11, 2025).

19 Menon, B. C., Morikawa, K., Tummala, S. V., Buckner-Petty, S., and Chhabra, A., "The Primary Risk Factors for Season-Ending Injuries in Professional Basketball Are Minutes Played Per Game and Later Season Games," *Arthroscopy: The Journal of Arthroscopic & Related Surgery* 40, no. 6 (2024): 1543–50, https://www.arthroscopyjournal.org/article/S0749-8063(24)00062-8/abstract (accessed July 11, 2025).

20 Steve Aschburner, "Adam Silver discusses new policy as load management goes 'too far,'" *NBA.com*, September 13, 2023, https://www.nba.com/news/adam-silver-load-management-bog-news-conference-2023 (accessed July 11, 2025).

21 Samantha Lewis, "How Sam Kerr's ACL injury puts the human back into her superhuman career," *ABC News*, January 8, 2024, https://www.abc.net.au/news/2024-01-08/sam-kerr-acl-injury-human-superhuman-career/103292600 (accessed July 11, 2025).

22 "Beth Mead: 'The people who understand ACL injuries are the players who have gone through it'" *FIFPRO*, https://fifpro.org/en/supporting-players/health-and-performance/beth-mead-the-people-who-understand-acl-injuries-are-the-players-who-have-gone-through-it (accessed July 11, 2025).

23 "Players share invaluable insights and experiences at Project ACL launch event," *FIFPRO*, https://fifpro.org/en/supporting-players/health-and-performance/players-share-invaluable-insights-and-experiences-at-project-acl-launch-event (accessed July 11, 2025).

24 "Barcelona's Alexia Putellas undergoes surgery in effort to resolve knee injury," *The Guardian*, December 26, 2023, https://www.theguardian.com/football/2023/dec/26/alexia-putellas-knee-problem-barcelona-spain (accessed July 11, 2025).

25 Blair Newman, "10 players who could define women's soccer in 2024," *Equalizer Soccer*, January 12, 2024, https://equalizersoccer.com/2024/01/12/10-players-who-could-define-womens-soccer-in-2024 (accessed July 11, 2025).

26 Sam Marsden, "UWCL final: Alexia Putellas shows she's 'queen of Barcelona'," *ABC News*, May 25, 2024, https://abcnews.go.com/Sports/uwcl-final-alexia-putellas-shows-shes-queen-barcelona/story?id=110563457 (accessed July 11, 2025).

Chapter 4

1 "Ryan Reynolds and Rob McElhenney: Hollywood stars to take over Wrexham," *BBC Sport*, November 16, 2020, https://www.bbc.co.uk/sport/football/54956962 (accessed June 19, 2025).

2 Kerry Martin, "Ryan Reynolds and Rob McElhenney announce 'Welcome to Wrexham' football club documentary," *Yahoo News UK*, https://uk.news.yahoo.com/ryan-reynolds-rob-mcelhenney-welcome-wrexham-football-club-documentary-153138330.html (accessed June 19, 2025).

3 Aled Williams, "Wrexham 4-5 Grimsby Town: Luke Waterfall's winner late in extra time seals thrilling win," *BBC Sport*, https://www.bbc.com/sport/football/61560268 (accessed June 19, 2025).

4 "Notts County: Alexander & Christoffer Reedtz complete takeover," *BBC Sport*, https://www.bbc.com/sport/football/48282230 (accessed June 19, 2025).

5 "About Us," *Football Radar*, https://www.footballradar.com/about (accessed June 19, 2025).

6 Evan Shaw, "Notts County: How did owners Christoffer & Alexander Reedtz make their cash," *Football League World*, https://footballleagueworld.co.uk/how-exactly-did-notts-countys-owners-the-reedtz-brothers-make-their-cash (accessed June 19, 2025).

7 Drew Palombi, Jeff Luini, and Aaron Lovell, "Nott Yet," Welcome to Wrexham, season 2, FX, September 19, 2023.

8 "Arrival | Armstrong Bolsters Spartans' Attacking Options with Langstaff Loan," *Blyth Spartans*, https://www.blythspartans.com/news/arrival-armstrong-bolsters-spartans-attacking-options-langstaff-loan (accessed June 19, 2025).

9 Simeon Gholam, "Macaulay Langstaff interview: Notts County striker on Erling Haaland, Jamie Vardy and being Wrexham's antagonist," *Sky Sports*, https://www.skysports.com/football/news/11095/13009526/macauley-langstaff-interview-notts-county-striker-on-erling-haaland-jamie-vardy-and-being-wrexhams-antagonist (accessed June 19, 2025).

10 Rory Smith, "The team trying to change the ending to Welcome to Wrexham," *The New York Times*, April 8, 2023, https://www.nytimes.com/2023/04/08/sports/soccer/welcome-to-wrexham-notts-county.html (accessed June 19, 2025).

11 Ryan O'Hanlon, "How Ryan Reynolds & Co. bought Wrexham's path to promotion," *ESPN*, https://www.espn.com/soccer/story/_/id/44940499/how-ryan-reynolds-co-bought-wrexhams-path-promotion (accessed June 19, 2025).

12 Leander Schaerlaeckens, "Wrexham's success shows that content is now truly king in football," *The Guardian*, May 13, 2025, https://www.theguardian.com/football/2025/may/13/welcome-to-wrexham-tv-series (accessed June 19, 2025).

13 Jared Evitts, "Wrexham: United Airlines replace TikTok on shirts," *BBC News*, https://www.bbc.com/news/uk-wales-65844028 (accessed June 19, 2025).

14 "Former Scottish International Steven Fletcher Signs for Wrexham AFC," *Wrexham AFC*, https://wrexham.com/news/steven-fletcher-signed-former-scottish-international-striker-snapped-up-on-free-transfer-239904.html (accessed June 19, 2025).

15 "County Trust deal is held up," *Manchester Evening News*, https://www.manchestereveningnews.co.uk/sport/football/football-news/county-trust-deal-is-held-up-1074548 (accessed June 19, 2025).

16 "Stockport enter administration after failing to pay creditors," *The Guardian*, April 30, 2009, https://www.theguardian.com/football/2009/apr/30/stockport-county-administration-football (accessed June 19, 2025).

17 "Second group in bid for Stockport," *Manchester Evening News*, https://www.manchestereveningnews.co.uk/sport/football/football-news/second-group-in-bid-for-stockport-886524 (accessed June 19, 2025).

18 Rob Dawson, "Nightmare ends with the dawn of new era," *Manchester Evening News*, April 22, 2013, https://archive.md/20130422042521/http://menmedia.co.uk/stockportexpress/sport/football/stockport_county/s/1263090_nightmare_ends_with_the_dawn_of_new_era (accessed June 19, 2025).

19 Beth Abbit, "Stockport County FC sold to businessman Mark Stott who was born and raised in the town," *Manchester Evening News*, https://www.manchestereveningnews.co.uk/news/greater-manchester-news/stockport-county-fc-sold-businessman-17582352 (accessed June 19, 2025).

20 "Roman Abramovich says he has not asked Chelsea to repay £1.5bn loan," *BBC Sport*, https://www.bbc.com/sport/football/61340324 (accessed June 19, 2025).

21 Brent Pilnick, "League One and Two owner investment to be restricted," *BBC Sport*, https://www.bbc.com/sport/football/articles/c36e4068113o (accessed June 19, 2025).

22 "Huddersfield Town: American businessman Kevin Nagle completes takeover," *BBC Sport*, https://www.bbc.com/sport/football/65992665 (accessed June 19, 2025).

23 "Carling Cup final: McLeish hails 'greatest achievement,'" *BBC Sport*, http://news.bbc.co.uk/sport2/hi/football/9407612.stm (accessed June 19, 2025).

24 "Birmingham City: Trillion Trophy Asia complete takeover of club," *BBC Sport*, https://www.bbc.com/sport/football/37677483 (accessed June 19, 2025).

25 Ged Scott and Richard Wilford, "Birmingham City: Blues owners 'have no intention to sell' Championship club—Zheng," *BBC Sport*, https://www.bbc.com/sport/football/60077060 (accessed June 19, 2025).

26 "Knighthead Capital Management LLC," *Fintel*, https://fintel.io/i/knighthead-capital-management-llc (accessed June 19, 2025).

27 Chris Wright, "What Birmingham fans think of co-owner, NFL legend Tom Brady," *ESPN*, https://www.espn.com/soccer/story/_/id/43819987/what-birmingham-fans-think-co-owner-nfl-legend-tom-brady (accessed June 19, 2025).

28 Brent Pilnick, "League One and Two owner investment to be restricted," *BBC Sport*, https://www.bbc.com/sport/football/articles/c36e4068113o (accessed June 19, 2025).

29 "Colchester boss Parkinson resigns," *BBC Sport*, http://news.bbc.co.uk/sport2/hi/football/teams/c/colchester_united/5081416.stm (accessed June 19, 2025).

30 Brent Pilnick, "League One and Two owner investment to be restricted," *BBC Sport*, https://www.bbc.com/sport/football/articles/c36e4068113o (accessed June 19, 2025).

31 Craig Johns, "Change in Championship's financial fair play rules provide a small boost for Middlesbrough," *Gazette Live*, https://www.gazettelive.co.uk/sport/football/transfer-news/change-championships-financial-fair-play-29254166 (accessed June 19, 2025).

32 Linda Yueh "Why on earth buy a football club?" *BBC News*, https://www.bbc.com/news/business-26365955 (accessed June 19, 2025).

33 Sean Ingle, Peter Walker, and Nick Ames, "European Super League collapsing as all six English clubs withdraw," *The Guardian*, April 20, 2021, https://www.theguardian.com/football/2021/apr/20/european-super-league-unravelling-as-manchester-city-and-chelsea-withdraw (accessed June 19, 2025).

Chapter 5

1 "The 10 most followed Instagram accounts in the world in 2025," *Forbes India*, https://www.forbesindia.com/article/explainers/most-followed-instagram-accounts-world/85649/1 (accessed June 23, 2025).

2   "Saudi Arabia's Eternal Rivalry: Al Hilal v Al Ittihad," *Asian Football Confederation*, https://www.the-afc.com/en/club/afc_champions_league/news/saudi_arabia%E2%80%99s_eternal_rivalry_al_hilal_v_al_ittihad.html (accessed June 23, 2025).

3   "Al-Ittihad," *Football History*, https://www.footballhistory.org/club/al-ittihad.html (accessed June 23, 2025).

4   Sulafa Alkhunaizi, "The long history of The Beautiful Game in Saudi Arabia," *Arab News*, https://www.arabnews.com/node/2572330/amp (accessed June 23, 2025).

5   "History of Arabia," *Encyclopædia Britannica*, https://www.britannica.com/EBchecked/topic/31568/history-of-arabia (accessed June 23, 2025).

6   Ofer Muchtar, "Saudi Arabia's Vision 2030: How soccer became the heart of a nation's ambition," *Ynet News*, https://www.ynetnews.com/article/s1b6qeji1g (accessed June 23, 2025).

7   Alistair Magowan, Dan Roan, and Laura Scott, "Newcastle United takeover deal worth £300m close," *BBC Sport*, https://www.bbc.co.uk/sport/football/52284645 (accessed June 23, 2025).

8   "A fit and proper Premiership?" *BBC Sport*, http://news.bbc.co.uk/sport2/hi/football/eng_prem/6923831.stm (accessed June 23, 2025).

9   Asa Bennett, "Louis Tomlinson's Doncaster Rovers Takeover Bid Falls Through," *Huffington Post UK*, https://www.huffingtonpost.co.uk/2014/07/17/louis-tomlinson-doncaster-rovers-deal_n_5595517.html (accessed June 23, 2025).

10 Paul MacInnes, "Premier League clubs ask government to block nation-state ownership," *The Guardian*, https://www.theguardian.com/football/2023/sep/07/premier-league-clubs-call-to-block-nation-state-ownership (accessed June 23, 2025).

11 Louise Taylor, "Bin Salman heavily involved in Newcastle takeover, messages suggest," *The Guardian*, https://www.theguardian.com/football/2024/oct/20/mohammed-bin-salman-newcastle-united-takeover-saudi-arabia-football (accessed June 23, 2025).

12 Alistair Magowan, "Newcastle takeover: Supporters' Trust wants Premier League 'transparency' on deal collapse," *BBC Sport*, https://www.bbc.com/sport/football/53662771 (accessed June 23, 2025).

13 "Newcastle: Boris Johnson backs calls for Premier League statement on failed takeover," *Sky Sports*, https://www.skysports.com/football/news/11678/12045046/newcastle-boris-johnson-backs-calls-for-premier-league-statement-on-failed-takeover (accessed June 23, 2025).

14 Steven Impey, "AFC cancels BeIN Sports rights in Saudi Arabia," *SportsPro*, https://www.sportspro.com/news/afc-cancels-bein-sports-rights-saudi-arabia (accessed June 23, 2025).

15 Steven Hawley, "MarkMonitor research released by UEFA & European football leagues traces beoutQ piracy," *Piracy Monitor*, https://piracymonitor.org/european-football-leagues-trace-beoutq-piracy (accessed June 23, 2025).

16 Alex Ritman, "Could This Be the World's Biggest State-Sponsored Piracy Operation?" *The Hollywood Reporter*, https://www.hollywoodreporter.com/business/business-news/could-be-worlds-biggest-state-sponsored-piracy-operation-1217919/ (accessed June 23, 2025).

17 "beoutQ: Notorious pirate is down, but its echo reverberates," *Piracy Monitor*, https://piracymonitor.org/the-impact-of-beoutq-piracy-on-bein-media/ (accessed June 23, 2025).

18 Martin Hardy and Martyn Ziegler, "Lawyers report urges Premier League to block Newcastle takeover," *The Times*, https://www.thetimes.co.uk/article/lawyers-report-urges-premier-league-to-block-newcastle-takeover-h5mv83jq3 (accessed June 23, 2025).

19 "Newcastle takeover: Premier League CEO Richard Masters breaks silence over Saudi-led deal," *Sky Sports*, https://www.skysports.com/football/news/11678/12049306/newcastle-takeover-premier-league-ceo-richard-masters-breaks-silence-over-saudi-led-deal (accessed June 23, 2025).

20 Alex Milne, "Richard Keys questions morality of proposed Newcastle United Saudi takeover," *Mirror*, https://www.mirror.co.uk/sport/football/news/richard-keys-questions-morality-proposed-21905507 (accessed June 23, 2025).

21 Martin Hardy and Martyn Ziegler, "Lawyers report urges Premier League to block Newcastle takeover," *The Times*, https://www.thetimes.co.uk/article/lawyers-report-urges-premier-league-to-block-newcastle-takeover-h5mv83jq3 (accessed June 23, 2025).

22 David Conn, "Revealed: government did encourage Premier League to approve Newcastle takeover," *The Guardian*, https://www.theguardian.com/football/2022/may/24/government-did-encourage-premier-league-to-approve-saudi-newcastle-takeover (accessed June 23, 2025).

23 David Conn and Lucas Amin, "Documents reveal Tory minister's push to smooth Saudi Newcastle takeover," *The Guardian*, https://www.theguardian.com/football/2022/sep/26/documents-reveal-tory-ministers-push-to-smooth-saudi-newcastle-takeover (accessed June 23, 2025).

24 Chi Onwurah, "Football: Takeovers," *UK Parliament*, https://questions-statements.parliament.uk/written-questions/detail/2021-04-15/181471 (accessed June 23, 2025).

25 "FP McCann Ltd directors disqualified over illegal construction cartel," *Scottish Construction Now*, https://www.scottishconstructionnow.com/articles/fp-mccann-ltd-directors-disqualified-over-illegal-construction-cartel (accessed June 23, 2025).

26. "Newcastle take Premier League to competition tribunal over takeover collapse," *BT Sport*, https://www.bt.com/sport/news/2021/may/newcastle-take-premier-league-to-competition-tribunal-over-takeover-collapse (accessed June 23, 2025).

27. "St James Holdings Limited v The Football Association Premier League Limited," *Competition Appeal Tribunal*, https://www.catribunal.org.uk/cases/14025721-st-james-holdings-limited (accessed June 23, 2025).

28. "Newcastle United: Club asks Premier League for arbitration claim against it to be heard in public," *BBC Sport*, https://www.bbc.com/sport/football/57689227 (accessed June 23, 2025).

29. "Newcastle fans 'kept in the dark' by Premier League amid ongoing takeover," *Sky Sports*, https://www.skysports.com/football/news/11678/12359153/newcastle-fans-kept-in-the-dark-by-premier-league-amid-ongoing-takeover (accessed June 23, 2025).

30. Louise Taylor, "Saudi Arabia takeover of Newcastle United will be decided in January," *The Guardian*, https://www.theguardian.com/football/2021/sep/29/saudi-arabia-takeover-of-newcastle-united-will-be-decided-in-january (accessed June 23, 2025).

31. "Newcastle takeover completed: Saudi-led consortium end Mike Ashley's 14-year ownership," Sky Sports, https://www.skysports.com/football/news/11678/12427983/newcastle-takeover-completed-saudi-led-consortium-end-mike-ashleys-14-year-ownership (accessed June 23, 2025).

32. Harry Booth, "Yasir Al-Rumayyan," *Time*, https://time.com/7012835/yasir-al-rumayyan-2 (accessed June 23, 2025).

33. "Market capitalization of Saudi Aramco," *Companies Market Cap*, https://companiesmarketcap.com/saudi-aramco/marketcap (accessed June 23, 2025).

34. "Fortune Global 500," *Fortune*, https://fortune.com/ranking/global500/ (accessed June 23, 2025).

35. James Chen, "Oil Reserves," *Investopedia*, https://www.investopedia.com/terms/o/oil-reserves.asp (accessed June 23, 2025).

36. Mark Schlabach, "Jay Monahan, Yasir Al-Rumayyan grouped together at Alfred Dunhill," *ESPN*, https://www.espn.com/golf/story/_/id/41586516/jay-monahan-yasir-al-rumayyan-grouped-together-alfred-dunhill (accessed June 23, 2025).

37. Shwetha Surendan, "What Messi's MLS, Apple, Adidas deal means for everyone else," *ESPN*, https://www.espn.com/soccer/story/_/id/37975000/lionel-messi-mls-apple-adidas-inter-miami (accessed June 23, 2025).

38. Adwaidh Rajan, "From Batistuta and Desailly to Xavi and Sneijder: Qatari football's highest-profile signings ever," *ESPN*, https://www.espn.com/soccer/story/_/id/37619440/batistuta-desailly-xavi-sneijder-qatari-football-highest-profile-signings-ever (accessed June 23, 2025).

39 Tommaso Fiore, "Cristiano Ronaldo: New Manchester United No 7 smashes shirt sale record and causes media frenzy," *Sky Sports*, https://www.skysports.com/football/news/11667/12400586/ronaldo-smashes-man-utd-shirt-sales (accessed June 23, 2025).

40 Ed Aarons, "Chelsea decide against signing Cristiano Ronaldo after talks with representatives," *The Guardian*, https://www.theguardian.com/football/2022/jul/14/chelsea-decide-against-signing-cristiano-ronaldo-after-talks-with-representatives (accessed June 23, 2025).

41 Tom Hamilton, "Man United manager Erik ten Hag: The 'tactically brilliant' coach who became a winner at Ajax," *ESPN*, https://www.espn.com/soccer/story/_/id/38680786/tactically-brilliant-coach-became-winner-ajax (accessed June 23, 2025).

42 "Cristiano Ronaldo: Erik ten Hag confirms striker refused to come on against Tottenham," *Sky Sports*, https://www.skysports.com/football/news/11667/12726200/cristiano-ronaldo-erik-ten-hag-confirms-striker-refused-to-come-on-against-tottenham (accessed June 23, 2025).

43 "Cristiano Ronaldo: Manchester United forward says he feels 'betrayed' and has 'no respect' for Erik ten Hag," *Sky Sports*, https://www.skysports.com/football/news/11667/12747058/cristiano-ronaldo-manchester-united-forward-says-he-feels-betrayed-and-has-no-respect-for-erik-ten-hag (accessed June 23, 2025).

44 Jamie Jackson, "Cristiano Ronaldo to leave Manchester United with immediate effect," *The Guardian*, https://www.theguardian.com/football/2022/nov/22/cristiano-ronaldo-to-leave-manchester-united-with-immediate-effect (accessed June 23, 2025).

45 "Kylian Mbappe beats Lionel Messi and Cristiano Ronaldo to top Forbes rich list," *BBC Sport*, https://www.bbc.com/sport/football/63178900 (accessed June 23, 2025).

46 Chris Burton, "Cristiano Ronaldo rules out January transfer: CR7 makes statement on Al-Nassr future as £177m contract in Saudi Pro League runs down," *Goal*, https://www.goal.com/en-us/lists/cristiano-ronaldo-rules-out-january-transfer-cr7-statement-al-nassr-future-177m-contract-saudi-pro-league-runs-down/blt82449f257e16ffbe (accessed June 23, 2025).

47 Fabrizio Romano, "Cristiano Ronaldo completes deal to join Saudi Arabian club Al Nassr," *The Guardian*, https://www.theguardian.com/football/2022/dec/30/cristiano-ronaldo-al-nassr-saudi-arabia (accessed June 23, 2025).

48 Justin Birnbaum, "The world's 10 highest paid athletes in 2024," *Forbes*, https://www.forbes.com/sites/justinbirnbaum/2024/05/16/the-worlds-10-highest-paid-athletes-2024/ (accessed June 23, 2025).

49 Ahmed Walid, "PIR to take control of Saudi Arabia's four biggest clubs as part of major shake-up in Pro League," *The New York Times*, https://www.nytimes.com/athletic/4581869/2023/06/05/saudi-arabia-pif-pro-league/ (accessed June 23, 2025).

50 Antonio Losada, "Saudi Arabia's PIF acquires Saudi Pro League four largest clubs," *Coming Home Newcastle*, https://cominghomenewcastle.sbnation.

com/2023/6/7/23750627/saudi-arabias-pif-acquires-saudi-pro-league-four-largest-clubs (accessed June 23, 2025).

51. Hall, S., Szymanski, S., and Zimbalist, A. S. "Testing causality between team performance and payroll: The cases of Major League Baseball and English soccer," *Journal of Sports Economics* 3, no. 2 (2002): 149–68.

52. Oliver Kay and Matt Slater, "Chinese Super League: From unprecedented salaries to uncertain restart dates, unpaid wages and deepening turmoil," *The New York Times*, https://www.nytimes.com/athletic/2981422/2021/11/28/the-chinese-super-league-from-unprecedented-salaries-to-uncertain-restart-date-unpaid-wages-and-deepening-turmoil/ (accessed June 23, 2025).

53. Dan Sheldon, "Saudi Pro League eyes global TV deal after Ronaldo and Benzema arrivals," *The New York Times*, https://www.nytimes.com/athletic/4643603/2023/06/27/saudi-pro-league-tv-deal-transfers/ (accessed June 23, 2025).

54. Christopher Harris, "Saudi Pro League signs FOX deal to bring Ronaldo to US TV," *World Soccer Talk*, https://worldsoccertalk.com/tv/saudi-pro-league-signs-fox-deal-to-bring-ronaldo-to-us-tv-20230809-WST-448998.html (accessed June 23, 2025).

55. Scott Polacek, "Cristiano Ronaldo Says 'Chapter Is Over' in IG Photo Amid Expiring Al Nassr Contract," *Bleacher Report*, https://bleacherreport.com/articles/25199525-cristiano-ronaldo-says-chapter-over-ig-photo-amid-expiring-al-nassr-contract (accessed June 23, 2025).

56. James Robson, "Ronaldo declares 'Al Nassr forever' after signing a two-year deal to stay in Saudi Arabia," *Yahoo Sports*, https://sports.yahoo.com/article/cristiano-ronaldo-signs-contract-al-135223195.html (accessed June 23, 2025).

57. Kyle Bonn, "Cristiano Ronaldo salary: How much CR7 is paid with reports of new Al Nassr contract in Saudi Arabia," *Sporting News*, https://www.sportingnews.com/us/soccer/news/cristiano-ronaldo-salary-saudi-arabia-contract-net-worth/acb5hk0gkqdl1yxwfmhrupfx (accessed June 23, 2025).

Chapter 6

1. "1885 Chicago White Stockings Statistics," *Baseball-Reference*, https://www.baseball-reference.com/teams/CHC/1885.shtml (accessed June 28, 2025).

2. "Thomas Sørensen—Detailed stats," *Transfermarkt*, https://www.transfermarkt.us/thomas-sorensen/leistungsdatendetails/spieler/3473/plus/0/saison/2003/wettbewerb/GB1/verein/405 (accessed June 28, 2025).

3. Cameron Smith, "How much have Man City spent on transfers under Sheikh Mansour?" *Football Transfers*, https://www.footballtransfers.com/us/transfer-news/uk-premier-league/2023/09/man-city-sheikh-mansour-abu-dhabi-group-total-spending-transfer-fees-signings-us (accessed June 28, 2025).

4   "Opportunities in Football," *Barclays Private Bank*, https://privatebank.barclays.com/news-and-insights/2019/december/opportunities-in-football/ (accessed June 28, 2025).

5   Owen Gibson & Philip Oltermann, "Is Katharina Liebherr, Southampton's owner, in it for the long term?" *The Guardian*, https://www.theguardian.com/football/2014/jan/16/katharina-liebherr-southampton-football-owner-german-markus (accessed June 28, 2025).

6   Ben Fisher, "Southampton sell 80% stake to Chinese businessman Gao Jisheng," *The Guardian*, https://www.theguardian.com/football/2017/aug/14/southampton-sell-80-stake-to-chinese-businessman-gao-jisheng (accessed June 28, 2025).

7   Ben Alamar, "Rockets, Spurs lead the way in NBA draft analytics," *ESPN*, https://www.espn.com/nba/story/_/id/23762871/rockets-spurs-celtics-most-analytical-draft-teams-nba (accessed June 28, 2025).

8   "The Great Analytics Rankings," *ESPN*, https://www.espn.com/espn/feature/story/_/id/12331388/the-great-analytics-rankings (accessed June 28, 2025).

9   Barry Anderson, "Inside Tony Bloom's algorithms: How it works & what Hearts can expect from Brighton's maths genius," *Edinburgh News*, https://www.edinburghnews.scotsman.com/sport/football/hearts/inside-tony-blooms-algorithms-how-it-works-what-hearts-can-expect-from-brightons-maths-genius-4786037 (accessed June 28, 2025).

10 Barry Anderson, "Inside Tony Bloom's algorithms: How it works & what Hearts can expect from Brighton's maths genius," *Edinburgh News*, https://www.edinburghnews.scotsman.com/sport/football/hearts/inside-tony-blooms-algorithms-how-it-works-what-hearts-can-expect-from-brightons-maths-genius-4786037 (accessed June 28, 2025).

11 Andy Naylor and Jay Harris, "'A Cold War' the rivalry between Brighton's Tony Blood and Matthew Benham at Brentford," *The Athletic*, https://theathletic.com/3029279/2021/12/24/cold-war-brighton-tony-bloom-matthew-benham-brentford (accessed June 28, 2025).

12 Kieran King, "Why Brighton and Brentford's Europe-chasing owners haven't spoken to each other since 2004," *Mirror*, https://www.mirror.co.uk/sport/football/news/brentford-brighton-premier-league-owners-29595764 (accessed June 28, 2025).

13 Andy Naylor and Jay Harris, "'A Cold War' the rivalry between Brighton's Tony Blood and Matthew Benham at Brentford," *The Athletic*, https://theathletic.com/3029279/2021/12/24/cold-war-brighton-tony-bloom-matthew-benham-brentford/ (accessed June 28, 2025).

14 Oscar Williams-Gut, "Inside Starlizard: The story of Britain's most successful gambler and the secretive company that helps him win," *Yahoo Finance UK*, https://uk.finance.yahoo.com/news/inside-starlizard-story-britains-most-090759947.html (accessed June 28, 2025).

15   "Opta Data," *Stats Perform*, https://www.statsperform.com/opta (accessed June 28, 2025).

16   Tom Hancock, "Germany 1-2 Japan: New World Cup, Same Opening Result for Four-Time Winners," *The Analyst*, https://theanalyst.com/2022/11/germany-japan-world-cup-2022-stats (accessed June 28, 2025).

17   "Brentford score in first minute for record third straight game," *ESPN*, https://www.espn.com/soccer/story/_/id/41491698/brentford-score-first-minute-record-third-straight-game (accessed June 28, 2025).

18   Stephen Gillett, "Quality over quantity: Brentford leading the way in Premier League xG per shot statistic," *Brentford FC*, https://www.brentfordfc.com/en/news/article/analysis-xg-per-shot-premier-league-brentford (accessed June 28, 2025).

19   Jayson Stark, "Theo Epstein and his historic journey back to Fenway Park," *The New York Times*, https://www.nytimes.com/athletic/5249104/2024/02/03/theo-epstein-historic-journey-red-sox (accessed June 28, 2025).

20   Sean Ingle, "Billy Beane can't get enough of soccer after revolutionising baseball," *The Guardian*, https://www.theguardian.com/sport/2014/oct/17/billy-beane-soccer-baseball-oakland (accessed June 28, 2025).

21   Tom Hamilton, "Moneyball guru Billy Beane buys minority stake in Dutch club Alkmaar," *ESPN*, https://www.espn.com/soccer/story/_/id/37586707/moneyball-guru-billy-beane-buys-minority-stake-dutch-club-alkmaar (accessed June 28, 2025).

22   Simon Stone, "West Ham v AZ Alkmaar: The Dutch Moneyball team chasing Europa Conference victory," *BBC Sport*, https://www.bbc.com/sport/football/65549007 (accessed June 28, 2025).

Chapter 7

1   "FIFA Club World Cup 2025™: Record prize money and unprecedented solidarity to benefit club football," *FIFA*, https://www.fifa.com/en/tournaments/mens/club-world-cup/usa-2025/articles/record-prize-money-solidarity (accessed June 28, 2025).

2   Matt Hughes, "Fifa ready to discuss staging 48-team Club World Cup after lobbying from Europe," *The Guardian*, June 11, 2025, https://www.theguardian.com/football/2025/jun/11/fifa-48-team-club-world-cup-europe (accessed June 28, 2025).

3   Kevin G. Quinn, *The Economics of the National Football League: The State of the Art* (New York: Springer Science & Business Media, 2011), 338.

4   Peter Ball, "Premier League unity is tested by an offer of £34m," *The Times*, April 18, 1992.

5   Jason Rodrigues, "Premier League football at 20: 1992, the start of a whole new ball game," *The Guardian*, February 2, 2012, https://www.theguardian.com/football/from-the-archive-blog/2012/feb/02/20-years-premier-league-football-1992 (accessed June 28, 2025).

6   T. H. Davenport and J. C. Beck, "The attention economy," *Ubiquity* 2001, May (2001): 1–es.

7   Paul MacInnes, "Premier League agrees new £6.7bn TV rights deal with Sky and TNT Sports," *The Guardian*, December 4, 2023, https://www.theguardian.com/football/2023/dec/04/premier-league-agrees-67bn-tv-rights-deal-with-sky-and-tnt-sports (accessed June 28, 2025).

8   Peter Scrimgeour, "NBA nets more media value with new domestic rights," *Sportcal*, https://www.sportcal.com/analyst-comment/nba-nets-more-media-value-with-new-domestic-rights (accessed June 28, 2025).

9   Charlotte Coates, "Premier League TV viewing figures drop on Sky and TNT," *BBC Sport*, https://www.bbc.com/sport/football/articles/cwyj7506y5jo (accessed June 28, 2025).

10 Adam White, "Ligue 1 clubs stare into financial abyss after huge TV deal collapses," *The Guardian*, December 15, 2020, https://www.theguardian.com/football/2020/dec/15/ligue-1-clubs-stare-financial-abyss-tv-deal-collapses-mediapro (accessed June 28, 2025).

11 "Mediapro CEO Jaume Roures on cancelling multi-billion pound Ligue 1 broadcast deal," *The New York Times*, February 2, 2023, https://www.nytimes.com/athletic/4130823/2023/02/02/jaume-roures-ligue-1-broadcast-deal/ (accessed June 28, 2025).

12 "Olympique Lyonnais provisionally relegated to Ligue 2," *One Football*, https://onefootball.com/en/news/olympique-lyonnais-provisionally-relegated-to-ligue-2-40313863 (accessed June 28, 2025).

13 Matt Hughes, "BBC and ITV opt against bids to televise Fifa Club World Cup in summer," *The Guardian*, April 4, 2025, https://www.theguardian.com/football/2025/apr/04/bbc-and-itv-opt-against-bids-to-televise-fifa-club-world-cup-dazn (accessed June 28, 2025).

14 Nick Vivarelli, "DAZN Sells Minority Stake to Saudi Arabia's Surj Sports Investment in Landmark $1 Billion Deal," *Variety*, https://variety.com/2025/tv/news/dazn-saudi-arabia-surj-sports-investment-1billion-deal-1236311715 (accessed June 28, 2025).

15 "FIFA adds Saudi Arabia's PIF as Club World Cup partner," *ESPN*, https://www.espn.com/soccer/story/_/id/45458889/fifa-club-world-cup-usa-saudi-arabia-sovereign-wealth-fund (accessed June 28, 2025).

16 José Escobar, "Messi No Longer Sells Tickets and Prices Drop for the Club World Cup Opener Between Inter Miami and Al-Ahly," *beIN Sports*, June 5, 2025, https://www.beinsports.com/en-us/soccer/fifa-club-world-cup/articles-video/messi-no-

longer-sells-tickets-and-prices-drop-for-the-club-world-cup-opener-between-inter-miami-and-al-ahly-2025-06-05 (accessed June 28, 2025).

17. The Clash, "London Calling," Epic Records, 1979.

18. Maxime Jody, "Welcome to the Kylian Mbappé era," *GQ Magazine UK*, https://www.gq-magazine.co.uk/article/kylian-mbappe-interview-2024 (accessed July 9, 2025).

19. Eric Fisher, "Yellow Card: Soccer Stars Warn of Load Management Concerns," *Front Office Sports*, https://frontofficesports.com/yellow-card-soccer-stars-warn-of-load-management-concerns/ (accessed July 9, 2025).

20. Jacob Schneider, "Former USMNT defender Jimmy Conrad: Christian Pulisic skipping Gold Cup is 'disappointing,' but spotlight should be on U.S. players on the roster," *Goal*, https://www.goal.com/en/lists/usmnt-jimmy-conrad-christian-pulisic-gold-cup/bltffde83cbb4ed3c26 (accessed July 9, 2025).

21. Jonathan Harding, "Bayern Munich's Kim Min-jae pushed beyond his limit," *Deutsche Welle*, https://www.dw.com/en/bayern-munichs-kim-min-jae-pushed-beyond-his-limit/a-72273074 (accessed July 9, 2025).

22. "Achilles Tendinitis," Cleveland Clinic, https://my.clevelandclinic.org/health/diseases/21553-achilles-tendinitis (accessed July 9, 2025).

23. "FC Bayern calls for more effective compliance with protection obligations by national associations," *FC Bayern*, June 2025, https://fcbayern.com/en/news/2025/06/fc-bayern-calls-for-more-effective-compliance-with-protection-obligations-by-national-associations-following-alphonso-davies-injury (accessed July 9, 2025).

24. "2020-2021 Premier League Salaries and Contracts," *Capology*, https://www.capology.com/uk/premier-league/salaries/2020-2021 (accessed July 9, 2025).

25. "FIFA Club World Cup 2025™: Record prize money and unprecedented solidarity to benefit club football," *FIFA*, https://www.fifa.com/en/tournaments/mens/club-world-cup/usa-2025/articles/record-prize-money-solidarity (accessed July 9, 2025).

26. Ed Dixon, "PIF sponsors Club World Cup as Fifa deepens Saudi ties," *SportsPro*, https://www.sportspro.com/news/club-world-cup-pif-fifa-saudi-arabia-sponsorship-gianni-infantino-june-2025 (accessed July 9, 2025).

27. Tom Bogert, Twitter post, https://twitter.com/tombogert?ref_src=twsrc%5Etfw%7Ctwcamp%5Etweetembed%7Ctwterm%5E1929299010814140492%7Ctwgr%5E6bab3bb09c1a846969a4abe57fc1ec2ae53c1237%7Ctwcon%5Es1_&ref_url=https%3A%2F%2Fwww.givemesport.com%2Fseattle-sounders-owner-angrily-confronts-players-for-club-world-cup-protest%2F (accessed July 9, 2025).

28. Chuck Booth, "Seattle Sounders' FIFA Club World Cup protest explained: MLS side accuse governing body of 'cash grab'," *CBS Sports*, https://www.cbssports.com/soccer/news/seattle-sounders-fifa-club-world-cup-protest-explained-mls-side-accuse-governing-body-of-cash-grab (accessed July 9, 2025).

29 Jayda Evans, "Sounders owner confronts team after Sunday's protest over Club World Cup payout," *Seattle Times*, https://www.seattletimes.com/sports/sounders/sounders-owner-angrily-addresses-team-after-sundays-protest-over-club-world-cup-payout/ (accessed July 9, 2025).

30 Alexander Abnos, "Players union condemns MLS's Club World Cup prize money offer," *The Guardian*, June 8, 2025, https://www.theguardian.com/football/2025/jun/08/mls-club-world-cup-prize-money-proposal (accessed July 9, 2025).

Chapter 8

1 Clay Johnson, "My favourite game: Liverpool v Wimbledon 1988 FA Cup final," *The Guardian*, May 2, 2020, https://www.theguardian.com/football/2020/may/02/my-favourite-game-liverpool-v-wimbledon-1988-fa-cup-final (accessed July 11, 2025).

2 Luke Reddy, "Wimbledon v Liverpool: How the Crazy Gang made FA Cup history," *BBC Sport*, https://www.bbc.com/sport/football/30637342 (accessed July 11, 2025).

3 Luke Reddy, "Wimbledon v Liverpool: How the Crazy Gang made FA Cup history," *BBC Sport*, https://www.bbc.com/sport/football/30637342 (accessed July 11, 2025).

4 Sandeep Menon, "The tale of Crazy Gang," *Deccan Herald*, https://www.deccanherald.com/sports/the-tale-of-crazy-gang-781390.html (accessed July 11, 2025).

5 Mihir Bose, "Inside Sport: Hammam cast in villain's role as Dons seek happy ending," *The Telegraph*, April 21, 2013, https://archive.md/20130421092913/http://www.telegraph.co.uk/sport/football/leagues/championship/3010879/Inside-Sport-Hammam-cast-in-villains-role-as-Dons-seek-happy-ending.html (accessed July 11, 2025).

6 Stephen Morrow, *The People's Game?: Football, Finance and Society* (Basingstoke: Palgrave Macmillan, 2003).

7 "WISA files," *Wimbledon Independent Supporters' Association*, May 30, 2002, https://web.archive.org/web/20120205212904/http://www.wisa.org.uk/cgi/l/files/20020530_fa.pdf (accessed July 11, 2025).

8 "Dons get Milton Keynes green light," *BBC Sport*, http://news.bbc.co.uk/sport2/hi/football/teams/w/wimbledon/2012312.stm (accessed July 11, 2025).

9 Jim White, "Pitch battle," *The Guardian*, January 11, 2003, https://www.theguardian.com/football/2003/jan/11/clubsincrisis.sport (accessed July 11, 2025).

10 Alastair Moffitt, "Dons chief shrugs off lowest ever crowd," *The Guardian*, October 31, 2002, https://www.theguardian.com/football/2002/oct/31/newsstory.

sport3 (accessed July 11, 2025).

11 "Wimbledon go into administration," *The Telegraph*, https://www.telegraph.co.uk/sport/2405494/Wimbledon-go-into-administration.html (accessed July 11, 2025).

12 "Spurs join Charlton in Wimbledon snub," *BBC Three Counties*, May 9, 2003, https://web.archive.org/web/20060619162326/http://www.bbc.co.uk/threecounties/sport/2003/05/09/spurs_snub.shtml (accessed July 11, 2025).

13 "Wimbledon get the OK," *BBC Three Counties*, September 18, 2003, https://web.archive.org/web/20050311222815/http://www.bbc.co.uk/threecounties/sport/2003/09/18/wimbledon_stadium_decision.shtml (accessed July 11, 2025).

14 "AFC Wimbledon set English record," *BBC Sport*, http://news.bbc.co.uk/sport1/hi/football/4010137.stm (accessed July 11, 2025).

15 Steve Marshall, "AFC Wimbledon 0-0 Luton Town (4-3 on pens)," *BBC Sport*, https://www.bbc.com/sport/football/13418508 (accessed July 11, 2025).

16 "Plough Lane: AFC Wimbledon say they need further £11m to complete new stadium," *BBC Sport*, https://www.bbc.com/sport/football/50564661 (accessed July 11, 2025).

17 "Borussia Dortmund: why are they the best-supported, most fun, coolest club in the world?" *Bundesliga*, https://www.bundesliga.com/en/bundesliga/news/why-are-borussia-dortmund-best-supported-most-fun-coolest-club-in-the-world-5582 (accessed July 11, 2025).

18 Richard J. Evans, *The Coming of the Third Reich* (New York: Penguin Press, 2003).

19 Ali Rampling, "Borussia Dortmund fans protest Champions League reforms with banners and fake money during Newcastle game," *The New York Times*, November 8, 2023, https://www.nytimes.com/athletic/5043334/2023/11/08/borussia-dortmund-champions-league-protest-reform (accessed July 11, 2025).

20 "Borussia Dortmund Fans Protest Against Possible Mario Gotze Return," *beIN Sports*, https://www.beinsports.com/en-us/soccer/bundesliga/articles/borussia-dortmund-fans-protest-against-possib (accessed July 11, 2025).

21 Constantin Eckner, "Dortmund fans riled by Klopp's Red Bull move," *BBC Sport*, https://www.bbc.com/sport/football/articles/c89l5xx8n1xo (accessed July 11, 2025).

22 "Rheinmetall sponsorship gnaws away at Borussia Dortmund fans," *Deutsche Welle*, https://www.dw.com/en/rheinmetall-sponsorship-gnaws-away-at-borussia-dortmund-fans/a-69215812 (accessed July 11, 2025).

23 Viktoria Koenigs, "Munition für die Ukraine: Rheinmetall baut Standort in Unterlüß aus," *NDR*, https://www.ndr.de/nachrichten/niedersachsen/lueneburg_heide_unterelbe/Rheinmetall-legt-Grundstein-fuer-neues-Munitionswerk-in-

Unterluess,rheinmetall260.html (accessed July 11, 2025).

24 Giovanna Coi, Joshua Posaner, and Ali Walker, "German weapons-maker loses Champions League final," *Politico*, https://www.politico.eu/article/german-weapons-maker-rheinmetall-borussia-dortmund-champions-league-final (accessed July 11, 2025).

25 "Borussia Dortmund members vote against Rheinmetall sponsorship deal," *Yahoo Sports*, https://sports.yahoo.com/borussia-dortmund-members-vote-against-172727005.html (accessed July 11, 2025).

26 Giovanna Coi, Joshua Posaner, and Ali Walker, "German weapons-maker loses Champions League final," *Politico*, https://www.politico.eu/article/german-weapons-maker-rheinmetall-borussia-dortmund-champions-league-final (accessed July 11, 2025).

27 Jonny Lambe, "The Kult club of German football are back in the big time: FC St Pauli 2024/25 season preview," *Vavel*, August 20, 2024, https://www.vavel.com/en/international-football/2024/08/20/germany-bundesliga/1193276-the-kult-club-of-german-football-are-back-in-the-big-time-fc-st-pauli-202425-season-preview.html (accessed July 11, 2025).

28 "The Reeperbahn: A walk along the once 'most sinful mile in the world,'" *Entdecke Deutschland*, https://entdecke-deutschland.de/en/bundeslaender/hamburg/the-reeperbahn-a-walk-over-the-most-successful-mile-in-the-world (accessed July 11, 2025).

29 "The Reeperbahn: A walk along the once "most sinful mile in the world,'" Entdecke Deutschland, https://entdecke-deutschland.de/en/bundeslaender/hamburg/the-reeperbahn-a-walk-over-the-most-successful-mile-in-the-world (accessed July 11, 2025).

30 "St. Pauli: German football's cult club explained" *Bundesliga*, https://www.bundesliga.com/en/bundesliga/news/st-pauli-hamburg-cult-club-explained-hurzeler-promotion-reeperbahn-millerntor-1471 (accessed July 11, 2025).

31 Uli Hesse, "St Pauli: the club that stands for all the right things ... except winning," *The Guardian*, September 6, 2015, https://www.theguardian.com/football/blog/2015/sep/06/st-pauli-club-that-stands-for-all-the-right-things-except-winning (accessed July 11, 2025).

32 Harry Poole, "St Pauli: The cult German football club that wants to change the game forever," *BBC Sport*, https://www.bbc.com/sport/football/53078948 (accessed July 11, 2025).

33 "Germany's cult clubs explained: St. Pauli, Union Berlin and Co.," *Bundesliga*, https://www.bundesliga.com/en/bundesliga/news/germany-s-cult-clubs-explained-st-pauli-union-berlin-and-co-19103 (accessed July 11, 2025).

34 "FC St. Pauli—The Original St. Pauli Skinheads," *JSTOR*, https://www.jstor.org/stable/community.13458838 (accessed July 11, 2025).

Notes

35 "FCSP cooperative raises almost 29.2 million euro," *FC St. Pauli*, https://www.fcstpauli.com/en/news/published/fcsp-cooperative-raises-almost-292-million-euros (accessed July 11, 2025).

36 Uli Hesse, "St Pauli: the club that stands for all the right things… except winning," *The Guardian*, September 6, 2015, https://www.theguardian.com/football/blog/2015/sep/06/st-pauli-club-that-stands-for-all-the-right-things-except-winning (accessed July 11, 2025).

37 Nick Ames, "'A hate machine': St Pauli become first major football club to leave X," *The Guardian*, November 14, 2024, https://www.theguardian.com/football/2024/nov/14/st-pauli-leave-x-first-major-football-club (accessed July 11, 2025).

38 "St Pauli to install rainbow-coloured solar panels on Millerntor-Stadion stand roof," *Bundesliga*, https://www.bundesliga.com/en/bundesliga/news/st-pauli-rainbow-solar-panels-millerntor-stadion-lgbtq-gay-pride-32424 (accessed July 11, 2025).

39 "Hosts appointed for FIFA World Cups 2030 and 2034," *FIFA*, https://www.fifa.com/en/tournaments/mens/worldcup/articles/2030-2034-host-nations-confirmed (accessed July 11, 2025).

40 Ryan Baldi, "Fifa again under scrutiny for World Cup's increased carbon footprint," *The Guardian*, June 18, 2025, https://www.theguardian.com/football/2025/jun/18/fifa-again-under-scrutiny-for-a-world-cups-increased-carbon-footprint (accessed July 11, 2025).

41 "Qatar World Cup: Fifa 'made false statements' about carbon-neutral tournament, says Swiss regulato," *BBC Sport*, https://www.bbc.com/sport/football/65834022 (accessed July 11, 2025).

42 Dominic Perry, "Ecojet delays launch until 2025 but insists it is building for the long term," *Flight Global*, https://www.flightglobal.com/air-transport/ecojet-delays-launch-until-2025-but-insists-it-is-building-for-the-long-term/159913.article (accessed July 11, 2025).

43 John Vidal, "'Smashing the Noddy stereotype'—UK's first green supercar takes to the roads," *The Guardian*, November 5, 2010, https://www.theguardian.com/environment/2010/nov/05/uk-first-green-supercar (accessed July 11, 2025).

44 Sarah Phaedre Watson, "Dale Vince on why he's launching vegan food in schools, and what he's up to next," *Stroud News and Journal*, https://www.stroudnewsandjournal.co.uk/news/17492491.dale-vince-launching-vegan-food-schools-next (accessed July 11, 2025).

45 "Burger ban begins at Forest Green Rovers football club," *BBC News*, https://www.bbc.com/news/uk-england-gloucestershire-12416671 (accessed July 11, 2025).

46 "Climate change: Do I need to stop eating meat?" *BBC News*, https://www.bbc.com/news/explainers-59232599 (accessed July 11, 2025).

47 "Forest Green Rovers spread manure on football pitch," *BBC News*, https://www.bbc.com/news/uk-england-gloucestershire-13776435 (accessed July 11, 2025).

48 "Forest Green Rovers football club installs solar panels," *BBC News*, https://www.bbc.com/news/uk-england-gloucestershire-16022775 (accessed July 11, 2025).

49 "Robot lawn mower used by Forest Green Rovers football club," *BBC News*, https://www.bbc.com/news/uk-england-gloucestershire-17791690 (accessed July 11, 2025).

50 "Football club goes vegan in 'world first,'" *BBC News*, https://www.bbc.com/news/uk-england-gloucestershire-34680213 (accessed July 11, 2025).

51 Steven Morris, "Forest Green Rovers named world's first UN certified carbon-neutral football club," *The Guardian*, July 30, 2018, https://www.theguardian.com/football/2018/jul/30/forest-green-rovers-named-worlds-first-un-certified-carbon-neutral-football-club (accessed July 11, 2025).

52 "Forest Green Rovers named 'greenest football club in world,'" *BBC News*, https://www.bbc.com/news/uk-england-gloucestershire-45677536 (accessed July 11, 2025).

53 David Ornstein and James McNicholas, "Exclusive: Hector Bellerin invests in Forest Green Rovers," *The New York Times*, September 8, 2020, https://www.nytimes.com/athletic/2048466/2020/09/08/hector-bellerin-arsenal-forest-green-rovers (accessed July 11, 2025).

54 "Dale Vince: Forest Green Rovers using 'Moneyball' model," *BBC Sport*, https://www.bbc.com/sport/football/34186514 (accessed July 11, 2025).

55 Rob Stevens, "Visit Rwanda signs new deal as Arsenal protests continue," *BBC Sport*, https://www.bbc.com/sport/football/articles/c15v10l5w2go (accessed July 11, 2025).

56 "DR Congo: Rwanda-backed M23 Executed Civilians in Goma," *Human Rights Watch*, June 3, 2025, https://www.hrw.org/news/2025/06/03/dr-congo-rwanda-backed-m23-executed-civilians-goma (accessed July 11, 2025).

57 Tim Wigmore, "Gambling has a stranglehold on football—and it is tightening," *The Telegraph*, February 17, 2025, https://www.telegraph.co.uk/football/2025/02/17/football-betting-gambling-premier-league-bookmakers (accessed July 11, 2025).

58 "AFC Wimbledon X War Child," *War Child UK*, https://www.warchild.org.uk/news/afc-wimbledon-x-war-child (accessed July 11, 2025).

Chapter 9

1 Josh Niland, "NEOM's The Line is getting its own $186M concrete factory," *Archinect*, https://archinect.com/news/article/150450143/neom-s-the-line-is-getting-its-own-186m-concrete-factory (accessed July 11, 2025).

2 "FIFA issues glowing Saudi 2034 World Cup report despite human rights fears," *The Guardian*, November 30, 2024, https://www.theguardian.com/football/2024/nov/30/fifa-saudi-arabia-2034-world-cup-football-evaluation-report (accessed July 11, 2025).

3   "'Die First, and I'll Pay You Later' Saudi Arabia's 'Giga-Projects' Built on Widespread Labor Abuses," *Human Rights Watch*, December 4, 2024, https://www.hrw.org/report/2024/12/04/die-first-and-ill-pay-you-later/saudi-arabias-giga-projects-built-widespread (accessed July 11, 2025).

4   "Saudi Arabia 2024," Amnesty International, https://www.amnesty.org/en/location/middle-east-and-north-africa/middle-east/saudi-arabia/report-saudi-arabia (accessed July 11, 2025).

5   "Saudi Arabia Events of 2023," *Human Rights Watch*, https://www.hrw.org/world-report/2024/country-chapters/saudi-arabia (accessed July 11, 2025).

6   Tom Dart, "How many migrant workers have died in Qatar? What we know about the human cost of the 2022 World Cup" *The Guardian*, November 27, 2022, https://www.theguardian.com/football/2022/nov/27/qatar-deaths-how-many-migrant-workers-died-world-cup-number-toll (accessed July 11, 2025).

7   Tom Pashby, "Saudi Arabia calls reports of 21,000 construction worker deaths 'misinformation,'" *New Civil Engineer*, November 6, 2024, https://www.newcivilengineer.com/latest/saudi-arabia-calls-reports-of-21000-construction-worker-deaths-misinformation-06-11-2024 (accessed July 11, 2025).

8   "United States of America 2024," *Amnesty International*, https://www.amnesty.org/en/location/americas/north-america/united-states-of-america/report-united-states-of-america (accessed July 11, 2025).

9   "Jamal Khashoggi: All you need to know about Saudi journalist's death" *BBC News*, https://www.bbc.com/news/world-europe-45812399 (accessed July 11, 2025).

10 Rachel Treisman, "5 years after Khashoggi's murder, advocates say the lack of justice is dangerous," *NPR*, October 2, 2023, https://www.npr.org/2023/10/02/1202937036/jamal-khashoggi-mbs-murder-saudi-arabia-human-rights (accessed July 11, 2025).

11 Phil Stewart, "U.S. imposes sanctions, visa bans on Saudis for journalist Khashoggi's killing," *Reuters*, https://www.reuters.com/article/us-usa-saudi-khashoggi-sanctions/u-s-imposes-sanctions-visa-bans-on-saudis-for-journalist-khashoggis-killing-idUSKBN2AQ2QI (accessed July 11, 2025).

12 J. Mahoney and K. Alboaouh, "Religious and Political Authority in The Kingdom of Saudi Arabia: Challenges and Prospects," *MANAS Sosyal Araştırmalar Dergisi* 6, no. 2 (2017): 241–57.

13 Borzou Daragahi, "'People are leaving': Gulf investors wary after Khashoggi murder and British 'spy' detention," *The Independent*, https://www.independent.co.uk/news/world/middle-east/gulf-investment-saudi-arabia-uae-khashoggi-murder-mattew-hedges-mbs-emirates-economy-a8711771.html (accessed July 11, 2025).

14 Ed Pilkington, "Sir Richard Branson suspends Saudi business talks over Khashoggi affair," *The Guardian*, October 11, 2018, https://www.theguardian.com/business/2018/oct/11/sir-richard-branson-suspends-saudi-business-talks-over-khashoggi-affair (accessed July 11, 2025).

15. Marwa Rashad and Stephen Kalin, "Foreign investment in Saudi Arabia more than doubled in 2018: minister," *Reuters*, https://www.reuters.com/article/economy/foreign-investment-in-saudi-arabia-more-than-doubled-in-2018-minister-idUSKBN1OI0QT (accessed July 11, 2025).

16. "Foreign Investment in Saudi Arabia," *Andersen*, https://sa.andersen.com/foreign-investment-in-saudi-arabia (accessed July 11, 2025).

17. Stefania Bianchi, "The Key Questions asked about Saudi Arabia's $2 Trillion fund," *Bloomberg*, May 25, 2016, https://www.bloomberg.com/news/articles/2016-05-25/key-questions-raised-by-the-2-trillion-saudi-wealth-fund-plan (accessed July 11, 2025).

18. Alexis Montambault Trudelle, "Towards a sociology of state investment funds? sovereign wealth funds and state-business relations in Saudi Arabia," *New Political Economy* 28, no. 3 (2023): 380–97.

19. Davide Barbuscia, "Abu Dhabi Power to take control of TAQA in asset swap," *Reuters*, https://www.reuters.com/article/us-taqa-m-a-adpower-idUSKBN1ZX0JB (accessed July 11, 2025).

20. Stefania Spezzati, Paritosh Bansal, and America Hernandez, "Exclusive: Qatar fund explored claims against Switzerland for Credit Suisse losses," *Reuters*, May 17, 2023, https://www.reuters.com/business/finance/qatar-fund-explored-claims-against-switzerland-credit-suisse-losses-2023-05-17 (accessed July 11, 2025).

21. "Credit Suisse: Saudi Arabia and Qatar set to lose big after UBS deal," *Middle East Eye*, https://www.middleeasteye.net/news/credit-suisse-saudi-arabia-qatar-lose-big-investment (accessed July 11, 2025).

22. Natasha Turak, "Saudi National Bank loses over $1 billion on Credit Suisse investment," *CNBC*, March 20, 2023, https://www.cnbc.com/2023/03/20/saudi-national-bank-loses-over-1-billion-on-credit-suisse-investment.html (accessed July 11, 2025).

23. Glenn Peoples, "Saudi Arabia's Public Investment Fund Sold Its Entire Live Nation Stake," *Billboard*, https://www.billboard.com/pro/saudi-arabia-public-investment-fund-sells-live-nation-shares (accessed July 11, 2025).

24. Sam Meredith, "World's largest sovereign wealth fund posts $138 billion in first-half profit as AI demand boosts tech," *CNBC*, August 14, 2024, https://www.cnbc.com/2024/08/14/worlds-largest-sovereign-wealth-fund-posts-138-billion-in-h1-profit.html (accessed July 11, 2025).

25. Kate Kelly and Vivian Nereim, "All about the deep pocketed Saudi wealth fund that rocked golf," *The New York Times*, June 7, 2023, https://www.nytimes.com/2023/06/07/world/middleeast/saudi-arabia-sovereign-wealth-fund.html (accessed July 11, 2025).

26. "Dragon Ball Theme Park," *Qiddiya*, https://qiddiya.com/qiddiya-city/dragon-ball (accessed July 11, 2025).

27 Emily Sullivan, "US Public Views Saudi Relationship as One of Necessity," *Global Affairs*, https://globalaffairs.org/commentary-and-analysis/blogs/us-public-views-saudi-relationship-one-necessity (accessed July 11, 2025).

28 Philip Chrysopoulos, "Giorgos Tromaras: Greece Loses its Modern Day Hercules," *Greek Reporter*, January 24, 2022, https://greekreporter.com/2022/01/24/tromaras-modern-day-hercules (accessed July 11, 2025).

29 "WWE Live Comes To Saudi Arabia," *WWE Corporate*, December 15, 2013, https://web.archive.org/web/20170829182249/https://corporate.wwe.com/news/company-news/2013/12-15-2013 (accessed July 11, 2025).

30 Chris Newbould, "WWE Wal300ha: the long wait is over for wrestling fans in the Middle East," *The National*, https://www.thenationalnews.com/arts-culture/television/wwe-wal300ha-the-long-wait-is-over-for-wrestling-fans-in-the-middle-east-1.64271 (accessed July 11, 2025).

31 Adam Silverstein, "WWE news, rumors: 'Greatest Royal Rumble,' NXT injury, Jericho-NJPW done?" *CBS Sports*, https://www.cbssports.com/wwe/news/wwe-news-rumors-greatest-royal-rumble-nxt-injury-Jericho-njpw-done (accessed July 11, 2025).

32 Garrett Martin, "WWE's 'Women's Evolution' Pauses For The Greatest Royal Rumble," *Paste Magazine*, https://www.pastemagazine.com/wrestling/wwe/wwes-womens-evolution-pauses-for-the-greatest-roya (accessed July 11, 2025).

33 Matty Paddock, "WWE Greatest Royal Rumble: Triple H defends hosting event in Saudi Arabia without women wrestlers," *The Independent*, https://www.independent.co.uk/sport/general/wwe-mma-wrestling/wwe-greatest-royal-rumble-saudi-arabia-triple-h-interview-defends-no-women-wrestlers-a8319446.html (accessed July 11, 2025).

34 "Women, children attend wrestling event in Saudi Arabia," https://apnews.com/general-news-a05bf0eea74b4a9a9a776ae5039c7066 (accessed July 11, 2025).

35 "Bret Baier previews 'historic moments' in first-ever all-English interview with Saudi Arabia's Crown Prince," *Fox News*, https://www.foxnews.com/video/6337512022112 (accessed July 11, 2025).

36 Paul MacInnes, "Mohammed bin Salman says he will 'continue doing sport washing' for Saudi Arabia," *The Guardian*, September 21, 2023, https://www.theguardian.com/world/2023/sep/21/mohammed-bin-salman-says-he-will-continue-doing-sport-washing-for-saudi-arabia (accessed July 11, 2025).

37 Joel Beall, "The LIV Golf series: What we know, what we don't, and the massive ramifications of the Saudi-backed league," *Golf Digest*, https://www.golfdigest.com/story/saudi-golf-league-2022-primer (accessed July 11, 2025).

38 "LIV Golf: Dustin Johnson, Sergio Garcia, Lee Westwood and Ian Poulter to play in first event," *BBC Sport*, https://www.bbc.co.uk/sport/golf/61641439 (accessed July 11, 2025).

39 Mark Schlabach, "Kevin Na resigns from PGA Tour, will participate in LIV Golf series," *ESPN*, https://www.espn.com/golf/story/_/id/34036642/kevin-na-resigns-pga-tour-participate-liv-golf-series (accessed July 11, 2025).

40 Josh Sens, "13 golf-loving CEOs who run Fortune 500 companies," *Golf.com*, https://golf.com/news/13-golf-loving-ceos-who-run-fortune-500-companies (accessed July 11, 2025).

41 Luke Kerr-Dineen, "Report: The 'mind-blowingly enormous' money Tiger Woods declined to join LIV Golf," *Golf.com*, https://golf.com/news/tiger-woods-liv-golf (accessed July 11, 2025).

42 Joseph Nye, "Soft Power and the Public Diplomacy Revisited," *Harvard Kennedy School*, https://www.hks.harvard.edu/publications/soft-power-and-public-diplomacy-revisited (accessed July 11, 2025).

43 Jamie Jackson, "Sir Jim Ratcliffe completes deal to buy Manchester United 25% minority stake," *The Guardian*, December 2, 2023, https://www.theguardian.com/football/2023/dec/24/sir-jim-ratcliffe-manchester-united-stake-announced (accessed July 11, 2025).

44 "What is Davos in the Desert?" *Saudipedia*, https://saudipedia.com/en/article/2173/economy-and-business/investment/what-is-davos-in-the-desert (accessed July 11, 2025).

45 Frank Kane and Lojien Ben Gassem, "MBS: Middle East can be the 'new Europe'," *Arab News*, https://www.arabnews.com/node/1393491/saudi-arabia (accessed July 11, 2025).

46 Adam Lyjak, "The Finances Behind the 2022 World Cup," *Michigan Journal of Economics*, January 10, 2023, https://sites.lsa.umich.edu/mje/2023/01/10/the-finances-behind-the-2022-world-cup (accessed July 11, 2025).

47 "World Economic Outlook Database," *International Monetary Fund*, October 2024, https://www.imf.org/en/Publications/WEO/weo-database/2024/October/weo-report?c=419,443,449,453,456,466,&s=NGDP_RPCH,NGDPD,PPPGDP,NGDPDPC,PPPPC,PCPIPCH,LP,&sy=2022&ey=2028&ssm=0&scsm=1&scc=0&ssd=1&ssc=0&sic=0&sort=country&ds=.&br=1 (accessed July 11, 2025).

48 Robert Livingstone, "Qatar Furthers Progress Towards 2036 Olympic Games Bid," *GamesBids.com*, https://gamesbids.com/eng/summer-olympic-bids/qatar-furthers-progress-towards-2036-olympic-games-bid (accessed July 11, 2025).

49 Dominic Fifield, "Chelsea's Antonio Conte: Chinese Super League is a danger to all teams," *The Guardian*, December 16, 2016, https://www.theguardian.com/football/2016/dec/16/antonio-conte-chinese-super-league-danger-oscar-move-chelsea (accessed July 11, 2025).

50 Tariq Panja and Kevin Draper, "U.S. says FIFA officials were bribed to award World Cup to Russi and Qatar," *The New York Times*, April 6, 2020, https://www.nytimes.

com/2020/04/06/sports/soccer/qatar-and-russia-bribery-world-cup-fifa.html (accessed July 11, 2025).

51   Ed Thomas, "Fifa corruption: Documents show details of Jack Warner 'bribes,'" *BBC News*, https://www.bbc.com/news/world-latin-america-33039014 (accessed July 11, 2025).

52   Tariq Panja and Kevin Draper, "U.S. says FIFA officials were bribed to award World Cup to Russi and Qatar," *The New York Times*, April 6, 2020, https://www.nytimes.com/2020/04/06/sports/soccer/qatar-and-russia-bribery-world-cup-fifa.html (accessed July 11, 2025).

53   "Officials arrested in Switzerland ahead of FIFA meeting," *Sky Sports*, https://www.skysports.com/football/news/11095/9866259/reports-fifa-officials-arrested (accessed July 11, 2025).

54   "Fifa announces deal with Saudi oil company Aramco," *BBC Sport*, https://www.bbc.com/sport/football/articles/c51n3ld43yro (accessed July 11, 2025).

55   Andy Brown, Philippe Auclair, Jack Kerr, Samindra Kunti, and Steve Menary, "FIFA ignores new sponsor Aramco's dismal record on carbon emissions," *Play the Game*, https://www.playthegame.org/news/fifa-ignores-new-sponsor-aramco-s-dismal-record-on-carbon-emissions (accessed July 11, 2025).

56   David Rumsey, "$1B Saudi Arabian-FIFA Deal Expected To Follow 2034 World Cup Bid," *Front Office Sports*, https://frontofficesports.com/1b-saudi-arabia-fifa-deal-expected-to-follow-2034-world-cup-bid (accessed July 11, 2025).

57   Vitas Carosella, "FIFA And Aramco Agree Global Partnership," *Forbes*, April 26, 2024, https://www.forbes.com/sites/vitascarosella/2024/04/26/fifa-and-aramco-agree-global-partnership (accessed July 11, 2025).

58   "FIFA end World Cup rotation policy," *IOL*, http://www.int.iol.co.za/index.php?set_id=6&click_id=19&art_id=qw962980020648B216 (accessed July 11, 2025).

59   Mark Ledsom, "Fifa end World Cup rotation policy," *Mail & Guardian*, October 29, 2007, https://web.archive.org/web/20100720070353/http://za.mg.co.za/article/2007-10-29-fifa-end-world-cup-rotation-policy (accessed July 11, 2025).

60   "FIFA Council takes key decisions on FIFA World Cup™ editions in 2030 and 2034," *FIFA*, https://inside.fifa.com/about-fifa/organisation/fifa-council/media-releases/fifa-council-takes-key-decisions-on-fifa-world-cup-tm-editions-in-2030-and-2034 (accessed July 11, 2025).

61   Gavin Mair, "FIFA's foul, irresponsible, farcical, and absurd approach to the climate," *Carbon Market Watch*, December 20, 2024, https://carbonmarketwatch.org/2024/12/20/fifas-foul-irresponsible-farcical-and-absurd-approach-to-the-climate (accessed July 11, 2025).

62   "Indonesia wants to co-host 2034 World Cup with Australia, Malaysia, Singapore," *Reuters*, October 11, 2023, https://www.reuters.com/sports/soccer/indonesia-wants-

co-host-2034-world-cup-with-australia-malaysia-singapore-2023-10-11 (accessed July 11, 2025).

63 Jack Snape, "Australia given 25-day deadline to challenge Saudi Arabia's 2034 World Cup bid," *The Guardian*, October 5, 2023, https://www.theguardian.com/sport/2023/oct/05/australia-fifa-world-cup-2034-bid-saudi-arabia-challenge (accessed July 11, 2025).

64 Tariq Panja, "Saudi Arabia confirmed as sole bidder for 2034 World Cup," *The New York Times*, October 31, 2023, https://www.nytimes.com/2023/10/31/world/middleeast/saudi-arabia-world-cup-2034.html (accessed July 11, 2025).

65 "AFC President welcomes FWC hosting decision, backs SAFF intent to bid for 2034 edition," *Asian Football Confederation*, https://www.the-afc.com/en/about_afc/about_afc/the_president/news/afc_president_welcomes_fwc_hosting_decision_backs_saff_intent_to_bid_for_2034_edition_3.html (accessed July 11, 2025).

66 "Saudi Arabian Football Federation submits official letter of intent to bid for 2034 FIFA World Cup™," Saudi Arabian Football Federation, https://www.saff.com.sa/en/news.php?id=2572 (accessed July 11, 2025).

67 "Norway's Klaveness asks question of 2034 World Cup vote process and Saudis' HR report," *Inside World Football*, November 4, 2024, https://www.insideworldfootball.com/2024/11/04/norways-klaveness-asks-question-2034-world-cup-vote-process-saudis-hr-report (accessed July 11, 2025).

68 Chitra Ramaswamy, "Hosting the Olympics: the competition no one wants to win," *The Guardian*, November 30, 2015, https://www.theguardian.com/sport/shortcuts/2015/nov/30/hosting-olympics-hamburg-drop-out-2024-games (accessed July 11, 2025).

69 Graham Dunbar, "Norway plans to protest FIFA and abstain from decision giving 2034 World Cup to Saudi Arabia," *AP News*, https://apnews.com/article/fifa-world-2034-cup-saudi-arabia-norway-cb686740643fbfb9ceec9ebe6c5d5d23 (accessed July 11, 2025).

70 "Argentina's junta used a plane to hurl dissident mothers and nuns to their deaths from the sky. Decades later, it returned home from Florida," *CBS News*, https://www.cbsnews.com/news/argentina-death-flight-plane-dictatorship-returned-home-florida (accessed July 11, 2025).

71 Owen Gibson, "FIFA's Sepp Blatter says 2018 World Cup in Russia will stabilise region," *The Guardian*, March 20, 2015, https://www.theguardian.com/football/2015/mar/20/fifa-sepp-blatter-2018-world-cup-russia-peace-region (accessed July 11, 2025).

72 "What Is a Malignant Narcissist? Definition, Signs & Traits to Know," *Charlie Health*, https://www.charliehealth.com/post/malignant-narcissism (accessed July 11, 2025).

73 Tom Levitt, "Top female footballers urge Fifa to end deal with Saudi 'nightmare sponsor,'" *The Guardian*, October 21, 2024, https://www.theguardian.com/global-

development/2024/oct/21/top-female-footballers-urge-fifa-end-deal-saudi-nightmare-sponsor-aramco-oil-human-rights (accessed July 11, 2025).

74 Tariq Panja, "FIFA bends own rules to give Saudi Arabia coveted 2034 World Cup," *The New York Times*, December 10, 2024, https://www.nytimes.com/2024/12/10/world/middleeast/saudi-world-cup-human-rights.html (accessed July 11, 2025).

75 Nicholas Utikal, "Does Home Advantage Really Matter for the FIFA World Cup?" *Medium*, https://medium.com/@nicholasutikal/does-home-advantage-really-matter-for-the-fifa-world-cup-d18489248391 (accessed July 11, 2025).

76 "'Incredible honour': Gianni Infantino thanks President Donald Trump for show of support," *FIFA*, https://inside.fifa.com/organisation/president/news/donald-trump-rally-gianni-infantino-world-cup-2026-mentioned (accessed July 11, 2025).

77 "Letter to FIFA Re. Impact of U.S. Immigration Policies on the 2025 FIFA Club World Cup and the 2026 FIFA Men's World Cup," *Human Rights Watch*, July 1, 2025, https://www.hrw.org/news/2025/07/01/letter-to-fifa-re-impact-of-us-immigration-policies-on-the-2025-fifa-club-world-cup (accessed July 11, 2025).

78 Andres Oppenheimer, "Trump's random immigration raids could ruin 2026 FIFA World Cup in U.S.," *Miami Herald*, https://www.miamiherald.com/news/local/news-columns-blogs/andres-oppenheimer/article309811715.html (accessed July 11, 2025).

79 Matt Slater, "FIFA opens New York office in U.S. president's Trump Tower," *The New York Times*, July 8, 2025, https://www.nytimes.com/athletic/6479639/2025/07/08/fifa-trump-tower-new-york-club-world-cup/ (accessed July 11, 2025).

Index

Abramovich, Roman 40–2, 85–6, 104
Al Nassr 22, 97–8, 100, 113–14, 116–17
Al-Rumayyan, Yasir 2, 108–9, 203
amortization 19, 43–5
analytics 3, 52, 61, 80, 119–41
Anterior Cruciate Ligament (ACL) 38, 51–71
Apple Inc. 22, 110
Arsenal Football Club 7, 10, 15, 40, 49, 74–5, 93, 101, 120, 123, 125, 132, 135, 145, 165–6, 169, 183, 185, 201, 211
Arsenal Women's Football Club 54–6, 64–6
Asian Champions League 99, 102–3, 115–17
Asian Football Confederation (AFC) 101–3, 105, 206

Ballon d'Or 16, 21, 51–2, 55, 70, 100
bankruptcy (administration) 2, 20, 28, 31, 42, 46, 78, 87, 124, 169–70
Bartomeu, Josep 17–18, 20
Beane, Billy 121, 123, 125, 128, 135, 138–41
Beckham, (Sir) David 1, 6–14, 16, 18, 21–5, 111
Beckham, (Posh Spice) Victoria 7–8
Benham, Matthew 128–9, 135–7, 141
beIN 105–8, 149–50
Birmingham City 75, 86–9, 91–3
Bloom, Tony 2, 127–9, 136, 140–1
Boehly, Todd 37, 39–46, 49
Borussia Dortmund 74, 158, 173–6, 178–9, 185

Brentford Football Club 79, 127–30, 134–40, 166
Brighton Hove Albion Football Club 42, 79, 124, 127–30, 140, 179

China 190, 201–3
Chelsea Football Club 9, 12, 18, 40–45, 49, 75, 81, 85–6, 93, 104, 112, 115, 124–5, 128, 132, 138
Chelsea Women's Football Club 44–5, 67, 69
City Football Group 39, 42, 48, 114
Club World Cup 1, 99, 117, 143–5, 151–3, 155, 157, 159–60, 162–3, 181
Coase, Ronald 5
Confederation of North, Central America and Caribbean Association Football (CONCACAF) 144, 162
Crystal Palace 47–9, 168, 172

DAZN 149–53
debt 18–20, 28–30, 37, 85–6, 91, 192
designated player rule 11, 23

EA FC Video Game (formerly called FIFA) 76, 195
English Football League (EFL) 74, 76–78, 80, 82–5, 87, 89–92, 94, 167, 170–3, 183
expected goals (xG) 119, 130–9

FA Cup 7, 48, 168
FC Barcelona 8, 15–21, 23–6, 73, 75, 110, 115, 139, 160

FC Barcelona Femení (Women) 44, 51–2, 54, 56, 65, 70
Fédération Internationale de Football Association (FIFA) 1, 2, 62, 68–9, 98, 100, 143–5, 151–4, 162–4, 175, 180–1, 183, 190, 203–10
Fédération Internationale des Associations de Footballeurs Professionnels (FIFPro) 54, 65, 158–9
Ferguson, (Sir) Alex 7–9, 27–8, 111, 113
Financial Fair Play (FFP) 33, 45, 85–7, 90–2
Forest Green Rovers 81–3, 180, 182–4, 186
FuboTV 47

Galácticos 8–9, 21, 24, 116
Glazer, Malcom 27–8, 49, 200
Guardiola, Pep 15

Henry, Thierry 10, 110, 147
human rights 114, 185, 190–1, 197, 208, 210

Infantino, Gianni 2, 203, 205, 207
Inter Miami CF 2, 5, 11–12, 22–3, 26, 110–11, 153

Kang, Michele 2, 34–9, 49
Khashoggi, Jamal 191–2, 196, 200

La Liga 8, 16, 20–1, 73
Leiweke, Tim 9–13
leveraged buyout (LBO) 28, 30–1, 33, 50
Lewis, Michael 120–1, 137
Ligue 1 25, 32, 34, 48, 149–52, 164
LIV Golf 109, 114, 198–9
load management 61–3, 67, 70, 156
Los Angeles Dodgers 30–4, 37, 39–41, 45, 49
Los Angeles Galaxy 10–13

Major League Soccer (MLS) 2, 5–6, 10–14, 21–3, 25, 110, 157, 162–3
marginal revenue product (MRP) 9, 13
Manchester City Football Club 14, 48, 84, 93, 112, 115, 117, 124–5, 137, 139, 165

Manchester City Women's Football Club 65–6
Manchester United Football Club 6–7, 12, 18, 27, 30, 32, 55, 78, 93, 111, 113, 119, 125, 130, 145, 154, 165, 181, 200
Manchester United Women's Football Club 55
Mbappe, Kylian 21, 111, 113, 139, 155
McCourt, Frank 30–4, 39–40, 49
Mead, Beth 54–6, 66–7, 69
Messi, Lionel 2, 5–6, 12, 14–17, 20–6, 35, 55, 98, 110–11, 113–14, 153
Miedema, Vivianne 55–6
Milton Keynes Dons 82, 169–72
Moneyball 116, 121–3, 125–6, 128–30, 135, 137–40, 183
multi-club ownership 39, 48, 114, 175, 186

National Basketball Association (NBA) 11, 23, 29, 32, 62, 67, 76, 122, 126, 148–9, 156
National Football League (NFL) 23, 27–30, 87, 146, 160
National Women's Soccer League (NWSL) 34, 36–8
Newcastle United 11, 97, 103–9, 115, 199–202, 204
Neymar 18–19, 21
North American Soccer League (NASL) 11

Oakland Athletics (A's) 121, 124, 128, 135, 137–8, 140
Olympics 38, 64–5, 70
Olympique de Marseille (OM) 32–4, 49
Olympique Lyonnais (OL Group) 34, 48, 149–50
Lyonnes 34–5, 37, 49, 55, 70

Paris Saint-Germain (PSG) 19, 21, 48, 110–11, 150, 160
Perez, Florentino 8–9, 24
player contracts 5, 10, 12–17, 19–23, 25, 43, 54, 56, 111, 113–14, 117

Premier League 1, 3, 8, 11, 14, 18, 28–9, 33, 40, 42–9, 58, 61, 73–7, 79–95, 100–11, 15, 123–9, 135–40, 144–51, 160, 166–70, 173, 181, 200–2
Profit and Sustainability Rules (PSR) 42–5, 91, 93
promotion 38, 74–5, 77–8, 80, 82–4, 88–94, 115, 127, 167, 171–3, 177, 183–4
Public Investment Fund (PIF) 22, 102–9, 114–17 152–3, 162, 193–6, 198–203
Putellas, Alexia 51, 53

Qatar 2, 102, 105, 107–8, 151, 162, 181, 191, 193–4, 200–1, 203–5, 209
Qatar Stars League 48, 101, 110

Ratcliffe, (Sir) Jim 55, 200
Real Madrid 8–10, 12, 15–16, 18, 23–5, 73–4, 100, 110, 117, 124, 139, 155, 165, 175
Real Madrid Women 51
relegation 29, 47, 82–4, 86–7, 93, 100, 116, 129, 150, 168, 172, 179, 184, 199
Reynolds, Ryan 76, 78–9, 83, 85
Ronaldo, Cristiano 22, 24, 55, 97–8, 100, 110–17, 202

Salman, (Crown Prince) Mohammed bin (MBS) 98, 104, 108–9, 191, 193–8, 200, 203, 206–7, 209
Saudi Arabia 2, 21–3, 97–118, 152, 176, 189–210
Saudi Pro League 22, 98–103, 109, 113–18, 135
Saudi Vision 2030 Plan 109, 192, 195
Seattle Sounders 162
sponsorship 24, 44, 73, 76–7, 80, 153, 162, 175–6, 178, 185–6, 204, 208–9
sportswashing 176, 197–8, 208
St. Pauli (FC) 176–9, 186
streaming 47, 76, 145, 150, 154
sustainability 179, 180, 183–4

television 1, 40, 73, 80, 93, 105–6, 145–6, 154, 165, 191, 194
 broadcast rights 22, 73, 105, 116, 144–52, 160, 164
 contracts/revenues 31, 33–4, 40, 44, 90, 145–6, 148–50, 152
Textor, John 37, 46–49
transfer 2, 6, 8–9, 14, 18–20, 24, 28, 33, 41–3, 47, 77–8, 83, 88–90, 111, 115–16, 125–6, 128, 131, 135, 137
Trump, Donald 210

Union of European Football Associations (UEFA) 1, 35, 42, 45, 48, 62, 73, 148, 161–2, 174–5
UEFA Champions League (UCL) 1, 16, 18, 21, 24, 28, 33–4, 42, 45, 48, 73, 111–13, 147–8, 150, 153, 158–62, 166, 173–5, 181, 201
UEFA Women's Champions League (UWCL) 35, 44, 51, 55, 70

wages 11, 12, 17, 19–23, 25, 28, 33, 40, 43–4, 61, 63, 73–4, 77, 81–3, 87, 92, 110, 114, 117, 160–1
Wenger, Arsene 123
Wimbledon (AFC) 77, 167–73, 185–6
Women's Super League (WSL) 35, 44, 54–5
World Cup, Men's 1–2, 8, 10, 98–9, 117, 134, 143–4, 151–2, 157, 159, 164, 180–1, 189–91, 195, 199–210
 1978 Tournament 208
 1994 Tournament 98–9
 2022 Tournament 98, 134, 181, 191, 201, 205, 209
 2026 Tournament 144, 157, 159, 191, 206, 210
 2030 Tournament 180–1, 205–7, 209
 2034 Tournament 152, 189–90, 202, 204–7, 209
World Cup, Women's 36, 55, 206
World Wrestling Entertainment 196–8
Wrexham AFC 75–93, 181

About the Author

Nicholas M. Watanabe is the Canteen Corporation Professor Endowed Chair in the David and Nicole Tepper Department of Sport and Entertainment Management at the University of South Carolina. Having previously worked for the Chicago Fire of Major League Soccer, Watanabe is an internationally recognized scholar whose research focuses on economics and management in the sport industry. His work has been featured in the *BBC*, *New York Times*, *USA Today*, *Washington Post*, *National Public Radio*, and numerous other media outlets. He is a co-author of the upcoming book *International Sport Economics*.

Watanabe spends his free time worrying about Arsenal while hiking through the swamps of South Carolina and the mountains of Japan.